Evaluation for Social Workers

Evaluation for Social Workers

A Quality Improvement Approach for the Social Services

Second Edition

PETER A. GABOR
YVONNE A. UNRAU
RICHARD M. GRINNELL, JR.

Faculty of Social Work
The University of Calgary

ALLYN & BACON

Boston London Toronto Sydney Tokyo Singapore

Executive Editor, Social Sciences: Karen Hanson
Series Editor: Judith Fifer
Editorial Assistant: Mary Visco
Marketing Manager: Quinn Perkson
Editorial Production Service: MARBERN HOUSE
Manufacturing Buyer: Suzanne Lareau
Cover Administrator: Suzanne Harbison

Library of Congress Cataloging-in-Publication Data
Gabor, Peter A.
    Evaluation for social workers: a quality improvement approach for the social
    services/Peter A. Gabor, Yvonne A. Unrau, Richard M. Grinnell, Jr.—2nd ed.
        p. cm.
    Rev. ed. of Evaluation and quality improvement in the human services / Peter
    A. Gabor, Richard M. Grinnell, Jr. © 1994.
    Includes bibliographical references and index.
    ISBN: 0-205-26481-6 (alk. paper)
    1. Human services—Evaluation. 2. Human services—Evaluation—Case
    studies. I. Unrau, Yvonne A. II. Grinnell, Richard M. III. Gabor, Peter.
    Evaluation and quality improvement in the human services. IV. Title.
HV40. G33 1998
361' .0068'4—dc21   96-52615
                                                        CIP

Printed in the United States of America
10 9 8 7 6 5 4 3 2 1   01 00 99 98 97

CONTENTS

PREFACE

T HIS BOOK is the second edition of *Evaluation and Quality Improvement in the Human Services*. With the help and encouragement of a new coauthor, our revisions became so extensive that we decided to retitle the book to more accurately reflect its contents. Nevertheless, the audience of this edition remains the same as in the first—social work students in addition to students in other related human service programs.

The book is designed to be used as a main text in introductory evaluation courses, case management courses, or applied research courses. It is also suitable as a supplementary text in practice methods and administration courses that place an emphasis on accountability.

GOAL AND OBJECTIVES

As with our first edition, our goal was to write a "user-friendly," straightforward introduction to evaluation. In addition, this book contains only the core material that students realistically need to know to appreciate and understand the role of evaluation in professional social work practice. Thus, unnecessary material is avoided at all costs. To accomplish this goal, we strived to meet three simple objectives:

- To prepare students to participate in evaluative activities within their organizations
- To prepare students to become beginning critical producers and consumers of the professional evaluative literature
- To prepare students for more advanced evaluation courses and texts

In a nutshell, our goal is to provide students with a sound conceptual understanding of how the concepts of evaluation can be used in the delivery of social services. In addition, this book will provide them with the beginning knowledge and skills that they will need to demonstrate their accountability.

CONCEPTUAL APPROACH

With our goal and three objectives in mind, we present a unique approach in describing the place of evaluation in the social services. Simply put, our approach is realistic, practical, applied, and most importantly, "user-friendly."

Over the years, little has changed in the way in which most evaluation textbooks present their material. A majority of texts focus on *program-level* evaluation and describe project-type, one-shot approaches, implemented by specialized evaluation departments or external consultants. On the other hand, a few recent books present *case-level* evaluation, but place most emphasis on inferentially powerful—but difficult to implement—experimental and multiple baseline designs.

As social work educators and evaluators, we are convinced that neither of these two distinct approaches adequately reflects the realities in the field or the needs of students and *beginning* practitioners. We describe how data obtained through case-level evaluation can be aggregated to provide timely and relevant program-level evaluation information. Such information, in turn, is the basis for a quality improvement process within the entire organization.

In short, we have blended the two distinct evaluation approaches to demonstrate how they complement one another in contemporary professional practice. The integration of case-level and program-level approaches is one of the unique features of this book; we are convinced that this integration will play an increasingly prominent role in the future.

We have omitted more advanced methodological and statistical material such as a discussion of celeration lines, autocorrelation, effect sizes, and two standard-deviation bands for case-level evaluation, as well as advanced statistical techniques for program-level evaluation.

Some readers with a strict methodological orientation may find some of the described approaches simplistic, particularly the material on the aggregation of case-level data. We are aware of the limitations of the approach described in this book, but we firmly believe that this approach is more likely to be implemented by beginning practitioners than other more complicated, technically demanding approaches.

It is our opinion that the aggregation of case-level data can provide valuable feedback about services and programs and be the basis of an effective quality improvement process. It is our view that it is preferable to have such data, even if it is not methodologically airtight, than to have no aggregated data at all.

THEME

The underlying theme of this book is that social work practitioners can easily use evaluation procedures in their practices and programs. We maintain that professional practice rests upon the foundation that practice activities must be linked to the client's objectives, which are linked to the program's objectives, which are linked to the program's goals, which are linked to the agency's goals, which represents the reason why the program exists in the first place. The evaluation process presented in this book heavily reflects these connections.

Pressures for accountability have never been greater. Organizations and practitioners of all types are increasingly required to document the impacts of their services not only at the program level, but at the case level as well. Continually, they are challenged to improve the quality of their services and they are required to do this with scarce resources. In addition, few social service organizations can adequately maintain an internal evaluation department or hire external outside evaluators. Consequently, we place a considerable emphasis on monitoring, an approach that can be easily incorporated into the ongoing activities of the practitioner and agency.

In short, we provide a straightforward view of evaluation while taking into account:

- The current pressures for accountability in the social services
- The current available evaluation technologies and approaches
- The present evaluation needs of students as well as their needs in the first few years of their careers

WHAT'S NEW IN THIS EDITION?

As we have mentioned, this book provides an applied approach to evaluation for social workers and other human service professionals. It represents a major revision of the first edition with extensive reworking and addition of its contents. Readers' comments on the first edition indicated that our approach—which emphasizes the integration of case-level and program-level activities, as well as the focus on decision making—was well received. In line with this feedback, we have maintained this unique focus.

At the same time, however, readers' comments suggested that more extensive treatment of types of program evaluations would be welcome. In revising the first edition, we have devoted Part I of this edition to the exposition of the various types of evaluations.

Another major change is that this edition is now produced in paperback, making it quite a bit less expensive than the first.

In short, we have responded to readers' comments by maintaining and emphasizing the perceived strengths of the book and adding contents to provide a greater emphasis on program evaluation. At the same time, through extensive reorganization, we have been able to delete material, thereby providing a sharper, more focused treatment. In making these revisions, we have responded to comments and suggestion to the extent possible and, at the same time have attempted to maintain the user-friendly approach that was characteristic of the first edition.

CONTENT AND ORGANIZATION

We have divided this book into two parts. Part I presents the various types of evaluations and helps students to obtain a sound conceptual knowledge of evaluation. Part II is concerned with the practical applications of the foundation information gleaned from Part I.

The sequencing of chapters reflects our experiences in teaching evaluation courses. We recognize that others may prefer to order the contents differently. As much as possible, we have written each chapter in a manner that will allow it to stand alone, thereby enabling instructors to alter the sequence suggested in this book.

In general, our problem was not so much what content to include but what to leave out. Every topic that we have touched on in passing has been discussed in depth elsewhere. The choices we have made have been guided by the fact that this book is designed to be an introduction to evaluation, intended to provide students with a sound conceptual understanding of the process as well as some basic practical skills. Meanwhile, those students who desire to undertake more advanced studies in evaluation will have obtained a sound foundation upon which to build.

PART I: TYPES OF EVALUATIONS

Program evaluation is usually a complex, large-scale activity. In contrast to case-level evaluation, where the focus is on change in indicators of needs, problems, or strengths, a variety of questions may be relevant in program evaluation. This section reflects the range of possible issues that may be addressed in program evaluation and, consistent with the usual practice in the field, differentiates these into five types of evaluations. As such, in contrast with the rest of the book, which combines program- and case-level evaluation approaches, Part I is devoted exclusively to program evaluations.

The first type of program evaluation (covered in Chapter 2), needs assessment, is concerned with examining the need for a social service program as well as existing resources in the community to meet that need. Usually, the evaluation of need is undertaken prior to the inception of a program. This type of evaluation, however, is also useful in the case of existing programs, to determine if needs, which the program seeks to address, have changed over time. Chapter 3 covers a second type of program evaluation, evaluability assessment. This type of evaluation is concerned with determining if program goals, objectives, and activities are stated in sufficiently clear and explicit terms to enable an evaluation to take place. Often, an evaluability assessment uncovers the need to work on defining and clarifying goals, objectives, and activities.

Chapter 4 covers outcome evaluation, which is concerned with changes in needs, problems, or strengths relating to service recipients. Because, ultimately, social service programs exist to bring about changes in these areas, this form of evaluation has moved to center stage with the current emphasis on accountability.

Process evaluation is covered in Chapter 5, the last chapter in Part I. This chapter focuses on program resources, structures, organization, and operations. Depending on the question of interest, process evaluation may focus on administrative or service aspects of a program or it may address staff or client issues.

PART II: IMPLEMENTING EVALUATIONS

The six chapters in this part describe the nuts and bolts of basic evaluation methods, both case-level and program-level evaluations.

Measuring objectives is a fundamental step in carrying out both types of evaluations: In case-level evaluations, in practice objectives, and in program evaluations, program objectives are measured. The measurement principles are similar in both situations and are described in Chapter 6. In Chapter 7, evaluation designs appropriate for carrying out case-level evaluations, usually called single-case designs, are outlined. In Chapter 8, research designs suitable for program-level evaluation are covered.

Chapter 9 illustrates how the information obtained through case-level and program evaluations can be used in decision making at all levels within the program, from the practitioner to the senior administrator. Chapter 10 describes how to use objective and subjective data to inform case- and program-level decision making. Finally, Chapter 11 discusses the implementation of evaluation systems in the social services, with a particular emphasis on politics, standards, and ethics. Because of the ever-present danger that evaluation results may be misused, this chapter emphasizes the use of practices that can ensure that evaluations make constructive contributions to social services and social programs.

INSTRUCTOR'S MANUAL AND TEST BANK IS NOW AVAILABLE

A complementary computerized *Instructor's Manual and Test Bank* is available with this edition. The *Manual and Test Bank* contains numerous questions for each chapter. Instructors who use this book in the classroom can receive a computer disk that contains the *Manual and Test Bank* by faxing a request on letterhead stationary to Richard M. Grinnell, Jr. (403) 949-4303, or by calling (403) 949-4303. Please state the platform (e.g., IBM, Mac, ASCII) and the word processing language (e.g., WordPerfect, Word) you desire, and allow two weeks for shipping.

ACKNOWLEDGMENTS

We would like to thank the following people for their thoughtful reviews of our initial manuscript for the first edition of this book:

- Richard L. Edwards
  University of North Carolina at Chapel Hill
- John L. Stretch
  St. Louis University

- Maria Roberts DeGennaro
  San Diego State University

This edition's reviewers included:

- Leon Ginsberg
  University of South Carolina
- Mike Jacobsen
  University of North Dakota
- Maria Roberts DeGennaro
  San Diego State University

We would also like to thank Ted Peacock for providing us with permission to adapt and modify: Chapter 10 from *Research in Social Work: An Introduction* (2nd ed., pp. 161-194) by Margaret Williams, Leslie M. Tutty, and Richard M. Grinnell, Jr. Copyright ©1995 by F.E. Peacock Publishers; and Chapter 11 ("Group Designs") from *Social Work Research and Evaluation: Quantitative and Qualitative Approaches* (5th ed., pp. 259-297) edited by Richard M. Grinnell, Jr. Copyright ©1997 by F.E. Peacock Publishers.

A LOOK TOWARD THE FUTURE

The field of evaluation and quality improvement in the social services is continuing to grow and develop. We hope this book contributes to that growth. If, at some time, we prepare a third edition, readers' feedback will be most appreciated. If you have suggestions for improvement in the next edition, or other comments, we would like to hear from you.

If this book helps students to acquire basic evaluation knowledge and skills and assists them in more advanced evaluation and practice courses, our efforts will have been more than justified. If it also assists them to incorporate evaluation techniques into their practice, our task will be fully rewarded.

January 1997   PETER A. GABOR
                                                     YVONNE A. UNRAU
                                                     RICHARD M. GRINNELL, JR.

CHAPTER 1

INTRODUCTION TO EVALUATION

T HE PROFESSION YOU HAVE CHOSEN to pursue has never been under greater pressure. Our public confidence is eroding, our funding is diminishing at astonishing rates, and the private and public calls for us to become more accountable are increasing more than we would like; the very rationale for our professional existence is being called into question. We have entered a new era in which only the best social service delivery programs—which can demonstrate they provide needed, useful, and competent services for our clients—will survive.

How do we go about providing these services? The answer is simple. We provide them utilizing the quality improvement process. This process is a philosophy; it is a commitment to continually look for and seek new ways to make the services we offer clients more responsive, more efficient, and more effective. Quality improvement means that we continually monitor and adjust (when necessary) our practices, both at a practitioner level and at a program level. Thus, evaluation simply provides the means to this end. In short, the goal of the quality improvement process is to deliver excellent client and program services. Evaluations provide the basic tools for us to engage in the quality improvement process.

QUALITY IMPROVEMENT AND THE DELIVERY OF SERVICES

The delivery of social work services can be viewed at two levels: at the case level and at the program level. It is at the case level that we actually provide services to clients—individuals, couples, families, groups, organizations, and communities. With this point in mind, and at the simplest level, a program-level evaluation is nothing more than aggregations of case-level evaluations. To put it another way, case-level evaluations evaluate the effectiveness and efficiency of our individual services while program-level evaluations evaluate the effectiveness and efficiency of our programs where we work.

MYTHS ABOUT QUALITY IMPROVEMENT AND EVALUATION

There are a few reasons why social work practitioners and the programs in which they are employed should embrace the concepts of "the quality improvement process" and "evaluation." In today's current political environment it is a matter of survival. Moreover, we believe it is ethically and professionally the right thing to do. Nevertheless some social work students, practitioners, and administrators resist performing or participating in evaluations that can enhance the quality of the services they deliver.

Why is there such resistance when, presumably, most of us would agree that the pursuit of quality improvement, through the use of evaluations, is a highly desirable aspiration? This resistance is essentially founded upon two interrelated myths: That evaluations cannot properly and usefully be applied to the art of social work practice, and that evaluation, by its very nature, is to be feared. Both myths undercut the concept of evaluation when they are used to develop quality social service programs. The myths spring from two interrelated sources: philosophy and fear.

PHILOSOPHICAL BIAS

Some of us maintain that the evaluation of social work services—or the evaluation of anything for that matter—is impossible, never really "objective," politically incorrect, meaningless, and culture-biased. This belief is based purely on a philosophical bias. Our society tends to distinguish between "art" and "evaluation"—sometimes incorrectly thought of as "science." This is a socially constructed dichotomy that is peculiar to industrial society. It leads to the unspoken assumption that a person may be an "artist" *or* an "evaluator" but not both, and certainly not both at the same time.

Artists, as the myth has it, are sensitive and intuitive people who are hopeless at mathematics and largely incapable of logical thought. Evaluators, on the other hand, who use "scientific research and evaluation methods" are supposed to be cold and insensitive creatures whose ultimate aim, some believe, is to reduce humanity to a scientific nonhuman equation.

Both of the preceding statements are absurd, but a few of us may, at some deep level, continue to subscribe to them. Some of us may believe that social workers are artists who are warm, empathic, intuitive, and caring. Indeed, from such a perspective, the thought of evaluating a work of art does seem almost blasphemous.

Other social workers, more subtly influenced by the myth, argue that evaluations carried out using appropriate evaluation methods do not produce results that are relevant in human terms. It is true that the results of some evaluations that are done to improve the quality of our social service delivery system are not directly relevant to individual line-level practitioners and their clients. This usually happens when the evaluations were never intended to be relevant to those two groups of people in the first place. Perhaps the purpose of such an evaluation was to increase our knowledge base in a specific problem area—it was simply more "pure" than "applied."

Or perhaps the data were not interpreted and presented in a way that was helpful to the line-level practitioners who were employed by the program. Nevertheless, the relevance argument goes beyond saying that an evaluation produces irrelevant data that spawn inconsequential information to line-level workers. It makes a stronger claim: That evaluation methods *cannot* produce relevant information, because human problems have nothing to do with numbers and "objective" data. In other words, evaluation, as a concept, has nothing to do with social work practice.

The previous paragraph used the words *data* and *information.* The two words are often used interchangeably. In this book, the term *data* signifies isolated facts, in numerical or descriptive form, that are gathered in the course of an evaluation: for example, the number and demographic characteristics of people in a specific lower socioeconomic community or the number of clients referred by a particular referral source.

How we interpret data when they have all been collected, collated, and analyzed is called *information.* For example, *data* collected in reference to client referral sources gathered from a program's intake unit may indicate that the program accepts 90 percent of those who were referred by other social service programs but only 5 percent of people who are self-referred. One of the many pieces of *information* (or conclusions or findings drawn from the data) generated by these data may be that the program is somehow discriminating between clients who were referred by other social service programs and those who were self-referred.

The simple reporting of data, however, can also be a form of information. The distinction we would like to make between data and information is simple—data are obtained to provide information to help guide various decision-making processes in an effort to produce more effective and efficient services to clients.

As we have previously mentioned, the idea that evaluation has no place in social work springs from society's perceptions of the nature of evaluation and the nature of art. Since one of the underlying assumptions of this book is that evaluation *does* belong in social work, it is necessary to explore these perceptions a bit more.

PERCEPTIONS OF THE NATURE OF EVALUATION

It can be argued that the human soul is captured most accurately not in painting or in literature, but in advertisements. Marketers of cars are very conscious that they are selling not transportation, but power, prestige, and social status; their ads reflect this knowledge. In the same way, the role of evaluation is reflected in ads that begin, "Evaluators say...." Evaluation has the status of a minor deity. It does not just represent power and authority; it *is* power and authority. It is worshiped by many and denigrated with equal fervor by those who see in it the source of every human ill.

Faith in the evaluation process can of course have unfortunate effects on the quality improvement process within our profession. It may lead us to assume, for example, that evaluators reveal "truth" and that conclusions (backed by "scientific and objective" research and evaluation methods) have an unchallengeable validity. Those of us who do social work evaluations sometimes do reveal "objective truth," but we also spew "objective gibberish" at alarming rates.

Conclusions arrived at by well-accepted evaluative methods are often valid and reliable, but if the initial conceptualization of the problem to be evaluated is fuzzy, biased, or faulty, the conclusions (or findings) drawn from such an evaluation are unproductive and worthless. Our point is that the evaluation process is not infallible; it is only one way of attaining the "truth." It is a tool, or sometimes a weapon, that we can use to increase the effectiveness and efficiency of the services we offer to clients.

The denigration of evaluation can have equally unfortunate results. If it is perceived as the incarnation of all that is materialistic, in possible opposition to common social work values, then either evaluative methods will not be applied or their results will not be believed and hence not incorporated into day-to-day practice activities. In other words, practitioners will have deprived themselves and their clients of an important source of knowledge. A great deal will be said in this book about what evaluation can do for our profession. We will also show what it cannot do, because evaluation, like everything else in life, has its drawbacks.

Evaluations are only as "objective" and "bias-free" as the evaluators who do them. For example, people employed by the tobacco industry who do "objective" evaluations to determine (1) if smoking causes lung cancer, or (2) whether the advertisement of tobacco products around school yards influences children's using tobacco products in the future, may come up with very different conclusions than will people employed by the American Medical Association to do the same studies. Get the point?

PERCEPTIONS OF THE NATURE OF ART

Art, in our society, has a lesser status than evaluation, but it too has its shrines. Those who produce art are thought to dwell on an elevated spiritual plane that is inaccessible to lesser souls. The forces of artistic creation—intuition and inspiration—are held to be somehow "higher" than the mundane, plodding reasoning of evaluative methods. Such forces are also thought to be delicate, to be readily destroyed or polluted by the opposing forces of reason, and to yield conclusions that may not (or cannot) be challenged.

Art is worshiped by many who are not artists and defamed by others who consider it to be pretentious, frivolous, or divorced from the "real world." Again, both the worship and the denigration can lead to unfortunate results. Intuition, for example, is a valuable asset for social workers. It should neither be dismissed as unscientific or silly, nor regarded as a superior form of "knowing" that can never lead us astray.

The art of social work practice and the use of concrete and well-established evaluative methods to help us in the quality improvement process can easily coexist. Social workers can, in the best sense and at the same time, be both "caring and sensitive artists" *and* "hard-nosed evaluators." Evaluation and art are interdependent and interlocked. They are both essential to social work practice.

FEAR (EVALUATION PHOBIA)

The second myth that fuels resistance to the quality improvement process via evaluations is that an evaluation is a horrific event whose consequences should be feared. Social workers, for instance, may be afraid of an evaluation because it is they who may be evaluated; it is their programs that are being judged. They may be afraid for their jobs, their reputations, and their clients, or they may be afraid that their programs will be curtailed, abandoned, or modified in some unacceptable way. They may also be afraid that the data an evaluation obtains about them and their clients will be misused. They may believe that they no longer control these data and that the client confidentiality they have so very carefully preserved may be breached.

In fact, these fears have some basis. Programs *are* sometimes curtailed or modified as a result of an evaluation. In our view, however, it is rare for a social service program to be abandoned because of a negative evaluation. They are usually shut down because they are not doing what the funders intended, or they are not keeping up with the current needs of the community and continue to deliver an antiquated service that the funding sources no longer wish to support. They can also be terminated because of the current political climate.

On the other side of the coin, a positive evaluation may mean that a social service program will be expanded or similar programs put into place. And those who do evaluations are seldom guilty of revealing data about a client or using data about a staff member to retard career advancement. Since the actual outcome of an evaluation is so far removed from the mythical one, it cannot be just the results and consequences of an evaluation that generate fear: It is the idea of being judged.

It is helpful to illustrate the nature of this fear using the analogy of the academic examination. Colleges and universities offering social work programs are obliged to evaluate their students so that they do not release unqualified practitioners upon an unsuspecting public. Sometimes, this is accomplished through a single examination set at the end of a course. More often, however, students are evaluated in an ongoing way, through regular assignments and frequent small quizzes. There may or may not be a final examination, but if there is one, it is worth less and feared less.

Most students prefer the second, ongoing course of evaluation. A single examination on which the final course grade depends is a traumatic event; a mid-term, worth 40 percent, is less dreadful; and a weekly, ten-minute quiz marked by a fellow student may hardly raise the pulse rate. So it is with the evaluation of anything, from social service programs to the practitioners employed by them.

An evaluation of a social service program conducted once every five years by an outside evaluator is traumatic. On the other hand, an ongoing evaluation conducted by the practitioners themselves as a normal part of day-to-day program operations becomes a routine part of service delivery. The point is that "evaluation phobia" stems from a false view of what an evaluation necessarily involves.

Of course, one of the disadvantages of an ongoing evaluation of a social service program is that the workers have to carry it out.

Some may fear it because they do not know how to do it: They may never have been taught the quality improvement process during their studies, and they may fear both the unknown and the specter of the "scientific." One of the purposes of this book is to alleviate the fear and misunderstanding that presently shroud the quality improvement process, and to show that some forms of evaluations can be conducted in ways that are beneficial and lead to the improvement of the services we offer clients.

WHY SHOULD WE DO EVALUATIONS?

We have discussed two major reasons why social workers may resist the concept of evaluation—philosophical biases and fear. The next question is, Why should evaluations *not* be resisted? Why are they needed? What are they *for*? We have noted that the fundamental reason for conducting evaluations is to improve the quality of services. More specifically, evaluations also: (1) increase our know-ledge base, (2) help guide decision making, (3) help demonstrate accountability, and (4) help assure that our clients are getting what they need.

INCREASE OUR KNOWLEDGE BASE

One of the basic prerequisites of helping people to help themselves is knowing what to do. Knowing how to help involves practitioners possessing both practice skills and relevant knowledge. Child sexual abuse, for example, has come to prominence as a social problem only during the past few decades, and many questions still remain to be answered. Is the sexual abuse of children usually due to the individual pathology in the perpetrators, to dysfunctions in the family systems, or to a combination of the two?

If individual pathology is the underlying issue, can the perpetrator be treated in a community-based program or would institutionalization be more effective? If familial dysfunction is the issue, should clients go immediately into family services or should some other form of help be offered? In order to answer these and other questions, we need to acquire general knowledge from a variety of sources in an effort to increase our knowledge base in the area of sexual abuse.

One of the most fruitful sources of this knowledge is from the practitioners who are active in the field. What do they look for? What do they do? Which of their interventions are most effective? For example, it may have been found from experience that family therapy offered immediately is effective only when the abuse by the perpetrator was affection-based, intended as a way of showing love. When the abuse is aggression-based, designed to fulfil the power needs of the perpetrator, individual therapy may be more beneficial. If similar data are gathered from a number of evaluation studies, theories may be formulated about the different kinds of treatment interventions most likely to be effective with different types of perpetrators who abuse their children.

Once formulated, a theory has to be tested. This, too, can be achieved by means of the evaluations using simple evaluation designs. It should be noted that in our profession, however, very few evaluations test theories because the controlled conditions required for theory-testing are more readily obtained in an artificial setting.

The data gathered to increase general knowledge are sometimes presented in the form of statistics. The conclusions drawn from the data apply to groups of clients (program-level evaluation) rather than to individual clients (case-level evaluation), and thus will probably not be helpful to a particular practitioner or client in the short term. However, many workers and their future clients will benefit in the long term, when evaluation findings have been synthesized into theories, those theories have been tested, and effective treatment interventions have been derived.

Knowledge-based evaluations, then, can be used in the quality improvement process in four ways:

- To gather data from social work professionals in order to develop theories about social problems
- To test developed theories in actual practice conditions
- To develop treatment interventions on the basis of actual program operations
- To test treatment interventions in actual practice settings

GUIDE DECISION MAKING

A second reason for doing evaluations to improve the quality of our services is to gather data in an effort to provide information that will help decision makers at all levels. The people who make decisions from evaluation studies are called *stakeholders*. Many kinds of decisions have to be made in social service programs, from administrative decisions about funding to a practitioner's decision about the best way to serve a particular client (e.g., individual, couple, family, group, community, organization).

Six stakeholder groups benefit from evaluations: (1) state and federal policymakers, (2) administrators of the programs, (3) practitioners who work within the programs, (4) funders of the programs, (5) the general public, and (6) the clients served by the programs.

- POLICYMAKERS   To policymakers in governmental or other administrative bodies, any particular social service program is only one among many. Policymakers are concerned with broad issues: How effective and efficient are programs serving women who have been battered, youth who are unemployed, or children who have been sexually abused? If one type of program is more effective than another but also costs more, does the additional service to clients justify the increased cost? Should certain types of programs be continued, expanded, cut, abandoned, or modified? How should money be allocated among competing similar programs? In sum, policymakers want comparative data about the effectiveness of different social service programs serving similar clients.

- ADMINISTRATORS   An administrator is mostly concerned with his or her own program. Administrators want to know how well the program operates as a whole, in addition to how well its components operate. Is the assessment process at intake (a specific component) successful in selecting only those referred persons who are likely to benefit from the program's services? Does treatment planning (a second component) provide for the integration of individual, dyadic, group, and family services in an order and time that consider the client's particular demographic characteristics? Does the discharge process (a third component) provide adequate consultation with other involved professionals? Like the policymakers mentioned above, a director may also want to know which interventions are effective and which are less so, which are economical, which must be retained, and which could be modified or dropped.

- PRACTITIONERS   Practitioners who deal directly with clients are most often interested in practical, day-to-day issues: Is it wise to include adolescent male sexual abuse survivors in the same group with adolescent female survivors, or should the males be referred to another service if separate groups cannot be run? What mix of role playing, educational films, discussion, and other activities best facilitates client learning? Will parent education strengthen families? Is nutrition counseling for parents an effective way to improve school performance of children from impoverished homes?

Of greatest importance to a practitioner is the question: Is my particular treatment intervention with this particular client working? A periodic evaluation of an entire social service program (or part of the program) cannot answer questions about individual clients. However, as we will see later in this book, case-level evaluations can be carried out by workers as a way of determining the degree to which their clients are reaching their practice objectives.

- FUNDERS   The public and private funding organizations who provide money to run social service programs want to know that their money is being spent wisely. If funds have been allocated to combat family violence, is family violence declining? And, if so, by how much? Is there any way in which the money could be put to better use? Often, the funder will insist that some kind of an evaluation of the program it is funding must take place. Administrators are thus made *accountable* for the funds they receive. They must demonstrate that their programs are achieving the best results for the least cost.

- GENERAL PUBLIC   Increasingly, taxpayers are demanding that state and federal government departments in turn be accountable to them. Lay groups concerned with the care of the elderly, support for families, or drug rehabilitation or child abuse are demanding to know what is being done about these problems: How much money is being spent and where is it being spent? Are taxpayers' dollars effectively serving *current* social

needs? In the same way, charitable organizations are accountable to donors, school boards are accountable to parents, and
so forth. These bodies require evidence that they are making
wise use of the money entrusted to them. An appropriate
evaluation can provide such evidence through evaluation data.

An evaluation can also be used as an element in a public
relations campaign. Programs want to look good in the eyes of
the general public or other parties. Data showing that a program is helping to resolve a social problem may, for example,
silence opposing interest groups and encourage potential
funders to give money. On occasion, an evaluation can help
highlight a program's strengths in an effort to improve its
public image. In other cases, however, administrators may
merely wish to generate support for what they believe to be a
good and beneficial program.

- CLIENTS   Only recently have the people who use social
  service programs begun to ask whether the program's services
  meet their needs. Does the program's intent (goal) reflect the
  needs of the people it serves? Are ethnic and religious issues
  being sensitively considered? Do clients *want* what program
  administrators and funding sources think they ought to want?
  In short, is the social service program actually in tune with
  what the clients really need?

  A factor relevant to serving client needs is whether the
  program is administered, to some degree, by the clients' social
  group. If a community is predominantly African American or
  Asian or Mormon, is the program operated, to some extent, by
  people from these respective groups? If it is not, how much
  input does the community have in setting the program's objectives and suggesting appropriate intervention strategies for
  achieving them? An evaluation study might look not only at
  how well the program's objectives are being achieved, but also
  at whether they are appropriate to the clients being served.

DEMONSTRATE ACCOUNTABILITY

A third purpose of how evaluations are used in the quality
improvement process is to demonstrate accountability. As men-

tioned, administrators are accountable to their funders for the way in which money is spent, and the funders are similarly accountable to the public. Usually, accountability will involve deciding whether money should be devoted to this or that activity and then *justifying* the decision by producing data to support it.

Demonstrating accountability, or providing justification of a program, is a legitimate purpose of an evaluation insofar as it involves a genuine attempt to identify a program's strengths and weaknesses. Sometimes, however, an evaluation of a demonstration project may be undertaken solely because the terms of the grant demand it. For example, a majority of state and federally funded social work projects are forced to have periodic evaluations or their funds will be taken away. In such cases, a program's staff, who are busy delivering services to clients, may inappropriately view the required evaluation as simply a data-gathering ritual that is necessary for continued funding. Accountability in our profession can take four forms:

- COVERAGE ACCOUNTABILITY   Are the persons served those who have been designated as targets? Are there beneficiaries who should not be served?

- SERVICE DELIVERY ACCOUNTABILITY   Are proper amounts of services being delivered?

- FISCAL ACCOUNTABILITY   Are funds being used properly? Are expenditures properly documented? Are funds used within the limits set by the budget?

- LEGAL ACCOUNTABILITY   Is the program observing relevant laws, including those concerning affirmative action, occupational safety and health, and privacy of individual records?

ASSURE THAT CLIENT OBJECTIVES ARE BEING ACHIEVED

The last purpose of evaluations in the quality improvement process is to determine if clients are getting what they need from a social service program. Responsible practitioners are interested in knowing to what degree each of their individual client's practice objectives, and those of their caseloads as well, are being achieved;

That is, they are interested in evaluating their individual practices.

Clients want to know if the services they are receiving are worth their time, effort, and sometimes money. Usually, these data are required while treatment is still in progress, as it is scarcely useful to conclude that services were ineffective after the client has left the program. A measure of effectiveness is needed while there may still be time to try a different intervention.

On a general level, our profession has the responsibility to continually improve our social service programs. On a more specific level, the ethical obligation to evaluate our programs is addressed in the *Specialty Guidelines for the Delivery of Services by Counseling Psychologists* (APA, 1981) which states:

> Evaluation of the counseling psychological service delivery system is conducted internally, and when possible, under independent auspices as well. This evaluation includes an assessment of *effectiveness* (to determine what the service unit accomplished), *efficiency* (to determine the total costs of providing services), *availability* (to determine appropriate levels and distribution of services and personnel), *accessibility* (to ensure that the services are barrier free to users), and *adequacy* (to determine whether the services meet the identified needs for such services).

FIVE TYPES OF EVALUATIONS THAT HELP IMPROVE CLIENT SERVICES

As can be expected by now, there are many types of evaluations that can be done to improve the delivery of our services. We will briefly present the five that are most relevant to our profession. Each one is expanded upon in detail in the following four chapters, Part I of this book: (1) establishing need, (2) assessing evaluability, (3) assessing outcome, (4) determining efficiency, and (5) specifying the process of the service delivery.

NEEDS ASSESSMENT

As we will see in Chapter 2, the first type of evaluation is needs assessment. These evaluations must take place *before* a program is conceptualized, funded, staffed, and implemented (the topic of

Chapter 3). In short, a needs assessment assesses the feasibility of (or need for) a given social service. A needs assessment is intended to verify that a social problem exists within a specific client population to an extent that warrants the implementation of a program.

To do this, a needs assessment must produce fairly precise estimates of the demographic characteristics of individuals exhibiting the problem believed to exist. A needs assessment seeks to answer such questions as:

- What is the socioeconomic profile of the community?
- What are the particular needs of this community with respect to the type of program being considered (e.g., physical health, mental health, employment, education, crime prevention)?
- What kinds of service are likely to be attractive to this particular community?
- Is the program meeting the needs of the people it believes it is serving?
- Is the program meeting the needs of people in the best possible way?
- Are there any other needs that the program could be meeting?

Social service programs should never gather data to justify their own maintenance needs. They must collect data to ascertain the *real* needs of the people they hope to serve and then tailor the structure of their service delivery to meet these needs.

As mentioned, an evaluation does not necessarily assess a whole program; particular parts of a program may be the focus, as in a needs assessment. For example, there may be some doubt that the program is currently addressing a specific community's needs. The composition of the community may have changed since the program was first established, and there may now be a high proportion of African-American children being referred for service whereas, before, the majority of referrals were Caucasian.

The goal of a needs assessment may be to determine to what degree the program is responsive to the special needs of African-American children and to the present concerns of the African-American community. This may involve conducting a needs assessment within the community and comparing the community's *current* perceived needs with the program's *original* intent.

Experienced program directors and their funding sources know that the demographic characteristics of communities tend to change over time. Perhaps there is now a higher proportion of senior citizens than formerly, or perhaps the closure of a large manufacturing plant has meant high unemployment and an increase in all of the problems associated with job loss. Changes may also have occurred in the community's social service delivery network.

Perhaps a program for pregnant teens has had to close its doors or a meals-on-wheels service has recently been instituted for disabled seniors. Perceptive program directors try to keep abreast of changes like these by becoming members on interagency committees, consulting with local advisory boards and funding sources, establishing contact with community organizations, talking with social work professors, and taking other like action.

Despite all such preemptive measures, however, there is occasionally some doubt that a program is meeting the *current* needs of the people it was funded to serve. On these occasions, a needs assessment may be an appropriate type of evaluation to conduct, as it can ascertain what the community currently needs (if any) in the way of social services.

It is possible to avoid periodic and disruptive evaluative efforts if a program's responsiveness to its community needs is continually monitored. Indications that a target population is changing can be seen in changing referral patterns, novel problem situations presented by clients, and unusual requests from other programs. We believe all social service programs should have monitoring systems through which such data are routinely collected and analyzed, and any lack of responsiveness to a community's needs can be easily picked up and dealt with immediately. We will return to needs assessments in much more detail in the following chapter.

EVALUABILITY ASSESSMENT

After a needs assessment has determined that a social service program is required to solve a perceived social need, we can do another type of evaluation—evaluability assessment. It is nothing more than the development of a specific program model(s) that is presumed to solve the social problem believed to exist as evidenced by the needs assessment. A program model is a diagram of the way in which the program itself is run and is intended to illuminate such questions as:

- What is the program's *goal*?
- What program *objectives* does the program hope to achieve in relation to its goal?
- What *practice activities* do line-level workers undertake in order to achieve practice and program objectives?

Since most social service programs are complex, with a number of interlinking parts, a program model can be developed only through careful study of a program's operations; once developed, of course, it has to be tested to ensure its accuracy. So far, it should be evident that evaluations can be used to increase our knowledge both about the existence of social problems (via needs assessments) and about the ways in which social service programs can address these problems (via evaluability assessments).

Another task of an evaluability assessment is to determine whether a program's objectives are conceptualized and operationalized in a way that would permit a meaningful evaluation. This is not, however, a black and white matter. Often, an evaluability assessment indicates areas of the program's conceptualization and/or organization that interfere both with the delivery of its services and with the program evaluation effort itself.

Many social service programs really cannot be evaluated as they are currently organized. Many do not have the objectives of their programs written in such a way that makes common sense, or they are written in a form whereby they cannot be evaluated—circumstances that apply not only to the evaluators but to their funding sources as well. These programs are not necessary ineffective or inefficient. They just have a great degree of difficulty proving otherwise, as we will see in Chapter 3.

Since it is the program's objectives that are always evaluated, it only follows that if a program's objectives are not clearly defined it is impossible to determine whether or not they are being achieved. In such situations, evaluators need to work closely with the program's staff to clarify the program's objectives so that the program can be properly evaluated. Chapter 3 explains in detail how to establish meaningful program objectives so that they are consistent with the program's intent.

OUTCOME ASSESSMENT

As we will see in Chapter 4, a third type of evaluation is outcome assessment. It is an evaluation that determines to what degree the program is meeting its overall program objectives. In a treatment program, this usually means the degree to which treatment interventions are effective. For example, a program in which a high proportion of clients achieve their individual practice objectives (sometimes referred to as treatment objectives, or client objectives) can be considered a successful program. If the majority of clients terminate unilaterally without reaching their practice objectives, the program can be considered less than successful.

An outcome evaluation indicates *whether* the program is working, but it says nothing about *why* it is working (or failing to work). Nor is there any mention of efficiency; that is, the time and dollar cost of client success. After all, if a program achieves what it is supposed to achieve, via the attainment of its program objectives, what does it matter how it achieves it? If the program is to be replicated or even improved, it does matter; nevertheless, client outcome alone is the focus of many outcome assessments. Questions related to outcome generally fall into four categories:

- First, the evaluator wants to know to what degree the program is achieving its program objectives: For example, do people who participate in a vocational training program have improved job skills, and by how much have their job skills improved (a program objective)?
- Second, the evaluator wants to know whether people who have been through the program have better job skills than similar people who have been through similar programs.
- Third, and highly related to the point directly above, there is the question of causality. Is there any evidence that the program caused the improved job skills?
- Fourth, how long does the improvement last? Many clients who are discharged from social service programs return to the environment that was at least partially responsible for the problem in the first place. Often, client gains are not maintained, and equally often, programs have no follow-up procedures to find out if they in fact have been maintained.

As we will see throughout this book, questions about how well the program achieves its objectives can be answered by aggregating, or bringing together, the data that individual social workers collect about their individual clients. Questions about how well client success is maintained can be answered in a similar way. However, comparisons between those who have and those who have not been through the program, as well as questions about causality, require a different sort of data, collected via descriptive and explanatory evaluation designs involving two or more groups of clients. These types of designs are presented in Chapter 7 for case-level evaluations and Chapter 8 for program-level evaluations.

EFFICIENCY ASSESSMENT

Also described in the later part of Chapter 4 is efficiency assessment—a fourth type of evaluation. These types of evaluations address such questions as:

- How many hours of therapy are generally required before clients reach their practice objectives?
- What do these hours cost in clinical and administrative time, facilities, equipment, and other resources?
- Is there any way in which cost could be reduced without loss of effectiveness, perhaps by offering group therapy instead of individual therapy?
- Is a particular program process—intake, say—conducted in the shortest possible time, at minimum cost?

If an outcome evaluation has shown the program to be effective in achieving its program objectives, the efficiency questions become:

- Does the program achieve its success at a reasonable cost?
- Can dollar values be assigned to the outcomes it achieves?
- Does the program cost less or more than other programs obtaining similar results?

Efficiency assessments are particularly difficult to carry out in social work because so many of our client outcomes cannot be realistically (socially and professionally) measured in terms of dollars. In fact, it would be unthinkable to measure some client outcomes in terms of efficiency—such as counseling terminally ill cancer patients. Efficiency in terms of what?

The benefits of a job-training program that removes its clients from welfare rolls can be more easily quantified in terms of efficiency (cost savings) than a program that is designed to reduce the feeling of hopelessness in terminal cancer patients. Nevertheless, there is only so much money available for social service programs, and decisions regarding which ones to fund, no matter how difficult, have to be made—especially if funding decisions are made on efficiency criteria. We do not need to put a price on program results in order to use costs in decision making, but it is necessary to be able to describe in detail what results have been achieved via the expenditure of what resources.

Note that the four focuses of evaluation listed so far are linked in an ordered sequence: Without a determination of need, programs to meet the need cannot be planned; without implementation of the planned program, there can be no meaningful outcome; and without a valued outcome, there is no point in asking about efficiency.

Process Analysis

A fifth type of evaluation that is highly related to evaluability assessment (discussed in Chapter 2) is process analysis (discussed in Chapter 5). Process analysis is the monitoring and measurement of treatment interventions—the assumed cause of client success or failure. As mentioned previously, an evaluation of efficiency determines the ratio of effectiveness or outcome to cost, but says nothing about *why* the program is or is not efficient, either overall or in certain areas. To answer that question, we need to consider program *process*: the entire sequence of activities that a program undertakes to achieve its objectives, including all the decisions made, who made them, and on what criteria they were based.

An evaluation of process might include the sequence of events throughout the entire program or it might focus on a particular program component: intervention, say, or follow-up. A careful examination of *how* something is done may indicate *why* it is more or less effective or efficient. To state the point another way: When a program is planned, via an evaluability assessment, it should have included a definition of the population the program serves, a specification of the client needs it will meet, and a description of the specific social work interventions it will undertake to meet the client needs within the population. If client needs are not being met, or the population is not being adequately served, it may be that the practitioner activities are not being carried out as originally planned. A process evaluation can ascertain whether this is so.

Sometimes, a needs assessment will have determined that the program is serving a sufficient number of the people it is meant to serve. If not, a process evaluation will determine this, and will also determine exactly what treatment interventions (activities) are being undertaken by its social workers with their clients. It addresses such questions as:

- What procedures are in place for assessment?
- Are staff members who do assessments thoroughly trained for the job?
- What modes of therapy are offered?
- What criteria are used to decide when a client should move from individual to family therapy, or into group therapy, or should be discharged or referred elsewhere?
- What follow-up procedures are in place?
- How much and what type of staff training is available?
- How are client records kept?
- What do staff do compared with what they are supposed to do?

In order for a process analysis to occur, however, the program has to be specifically delineated in a written form that makes it extremely clear how a client goes through the entire program. In short, a client path flow must be established that depicts the key activities, decision points, and client flow through the program in a graphic format. We need to present a detailed diagram, sometimes called a *client path flow*, of the chronological order of how a client comes into and goes through our program.

The data necessary for a process evaluation will generally be available within the program itself, but rarely in usable form. Client demographic and assessment data may be on file but will probably not be summarized. Services provided to clients are typically recorded by social workers in handwritten notes deposited in client files. Training courses taken by staff may be included in staff files, or general training files or may not be recorded at all.

Where no systematic management data system (sometimes incorrectly referred to as Management Information System) is in place (see Chapter 9), gathering, summarizing, and analyzing data are extremely time-consuming endeavors. As a result, of course, it is rarely done until someone outside the program insists on it. Again, the use of routine monitoring procedures will avoid the need for intrusive evaluations initiated by outside sources.

We have assumed that both outcome and process evaluations are necessary components of any comprehensive program evaluation. If, however, we are concerned only with the client outcome of a specific program, it might be asked why we need to monitor the program's implementation. The answer is simple: An outcome analysis investigates any changes that are believed to be brought about by an orderly set of program activities. We cannot be certain, however, that any change was caused by the program's activities unless we know precisely what these activities were. Therefore, we need to study the program operations via process evaluations.

INTERNAL AND EXTERNAL EVALUATORS

Each one of the five types of evaluations mentioned in the previous section can be done by an internal and/or external evaluator. In short, any evaluation may be *internally driven,* that is, initiated and conducted by staff members who work within a program. In other cases, the evaluation may be *externally driven*—initiated by someone outside the program to be evaluated, often a funding source.

The main motive behind internal evaluations is usually to improve the quality of services to clients immediately. A distinct advantage of internal evaluations is that the evaluation questions framed are likely to be highly relevant to staff members' interests. This is hardly surprising; staff members are responsible for conducting the evaluation and, with their firsthand knowledge of the program, they are in a position to ensure that the evaluation addresses relevant issues. Thus, feedback from an evaluation nurtures the quality improvement process. Moreover, a practitioner (or organization) who evaluates his or her practice is in a position to demonstrate accountability to funders and other stakeholders.

A drawback to internal evaluations is that they may be viewed as lacking the credibility that comes with independent, outside evaluations. Sometimes, therefore, funding bodies are not content with data from internal evaluations and request external ones. Because they are carried out independently of the programs to be evaluated, external evaluations are often perceived to be more credible. Because they are commissioned by people outside social service programs, however, they tend to reflect those interests and may not address questions that are most relevant to program staff. As well, outside evaluations often impose an onerous data collection burden on staff and tend to be disruptive to normal program operations.

When externally driven evaluations are to occur, organizations that conduct internal evaluations are in an advantageous position. *A priori*, internal evaluations may identify some things that need to be improved before the outside evaluators appear. They may also identify programs' strengths, which can be displayed. As well, staff members are likely to be conversant with evaluation matters, allowing them to engage in knowledgeable discussions with outside evaluators and thus help ensure that the evaluation process will deal fairly with the programs' interests.

SCOPE OF EVALUATIONS

The word *program* can refer to many different things. It may refer to something small, specific, and short term, such as a film developed for use during a training session on AIDS. It may refer to a nationwide effort to combat family violence, and include all the diverse endeavors in that field, with different practice objectives and their corresponding intervention strategies. Or, it may refer to a specific treatment intervention used with a specific social worker and undertaken with a specific client.

Obviously, these different types of programs need to be evaluated using different evaluative methods. Thus, we need to know what the characteristics of the program are. The scope of any evaluation has to be sensitive to the following program characteristics:

- BOUNDARY   The program may extend across a nation, region, state, province, city, parish, county, or community; or it may be extremely limited—for example, a course presented in an individual agency or school.
- SIZE   The program may serve individual clients, such as people seeking individual therapy, or many clients, such as people infected with the HIV virus.
- DURATION   The program may be designed to last for half an hour—a training film, for example—or it may be an orientation course on child safety lasting for two days, a group therapy cycle lasting for ten weeks, or a pilot project designed to help the homeless being evaluated after two years. Or, as in the case of a child protection agency, it may be intended to continue indefinitely.
- COMPLEXITY   Some programs offer integrated components, combining, for instance, child protection services, individual therapy, family therapy, and educational services under one common umbrella. Such a program is obviously more complex than one with a simpler, singular focus—for example, providing nutrition counseling to pregnant adolescents.
- CLARITY AND TIME SPAN OF PROGRAM OBJECTIVES   Some programs have objectives that can readily be evaluated: for example, to increase the number of unemployed adolescents who find full-time jobs two months after a six-week training course (the intervention). Others have objectives that will not become evident for some time: for example, to increase the utilization by seniors of a meals-on-wheels program.
- INNOVATIVENESS   Some social service programs follow long-established treatment interventions, such as individual treatment; others are experimenting with new ones designed for use with current social problems, such as AIDS.

TWO APPROACHES TO QUALITY IMPROVEMENT

As we have seen, there are many types of evaluations that can be done to improve the quality of the services we offer to clients. Each type can be classified under the project approach or the monitoring approach to quality improvement. Sometimes, a particular type of evaluation can be classified under both approaches, depending on how often it is done within a social service program.

An evaluation whose purpose is to assess a completed social service program (or project) has a *project* approach to quality improvement. Complementary to the project approach, an evaluation whose purpose is to provide feedback while a program is still under way has a *monitoring* approach to quality improvement; that is, it is designed to contribute to the ongoing development and improvement of the program as it goes along. In addition, the data generated by both approaches must be utilization-focused. That is, the data must be useful to one or more of the stakeholders, or the evaluation effort is a waste of time and money and is really unethical! Let us now turn our attention to the first approach to quality improvement—the project approach.

THE PROJECT APPROACH TO QUALITY IMPROVEMENT

As we have seen, evaluations that enhance the quality improvement process in our profession may be carried out daily or they may not be initiated until the program has been in operation for a number of years. A substantial evaluation carried out periodically, at long intervals, illustrates the *project approach* to quality improvement. This approach tends to give rise to evaluations with the following eight characteristics:

- EXTERNALLY DRIVEN   The evaluation will almost certainly be externally driven, that is, it will be initiated by someone outside the program who more often than not will decide on the evaluation questions to be answered and the data to be collected that will presumably answer the questions.
- RESISTANT STAFF   Program staff may react badly to the idea of an evaluation that is externally driven and may see it as unnecessary, intrusive, irrelevant, and judgmental.
- INTRUSIVENESS   Evaluation procedures are very likely to be intrusive, no matter how hard the person doing the evaluation works to avoid this. Because the procedures are not a part of a program's normal day-to-day routine but must be introduced

as additional tasks to be performed, staff usually have less time to spend on normal, client-related activities. This diversion of attention may be resented when workers prefer to spend more time with clients rather than participating in an evaluation process that was mandated "from above," or "from outside the program."

- PERIODIC OR NO FEEDBACK TO STAFF   The data obtained from a project-type approach to quality improvement, even if shared with the practitioners, is usually not directly or immediately relevant to them or to their current clients. This is particularly the case if an evaluation is designed to answer questions posed by administrators or funders, and workers' practice concerns cannot be addressed using the same evaluation methods.

  If, as sometimes happens, the project-type approach does yield useful information (via the data collected) for the staff, and changes are made on the basis of this information, the next evaluation may not take place for a long time, perhaps for years. If the evaluator is not on hand to analyze the benefits resulting from the changes, staff members may not be sure that there *were* any benefits.

- RESISTANCE TO IMPLEMENTATION   When an evaluation is externally driven, staff may resist implementation of an evaluator's recommendations, even if the program's administration insists that changes be made. By the time that a project approach is initiated, day-to-day program procedures, both good and bad, may have become set. It is virtually a law of nature that the longer a routine has been in operation, the more difficult it is to change.

- LARGE RECOMMENDED CHANGES   The changes recommended as a result of a project approach to quality improvement can be enormous. Administrators and evaluators may feel that since an evaluation occurs only once in a number of years, it is a major event that requires drastic findings and recommendations to justify it. When a program is monitored continually, errors can be caught at once and can be corrected with minimal effort. Periodic evaluations, on the other hand, often result in more sweeping recommendations.

- NOT PRACTICAL IN APPLIED SETTINGS   All evaluations must be based on well-established evaluation principles and methods.

However, the rigorous techniques necessary to obtain cause-and-effect knowledge may not be practical in a normal program setting. Chapter 8 discusses the basic types of evaluation designs that can be used to obtain knowledge at different levels. For now, it is enough to point out that evaluation designs used to obtain higher levels of quality improvement recommendations may require that clients be randomly assigned to experimental or control groups without regard for their special needs. Similarly, evaluation designs to measure client change may require that measurement be carried out both before and after the treatment intervention, without regard to clinical time restraints or the client's emotional condition.

Usually, rigorous experiments for the purpose of increasing knowledge are carried out in laboratories, not in applied practice settings. However, the same rigorous conditions may be suggested if the purpose is, for example, to evaluate the effectiveness and efficiency of a therapy group. The worker might argue that more time will be spent administering measuring instruments than conducting therapeutic work; the evaluator can easily reply that results will be valid only if experimental conditions are observed. The issue here is: Whose interests is the evaluation intended to serve? Who is it *for*—the social work practitioner or the external evaluator?

In a project approach to quality improvement the answer is that it is sometimes for the evaluator, or for the administrative, academic, or funding body that has employed the evaluator. It should be stressed that this is not always the case. Many project approaches use unobtrusive evaluation techniques geared to actual practice situations. If, however, the evaluation is undertaken only once in a number of years, intrusion can be considered warranted in order to obtain reliable and valid results.

- DIFFICULT TO INCORPORATE IN PRACTICE SETTINGS   A final characteristic of a project approach to quality improvement is that the methods used by the evaluator are difficult for staff to learn and almost impossible for them to incorporate into their normal day-to-day practices. In fact, staff are not expected to learn anything about evaluation procedures as a result of the program being evaluated. Nor is it expected that the evaluation methods employed will be used again before the next major periodic evaluation. The project approach is carried out by the evaluator and, essentially, until the next time, that is that.

The reader may have noticed that all the preceding characteristics we listed for the project approach to quality improvement can be viewed as negative; without a doubt, the project approach is intrusive and traumatic, fails to meet the immediate needs of the workers, and may engender resentment and fear. Nevertheless, this approach must be periodically performed in order to improve the quality of services that clients receive. We now turn to a second approach to quality improvement that complements the project approach and is the focus of this book—the monitoring approach.

THE MONITORING APPROACH TO QUALITY IMPROVEMENT

The monitoring approach to quality improvement is based on reliable and valid evaluation methods that can be integrated into a social service program as a part of its normal operating routine. This approach measures the extent that a social service program is reaching its intended population and the extent to which its services match those that were intended to be delivered. In addition, this approach provides immediate and continual feedback on client progress to practitioners.

The monitoring approach is nothing more than the continual collection, analysis, reporting, and use of program data. This ongoing and dynamic approach to evaluation within a program contrasts with the periodic approach, in which evaluations are conducted on an infrequent, interval basis.

A program's administrator, for example, might decide to have a day-care program evaluated, receive the results, and then not have any further evaluations conducted for several years, if ever again. The program can be said to have been evaluated, if only on a one-time basis. But it is likely to change over time; years after the original evaluation was done, there are likely to be important new data needs that go unattended.

The alternative is to implement an ongoing monitoring system that provides continuous program data. Ideally, such a system would be integrated with the program's records system so as to avoid duplication and enhance efficiency. For example, demographic data on clients referred to the program can be collected at intake. Data on the services provided to clients can also be collected throughout their involvement with the program.

Finally, data on the changes the program aims to effect can be collected at intake, at specified times during treatment, at termination, and at follow-up. In this way, a constant stream of systematic data are collected, analyzed, and reported in an effort to help the program focus client-orientated interventions as they come into (intake), go through (treatment), and leave the program (termination), and go on with their lives (follow-up).

Evaluations resulting from a monitoring approach to quality improvement tend to have the seven characteristics described below:

- INTERNALLY DRIVEN   Continuous routine use of evaluation methods may have been initially suggested by an administrator or an outside consultant or funder. However, the evaluation methods are put into place and used by practitioners for their own and their clients' benefit without the request (or demand) from any outside source. The evaluation may thus be said to be internally driven.

- COOPERATIVE STAFF   When evaluation is a process instead of an event, practitioners generally do not resent it because it is an accepted part of the daily routine of delivering high-quality services to clients.

- NONINTRUSIVENESS   By definition, an intrusion is something unrelated to the task at hand that interferes with that task. Evaluation methods that are routinely used to improve services to clients are certainly relevant to our profession. Such methods do not interfere with the task at hand because they are an integral part of that task.

- ONGOING CONTINUOUS FEEDBACK   There are some activities in a social service program that need to be monitored on a continuing basis. For example, client referrals are received daily and must be processed quickly. In order to estimate remaining program space, intake workers need a list of how many clients are presently being served, how many clients will be discharged shortly, and how many clients have recently been accepted into the program. This continually changing list is an example of a simple evaluative tool that provides useful data. The resulting information can be used to compare the actual number of clients in the program with the number the program was originally designed (and usually funded) to serve.

In other words, the list can be used to fulfill a basic evaluative purpose: comparison of what is with what should be, of the actual with the ideal. It might be found, in some programs, that the arithmetic of intake is not quite right. For example, suppose that a program has space for 100 clients. At the moment, 70 are being served on a regular basis. In theory, then, the program can accept 30 more clients. Suppose also that the program has five social workers; each will then theoretically carry a maximum caseload of 20.

In the caseloads of these five workers there ought to be just 30 spaces. But for some reason, there are more than 30. The supervisor, who is trying to assign new clients to workers, discovers that the workers can muster 40 spaces between them. In other words, there are 10 clients on the computer who are theoretically being served, but who are not in any of the five workers' caseloads. What has happened to these 10 clients?

Investigation brings to light the fact that the workers and the intake computer keep their records in different ways. The computer assumes that every client accepted will continue to be served until formally discharged. However, the practitioner who has not seen Ms. Smith for six months, and has failed to locate her after repeated tries, has placed Ms. Smith in the "inactive" file and accepted another client in her place. The result of this disparity in record keeping is that the program seems to have fewer available spaces, and clients who might be served are being turned away.

The problem might be solved simply by discussing inactive files at a staff meeting. What steps will be taken to locate a client who does not appear for therapy? How long should attempts at contact continue before the client is formally discharged? Which other involved professionals need to be informed about the client's nonappearance and the discharge? When and how should they be informed? Is it worth modifying the intake computer's terminal display to include inactive files, with the dates they became inactive and the dates they were reactivated or discharged? Once decisions have been made on these points, a straightforward procedure can be put in place to deal with the ongoing problem of inactive files.

Other problems may also come to light. It may be found, for example, that a continual source of inappropriate referrals is the result of inaccurate information about the program's eligibility criteria. Neither the problem nor the solution can be identified unless data are routinely collected about the characteristics of clients referred by various sources. This sort of continuous feedback is obtained through the monitoring approach; problems that would otherwise continue to trouble staff can be immediately identified and solved.

Many social service programs routinely go through similar processes in order to identify and solve operational problems. They do not dignify them with the term "evaluations," but that is nevertheless what they are.

- ACCEPTANCE OF CHANGES   Necessary client-centered changes for solving problems are usually agreed upon by line-level practitioners and are usually accepted without difficulty. Resistance arises only when practitioners are not consulted about the changes or cannot see that they solve any specific problem. This is a fairly common occurrence in the project approach to quality improvement. A monitoring approach, on the other hand, usually allows the workers themselves to identify the problems and suggest tentative solutions.

- MINOR RECOMMENDED CHANGES   When changes occur constantly as a result of an ongoing monitoring process, they tend to be small. Of course, continual monitoring can suggest that fundamental changes are needed in the way that the program is conceptualized or structured, but such large changes are rare. Most often, monitoring gives rise to continual minor adjustments instead of the larger, more traumatic changes that may result from the project approach.

- EASY TO INCORPORATE IN PRACTICE SETTINGS   The monitoring approach, like the project approach to quality improvement, is based on well-established evaluation methods. The difference between them can lie in whom the evaluation is intended to serve: the line-level worker or the evaluator. When evaluation is undertaken by the workers themselves for their own and their clients' benefit, there is no doubt about whom the evaluation is intended to serve.

ADVANTAGES OF THE MONITORING APPROACH

Social workers who are interested in improving the quality of the services they offer via evaluations are well on their way to becoming self-evaluating professionals, or members of a self-evaluating organization. In other words, they are taking responsibility for providing the best possible service to clients through systematic examinations of their strengths and weaknesses via the quality improvement process. Becoming a self-evaluating social work professional (or program) has definite advantages not only for clients, but also for workers. Some of these advantages are:

INCREASED UNDERSTANDING OF PROGRAMS   A social service program is often a complex entity with a large number of interlinked components. Practitioners' main concerns usually have to do with the effectiveness of their treatment interventions. How can the confused sexual identity of an adolescent who has been sexually abused best be addressed? What teaching technique is most effective with children who have learning disabilities? Is an open-door policy appropriate for group homes housing adolescents who are mentally challenged? Answers come slowly through study, intuition, hunches, and past experience, but often the issues are so complex that practitioners cannot be sure if the answers obtained are correct.

Many social workers stumble onward, hoping their interventions are right, using intuition to assess the effectiveness of their particular interventions (or package of interventions) with a particular client. Chapter 7, on case-level evaluation, shows how the use of simple evaluation designs can complement a worker's intuition so that an inspired guess more closely approaches knowledge. However, no amount of knowledge about how well an intervention worked will tell the worker *why* it worked or failed to work. *Why* do apparently similar clients, treated similarly, achieve different results? Is it something about the client? About the worker? About the type of intervention?

It is always difficult to pinpoint a reason for unsatisfactory achievement of program objectives because there are so many possible overlapping and intertwined reasons. However, some reasons may be identified by a careful look at the program stages leading up to the interventions. For example, one reason for not attaining a client's practice objective may be that the client was unsuited for the program and ought never have been admitted in the first place. Or, perhaps the program's assessment procedures are inadequate; perhaps unsuitable clients are accepted if the referral comes from a major funding body. In other words, perhaps the lack of client success at the intervention stage derives from problems at intake.

Social workers who have been involved with a do-it-yourself evaluation may become familiar with the program's intake procedures, both in theory and in reality. They may also become familiar with the planning procedures, discharge procedures, follow-up procedures, staff recruitment and training procedures, recording procedures, and so on. The worker will begin to see a link between poor client outcomes at one program stage and inadequacies at another, between a success here and an innovation somewhere else. In sum, practitioners may be able to perform their own tasks more effectively if they understand how the program functions as a living organism. One way to gain this understanding is to participate in a hands-on, do-it-yourself evaluation.

RELEVANT FEEDBACK   A second advantage of internally driven evaluations is that meaningful and relevant questions can be formulated by the workers within the program. They can use evaluation procedures to find out what they want to know, not what the administrator, the funder, or a university professor wants to know. If the data to be gathered are perceived as relevant, staff are usually willing to cooperate in the evaluation. And if the information resulting from that data *is* relevant, it is likely to be used by the practitioners.

It is our belief that all evaluative efforts conducted in our profession provide feedback loops that improve the delivery of services. Feedback provides data about the extent to which a program's goal is achieved or approximated. Based on these data, services may be adjusted or changed to improve goal achievement.

TIMELY FEEDBACK   A third advantage is that the workers can decide when the evaluation is to be carried out. Evaluation procedures can be carried out daily, weekly, monthly, or only once in five years, as will be discussed in the following chapters. The point here is that data are most useful when they help to solve a current problem, less useful when the problem has not yet occurred, and least useful after the event.

SELF-PROTECTION   Most social service programs are evaluated eventually, often by outside evaluators. If staff have already familiarized themselves with evaluation procedures and with the program's strengths and weaknesses, they are in a better position to defend the program when an externally driven evaluation occurs. In addition, because improvements have already been made as a result of their self-evaluations, the program will be more defensible. In addition, the staff will indirectly learn about evaluation designs and methodology by monitoring their practices on a regular basis. Modifications recommended by an outside evaluator are hence likely to be less far-reaching and less traumatic.

An additional consideration is that staff members themselves are likely to be less traumatized by the idea of being evaluated: Evaluation is no longer a new and frightening experience, but simply a part of the routine—a routine that tries to improve the quality of services for clients.

PRACTITIONER AND CLIENT SATISFACTION   A case-level evaluation can satisfy the worker that an intervention is appropriate and successful, and it can improve a client's morale by demonstrating the progress that has been made toward his or her practice objective. Moreover, data gathered at the case level can always be used at the program level. Improvement of the program as a whole can follow from an improvement in one worker's practice.

SUMMARY

This chapter introduced the concept of quality improvement and explained how evaluation provides tools for the quality improvement process. The complete case- and program-level evaluative processes as explained in this chapter can be seen in Figure 1.1. Note how the stakeholders play an important role in the entire evaluative

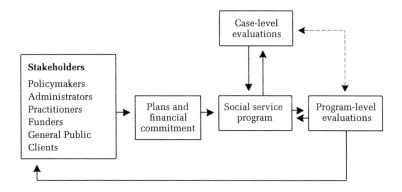

FIGURE 1.1   THE USE OF CASE- AND PROGRAM-LEVEL
EVALUATIONS IN SOCIAL WORK

effort. We presented a brief introduction to why our profession needs evaluations: to increase our knowledge base; to guide decision making for policymakers, administrators, practitioners, funders, the general public, and clients; to demonstrate accountability; and to assure that clients' practice objectives are being met.

We have presented five non–mutually exclusive types of evaluations that can be used to improve the quality of our services: needs assessment, evaluability assessment, outcome assessment, efficiency assessment, and process analysis. We did not attempt to classify the various types of evaluations into a project approach to quality improvement or into a monitoring approach to quality improvement. The types of evaluations cannot be meaningfully classified by approach. The needs assessment project-type of evaluation, for example, can be used in a monitoring fashion if it is undertaken on a regular and systematic basis. The point we want to make is simply that there are advantages and disadvantages to each quality improvement approach and one is not inherently better than the other; they complement one another, and each has its place in the evaluative process. That is, they are both used to improve the quality of services delivered by social work professionals.

External and internal evaluations were introduced with the notion that internally driven evaluations are usually concerned with the improvement of services and external evaluations are usually required by funding sources who want to know about effectiveness and/or efficiency issues. With this background, the next four chapters present five complementary types of evaluations and will show how each one can provide data to fill our profession's evaluative needs as just outlined.

C H A P T E R 2

EVALUATION OF NEED

AS PRESENTED IN THE PREVIOUS CHAPTER, there are many big and small social problems we can help solve. All of them cannot be solved at once, however, and given that our efforts will take considerable time, energy, and resources, how do we decide which problem(s) to tackle first? Additionally, how do we determine what social service program(s) is best suited to address the social problem(s) we have identified for solution?

The evaluation of need, more commonly called "needs assessment," is a type of evaluation that aims to establish, with some degree of certainty, that a social need actually exists and ultimately that the establishment of a social service program will address the identified need. Thus, a social need consists of two interrelated parts. First, a social need must actually exist and second, the development of a social service program will theoretically help solve the need. When conducting a needs assessment, it is not enough to establish that a social problem exists (e.g., child prostitution, drug abuse, discrimination) without also identifying possible ways to address the social concern.

All types of needs assessments begin by asking social problem–based evaluation questions. Paula, for example, a social work student who did a needs assessment–based masters thesis, asked the following needs assessment question:

- What social problem(s) (or issues) exist within Airdrie?

Airdrie is a small city of a population of 10,000. Paula's evaluation question was initially sparked by Airdrie's city planners because Airdrie is located only 12 miles from Calgary, a major city with a population of 750,000. In a very real way, the close proximity of Airdrie to Calgary forced Airdrie residents to rely on the social services offered in Calgary. By asking the needs assessment question from a problem focus, Paula allowed for a variety of scenarios (social problems) to emerge and left open many possible solutions (social programs to address the social problems). If Paula had approached the question with "the" solution first, she would have worded her question differently, such as:

- Does Airdrie need more social services?

This question would have assumed that a social problem existed in the first place, and thus is more narrowly focused because "the" solution is implied. This question may have led Paula to recommend more of the same social services without, for example, considering other problems within the small community. It goes without saying that the conclusions reached from a needs assessment must be useful for decision making. In fact, a needs assessment may determine that no additional social services are required.

The generic process of conducting all types of needs assessments, as illustrated in Figure 2.1, can be done with a little planning and forethought. This chapter uses Paula's study as an example of how to conceptualize, operationalize, and implement a simple needs assessment. Let us now turn our attention to a brief discussion of the purpose of needs assessments.

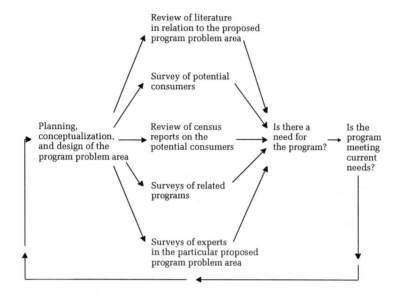

FIGURE 2.1   NEEDS ASSESSMENT EVALUATION PROCESS

PURPOSE OF NEEDS ASSESSMENTS

As previously mentioned, the main purpose of all needs assessments is to determine the nature, scope, and locale of a social problem (if one exists) *and* to identify a feasible, useful, and relevant solution(s) to the problem(s). In a nutshell, the ultimate goal of all needs assessments is to improve the human condition by identifying a social problem(s) and proposing a solution(s) to the problem(s). As we will see, all social problems are viewed from many different perspectives. This in turn leaves open the possibility of many potential solutions—one solution for each perspective.

These solutions come in the form of social policies and social service programs that are aimed at improving the quality of life for people. This can be done either by proposing an existing social service in a location where it has not previously been provided, or by suggesting new or alternative services where other services may not have proved to be adequate.

Like all types of evaluations, needs assessments achieve their purpose through well-established evaluative methods. They are nothing more than applied research efforts, and are typically done to examine a social problem(s) within a defined geographical area. Like any other type of evaluation, the steps used to carry them out must be clearly documented so other interested parties can evaluate the study's credibility. And, since there is a great deal of flexibility in conducting any needs assessment, we must have a clear rationale for each step taken.

All social problems and their tentative solutions are subject to politics, trends, biases, and opinions. The climate surrounding a particular social problem can support or supplant our efforts to ascertain whether a social need really exists. Examples of events that can influence a needs assessment are political elections, heightened awareness of a social problem in the local media, lobbying from interest groups about a particular social problem, and economic change.

USES OF NEEDS ASSESSMENT

Before we discuss the steps of conducting a needs assessment, it is first useful to consider how one can be used. They have four highly related uses: (1) justifying an initial need for a social service program, (2) educating people, (3) budgeting and planning, and (4) marketing future needs.

JUSTIFYING AN INITIAL NEED
FOR A SOCIAL SERVICE PROGRAM

The first use of a needs assessment is to justify the initial need for a social service program. A needs assessment is a proactive process and should ideally be undertaken before conceptualizing, designing, and implementing any type of social service program. A program that is based on the findings derived from a thorough needs assessment has a much clearer goal than a program that is implemented without one.

In Paula's needs assessment study, for example, she used the term "program" in the broadest sense of the word. Because she was looking at a variety of *potential* social problem areas (and *possible* solutions), she was, in effect, establishing what social services were a priority for the residents of the city based on the people's perceptions of social problems. Thus, her needs assessment was aimed at defining a "social service delivery program" for the city of Airdrie.

The social problem and potential solutions were geographically bound. Paula could have concluded, for example, that the existing social services were adequate or that the city may have required additional ones. On the other hand, she could have come up with other creative, very simple solutions, such as making free transportation available for the residents of Airdrie in order for them to use the social services in Calgary. The data collected in Paula's needs assessment study could have also justified the establishment of new or additional social services.

Needs assessments can be used to justify the initial need for social service programs that focus on a specific client population (e.g., high school dropouts, children with disabilities, adults with mental illness) or a social problem (e.g., crime, alcohol and drug abuse, child abuse, homelessness). The geographical boundaries for a needs assessment in these instances can be broad, such as when social service needs are assessed nationally, or narrow, such as when social service needs are assessed within a single community. In all of these examples, the results from a needs assessment can readily provide data to justify expenditures for new or additional social services.

EDUCATING PEOPLE

Needs assessments can be used as simple educational tools. The very nature of a needs assessment is to find out the magnitude of an identified social problem(s). In the absence of any data (as collected by a needs assessment), we are left with our personal opinions, values, and beliefs about the presence or absence of a social problem. With the data collected from a needs assessment, we can determine whether the popular opinions of residents expressed "on the street," in the media, by shop owners, and so on, matches what we find through a needs assessment.

Suppose that there was a general belief among Airdrie residents that social services in their city were sporadic and did not serve residents well. Through conducting a needs assessment evaluation, however, Paula could have found not only that people reported getting the services they needed but also that Airdrie's social services were comparable to those of other cities of the same size. Paula may have also found that her study's findings highlighted additional concerns that did not receive much previous public attention. Or, perhaps she found that the social service needs of Airdrie were expressed in a different way than they were before. Thus, the results of such a needs assessment can serve to educate people about the magnitude and nature of a social problem, gaps in public opinion, and forecasting for the future.

BUDGETING AND PLANNING

Needs assessments can be used for the budgeting and planning process within a program. The data obtained can help estimate the magnitude of a social problem and thus, may provide clues about the types of social service programs and the amount of resources needed to tackle the problem. Needs assessments do not necessarily produce detailed data that are needed for budgetary planning. They do, however, give strong clues about how money and other resources might be allocated and identify other budgetary priorities.

In the city of Airdrie, for example, Paula may have found that 50 percent of the people she surveyed had the opinion that job search assistance programs for people seeking employment were inadequate, whereas 10 percent may have felt that family life education programs were inadequate. Thus, in planning a package of social services, she would have given funding priority to a job search assistance program. She simply used data—generated by local Airdrie residents—to create social service priorities.

MARKETING FUTURE NEEDS

Another use of a needs assessment is to market future needs in relation to a specific social problem. Given that all needs assessments are supposed to focus on improving the human condition, a needs assessment, by definition, is future oriented. If a social problem is not dealt with, for example, then a needs assessment might estimate (or forecast) the consequences of taking no action to address the problem.

Suppose, for example, Paula's study showed that the residents of Airdrie perceived unemployment as a major social problem. Furthermore, suppose she collected data to show that the city's population had doubled in the past six years and that there had been a steady economic downturn over the past 10 years. These data alone could help Paula both to project social problems for the city's future and to provide recommendations to plan for more unemployment or preferably to prevent the problem from reaching major proportions. The growth of the city and the unemployment rate gave her a clue that the current unemployment rate was likely to become higher at a future date.

STEPS IN DOING A NEEDS ASSESSMENT

As with all types of evaluations, needs assessments do not develop out of thin air. They are born out of gaps in existing social services (or lack of them), public unrest, landmark cases, fluctuations in political and economic conditions, and changes in basic demographic trends. As such, the initial steps of conducting a needs assessment are in some ways predetermined.

A director of a family social service agency, for example, may notice that attendance at its parent support groups is low. The director then requests the line-level workers within the program to ask parents about the attendance problem and to see if there are any concerns about access to the program. Or, a child may be abducted from a public school ground during the lunch hour and an inquiry may be called to look into the general safety of children and supervision practices at all public schools. A third scenario could be that the number of street panhandlers may be perceived to be growing, so a municipal task force is formed to learn more about "the problem" and to decide what action, if any, the city should take.

In Paula's study, her particular needs assessment came from observations that Airdrie's population had doubled and economic conditions deteriorated in a relatively short amount of time. These simple straightforward examples illustrate that once a needs assessment begins, there is a certain amount of momentum that has already been established. Nevertheless, we must be able to take a step back and see if we have used a well-thought-out evaluation approach in examining the perceived need.

While the entire process of conducting a needs assessment, as outlined in Figure 2.1, requires a certain amount of knowledge, skill, and finesse, the process can be summarized into six highly interrelated steps: (1) defining a need, (2) developing needs assessment questions, (3) identifying targets for intervention, (4) developing a data collection plan, (5) analyzing and displaying data, and (6) disseminating and communicating findings.

STEP 1: DEFINING A NEED

Before we start a needs assessment, we must give considerable thought to how a particular need is to be defined. As we know, a needs assessment has two components: a specific social problem(s) *and* a possible solution(s). How we define a specific social problem has a major impact on the types of data that we gather and how we proceed in collecting the data. Our definition of the social problem also has a great deal of influence on our proposed solutions to resolve the problem. Thus, it is imperative to consider the social problem first and then, and only then, consider the scope of possible solutions to help solve the problem.

Suppose, for example, a runaway shelter for teens reports that they are filled to capacity and are turning *away* runaways on a regular day-to-day basis. It is tempting and easy to believe that more shelter space is needed to accommodate the teens who are being turned away. The solution is more space. Is the problem fixed? No! We can step back a bit more and ask more mature questions such as:

- Who are the teens using the shelter?
- Why are the teens running away?
- What are the teens running away from?

The answers to these questions may suggest that providing more space is not the solution to the problem. A crisis counseling program could be added to the shelter, for example, to help teens negotiate with their parents to return home, or to stay with friends or relatives. There are many more possible solutions as well, inasmuch as the definition of a need (social problem) is crystallized by the assumptions and questions we ask about it.

Defining a need is a slippery process at best, as it requires us to come up with a meaningful and specific statement that brings clarity to a vague and problematic situation. As we know from our social work practice classes, what is meaningful to one person is not necessarily meaningful to another. It is sometimes much easier for us to reach agreement about whether a social problem exists than it is for us to decide what, if anything, ought to be done about it.

The overcrowding of prisons is often identified as a social problem, for example, by the inmates within the prisons. Whether the general public feels that a solution to "the problem" is warranted is a matter of opinion. Deciding to invest time, energy, and resources to solve a social problem is related to how close we are to the problem. Deciding on whether something should be done about it is value-based and is a part of all needs assessments.

The residents of Airdrie, for example, may have felt strongly that they required more social services within their community. Social services, however, are largely funded by government moneys, and citizens, politicians, and funders in other communities. Thus, these funding sources may not have provided the same level of support for funding the additional social services that the residents of Airdrie would have liked. Clarifying our value position increases the likelihood of producing a meaningful needs assessment.

WANTS, DEMANDS, AND NEEDS

In developing a definition of need, it is helpful to distinguish among the terms *wants, demands*, and *needs*. A want is something people are willing to pay for and a demand is something people are willing to march for. These two definitions differentiate wants and demands by people's actions—that is, what people are willing to do for a particular situation or cause. These two definitions help define a "need," which is a basic requirement necessary to sustain the human condition, to which people have a right.

Clearly, what is defined as a want, demand, or a need is open to considerable debate depending on a person's views and beliefs. Inmates, for example, may protest the removal of televisions from their cells, thereby *demanding* that televisions are a necessary part of their recreational outlets. The public, on the other hand, may not see a *need* for televisions and feel that inmates' basic recreational outlets are met through various educational magazines and radio programming.

In Paula's study, she wanted to know what social problems, if any, existed within the Airdrie community. As could be expected, there were differing levels of commitment and interest, depending on whom she talked with and whether there were any upcoming special events such as political elections or major fund-raising campaigns.

THE VISIBILITY OF SOCIAL PROBLEMS

Some social problems present a visible and real threat to how society is organized and to what people believe is necessary for a basic level of well-being. Domestic violence, delinquency, child abuse, unemployment, racism, poverty, and suicide are examples of social problems that are presented in the media, have books written about them, and generally have been given a great deal of attention. These visible problems have been the traditional focus of our profession for over a century. They are the problems for which our society has drawn a minimum line of acceptability. Once the line is crossed—a child is physically abused, a teenager is caught selling drugs—there is some societal action that takes place. Generally, the more visible the social problem, the more aware people are of it.

Other less explicit problems have become more visible with the help of social workers. These problems do not have a definite "bottom-line" to indicate when and what action ought to take place. Children with behavior problems, individuals with low self-esteem, marital dissatisfaction, and unfair employment policies are examples of problems that might be considered part and parcel of daily life. Further, these problems are less likely to receive the attention of public money unless they are paired with more visible needs. Less visible social problems fall into the "prevention" category, where the focus is to establish a connection between an identified problem and the prevention of an undesired outcome. Take children with behavior problems. These children are more than likely to experience problems at home, at school, and in the community. Because their behavior can be disruptive to family relationships, classroom instruction, and community harmony, these children can be at-risk for out-of-home placement, school drop-out, and delinquency.

No matter what the degree of visibility, most people become aware of a social problem through the media and campaigning. The residents of Airdrie, for example, may have heard about an increase in the number of people who are HIV positive through reports on the news or a television talk show. Moreover, in the past decade, social problems have come to our attention through street-level campaigning. Troubled youth, for example, sell chocolate bars door-to-door in an attempt to keep the youth off the streets. Community fund-raising efforts have increased as the requirements associated with applications for public funds become more strict. Topical Awareness Weeks, where a specific social problem is discussed, are also common to raise either awareness, funds, or both.

PERCEIVED VERSUS EXPRESSED NEEDS

When considering any social problem we must consider perceived needs and expressed (or felt) needs. Perceived needs are the opinions and views of people who are not directly experiencing the problem themselves. In Paula's study, for example, perceived needs were shared by politicians, funders, agency directors, and helping professionals.

Expressed needs (or felt needs), on the other hand, were made known when the people experiencing the problem talked about how the problem impacted them and, perhaps, what they felt should be done about it. This group would be represented by the citizens of Airdrie and, more specifically, the users of Airdrie's social services. Because one individual can have two perspectives, we must be clear about which perspective we are interested in. A politician, for example, can comment on the perceived needs of a particular community by hearing from its members but may also express personal views about services he or she had received from a family counseling agency.

Thus, determining who is defining a need helps us to become

...at perspective is mostly represented. If possible, it is ...able to include both perspectives (perceived and expressed) in a single needs assessment. If the two different perspectives agree, then we obviously have stronger support for the social needs that we determine to exist. On the other hand, when perceived needs and expressed needs differ to some extent, it is usually necessary to include an educational component as part of our proposed solution.

Social workers at an AIDS clinic, for example, may have concerns about an increasing number of sexually active youth who are not practicing "safe sex" (perceived need). While adolescents may admit to being sexually active, they may not express any concerns about sexually transmitted diseases, pregnancy, or AIDS (expressed need). A reasonable solution to this mismatch of perceptions is to educate the youths in the community about the risks of unprotected sex and how to practice "safe sex."

So how do we come up with a definition of need? The most important thing to remember when answering this question is to include input from the various people who have a stake in the social problem being investigated. We might solicit the views of professionals, researchers, clients, and so on. It is a big mistake to develop a definition of need in isolation from other people. Because a needs assessment is usually conducted within a specific community (geographic or population), we must include as many divergent perspectives as possible.

In Paula's needs assessment, for example, she was able to clarify "the need" by talking with city officials, representatives of social service agencies, citizens of Airdrie, and by looking at other similar published and unpublished studies. The actual need she addressed, however, was clarified by developing a few well-thought-out guiding questions about a potential social problem(s).

STEP 2: DEVELOPING NEEDS ASSESSMENT QUESTIONS

The type of questions asked in a needs assessment can shift the study's initial focus, which means it will take a different direction. Let us suppose Paula wanted to examine a specific social problem in Airdrie—rising delinquency rates.

She could have asked *youth-focused questions:*

- Do youth perceive that they are a part of the community?
- What do the youths perceive their role in the community to be?

She could have asked *family-focused questions:*

- Are parents aware of their children's whereabouts and activities?
- Do parents feel they are responsible for their children's behavior in the community?

She could have asked *legal questions:*

- How are status offenses defined?
- Are the penalties for juvenile crime adequate?

She could have asked *intervention questions:*

- Is the probationary system able to accommodate the current number of juvenile delinquents?

Each of the above types of questions (i.e., youth, family, legal, and intervention) frame the social problem from a different angle. They also imply that a different intervention approach is warranted. The youth-focused questions suggest solutions such as a campaign for recognizing the roles that youth play in the community. The family-focused questions hint that parent training and education might be in order. The legal questions target change for legislation, and the intervention questions shift focus to the operations of existing social services. In short, it is always necessary to examine the problem from many different possible dimensions; otherwise we run the risk of offering biased solutions.

Other considerations for developing needs assessment questions are:

- Is the social problem acute or chronic?
- Is the problem long-standing or one that was brought about by some recent change?

BOX 2.1
NEEDS ASSESSMENT QUESTIONS

1. With what social problems or issues are Airdrie residents confronted?
2. What perceptions do residents have regarding their community?
3. What types of services are viewed by residents as being important?
4. Which services are needed most?
5. To what extent are residents satisfied with the present level of social services in Airdrie?
6. Is there a transportation problem for residents who use services that are available in Calgary?

The questions that guided Paula's needs assessment for the city of Airdrie are presented in Box 2.1 above. Questions 1 and 2 were designed to find out more about the social problems, if any, within the community. Questions 3–6 were specifically geared toward possible solutions to the problems.

STEP 3: IDENTIFYING TARGETS FOR INTERVENTION (UNIT OF ANALYSIS)

As we have seen, how a social problem is defined is clearly influenced by a multitude of factors. The specific definition of need, however, is clarified by developing questions that guide the remaining steps of a needs assessment. The final questions developed are particularly useful in telling us who, or what, will be the target for the proposed solution(s), or proposed social service program(s).

ESTABLISHING TARGET PARAMETERS

Targets for intervention can take many forms. In reviewing the questions contained within Paula's needs assessment, her target was the residents living in Airdrie; that is, she was interested in what people living in Airdrie thought about their community, the social problems they experienced (if any), and the social services that were available to them. She simply used a geographical boundary to define her target for intervention.

All targets for intervention ultimately involve individuals, groups, organizations, and communities. In each case, it is necessary to develop explicit criteria so that there is no question as to who a target is, or is not. Criteria that help define targets often include things such as:

- *demographics* (e.g., age, gender, race, socioeconomic status)
- *membership in predefined groups* (e.g., families, professional work teams, and members in an organization)
- *conditions* (e.g., people receiving public assistance, residents of low-cost housing, hospice clients)

Once a target for an intervention is defined, it can be tackled directly or indirectly. Proposed solutions can include direct services through social service programs established for the specified target. If we defined adolescents between 12–17 years of age who are at-risk for alcohol and drug abuse (the target), for example, we might suggest that outreach services (the intervention) be established to reach them at their "hang-out" places, such as shopping malls.

On the other hand, and complementary to direct solutions, are indirect solutions, which focus on changing policies and procedures that, in turn, affect the target. A possible indirect solution could be to institute a policy that increases the legal consequences (the intervention) for teens who are caught using drugs or alcohol (the target).

It should be clear by now that how we define a need and pose needs assessment questions logically lead us to determine the target for intervention. In the case of Paula's needs assessment, she was targeting the Airdrie residents because they were all considered potential users of social services. Another strategy might have been to target existing social service agencies (organizations) or specific neighborhoods (communities). She could have targeted the social services by asking questions such as:

- What is the profile of clients currently served?
- Do social service programs have waiting lists?
- How many clients are turned away because of inadequate resources?

- How many clients asked for services that were not available? What are these services?

Targeting neighborhoods may have led Paula to examine the number and type of social problems in each neighborhood. She could then have asked questions such as:

- What concerns do neighborhood residents have about the local area they live in?
- What were the existing social services in each neighborhood?
- What, if any, informal helping services existed in each neighborhood?

By selecting a different target and developing different needs assessment questions, Paula could have completely changed the direction of her study.

SAMPLING (DATA SOURCES)

Defining a target logically leads us to defining our data sources; that is, who (or what) we will collect data from. Therefore, it is necessary to apply basic sampling principles if our study's findings are to have any generalizability. In order to have this generalizability, however, we need to have a representative sample of data sources. For now, lets take a closer look at how Paula arrived at a representative sample for the Airdrie residents (her target).

Paula defined the pool of residents who were eligible to participate in her needs assessment study. She defined the parameters of her sampling frame as all people over 18 years of age who resided within the city limits of Airdrie. While it may have been useful to collect data from youth as well (those under 18 years of age), Paula was able to exclude them because the Boys and Girls Clubs in Airdrie was also conducting a similar survey with this younger age group. Therefore, her efforts were better spent targeting the older group.

Given that the population of Airdrie was a little over 10,000, it was necessary for Paula to use random sampling procedures to select her sample of people. How many people she sampled was influenced by time, money, resources, and the various possibilities on how to collect her data (Step 4). To gather a random sample, Paula obtained a complete list of Airdrie residents from the electric company, as everyone living in Airdrie is billed for electricity use. She then took a random sample of 300 people from this list.

When deciding whom to include in the pool of data sources, we want to cast our net as far as possible. Ideally, we want to choose from everyone who fits within the boundaries of those we have defined as a target.

STEP 4: DEVELOPING A DATA COLLECTION PLAN

There is a critical distinction between a data collection method and a data source that must be clearly understood before developing a viable data collection plan—the purpose of Step 4. A data collection method consists of a detailed plan of procedures that aims to gather data for a specific purpose; that is, to answer our needs assessment question(s). There are various data collection methods available to be discussed shortly (i.e., reviewing existing reports, secondary data analyses, individual interviews, group interviews, telephone and mail surveys). Each data collection method can be used with a variety of data sources, which are defined by who (or what) supplies the data. Data can be provided by a multitude of sources such as people, existing records, and existing databases.

Before we discuss the various data collection methods, we must remember once again that a need assessment has two parts (the social problem *and* the proposed solution). Thus, it is important to collect data for each part. If we collect data only about a potential social problem(s) for example, then we can only guess at its potential solution(s). If Paula asked only Questions 1 and 2 (see Box 2.1), for example, she would not have gathered any data to help decide what ought to be done about the social problems that Airdrie residents identified. Alternatively, if she only asked Questions 3–6 (see Box 2.1), she would have data to determine only what Airdrie residents think about the social services in their community and would not have a clear indication about what social problems they perceived to exist, if any.

It should be clear by now that how a needs assessment question is defined guides the selection of the data collection method(s). This seemingly unimportant fact is actually quite critical in developing the best possible needs assessment. We must be careful not to subscribe to any one data collection plan in an effort to change our needs assessment questions to fit a preferred data collection method and/or data source. Put simply, the combination of data collection method(s) and data source(s) that we choose influences the nature and type of data collected. Therefore, it is important that well-thought-out and meaningful questions are developed before plans to collect the data are set in stone.

How we go about collecting data to answer needs assessment questions depends on many practical considerations—such as how much time, money, and political support is available at the time of the study. Since financial resources are usually limited, it is worthwhile to begin a study using data that have already been collected by someone else. If existing data are not adequate to answer the needs assessment questions, however, then new data must be collected. To gain a broader understanding of the needs being examined, it is worthwhile to use numerous multiple data collection methods and data sources as possible.

There are many different ways to collect data for a needs assessment. The needs assessment questions posed in Step 2 of Paula's study can be tackled in a variety of ways. The approach eventually taken shapes the type of data collected and influences the flavor of the study's results. As mentioned, we can make use of data that already exist, or collect new data when there are none. There are many ways to collect data. They are: (1) reviewing existing reports, (2) secondary data analyses, (3) individual interviews, (4) group interviews, and (5) telephone and mail surveys.

REVIEWING EXISTING REPORTS

Reviewing existing reports is a process whereby we closely examine data and information that are presented in existing materials such as published research studies, government documents, news releases, social service agency directories, agency annual reports, minutes of important meetings, and related surveys, to name a few. The data provided from these many existing sources are generally descriptive and in the form of words.

While raw data may be presented in these existing sources, most are presented in the form of information. That is, someone else has interpreted the data and drawn conclusions from them. Paula, for example, could have accessed information about her particular community through professional journals and government reports. She might also have had access to another needs assessment previously conducted in Airdrie. At first glance, reviewing existing reports might seem like a time-consuming, academic task, but it can be a real time-saver in the long run.

By looking over what others have already done, we can save valuable time by learning from their mistakes and avoid unnecessarily reinventing the wheel. By taking the time to review existing documentation and reports at Airdrie's city planning office, for example, Paula was able to narrow the focus of her study by asking more specific questions, which she addressed in Step 2.

Data and information gleaned from existing published reports and articles provide us with a picture of how much attention our "social problem" has previously received. What other similar studies have been undertaken? In Paula's study, for example, she found that city residents have been polled about their opinions in the past. The city had previously commissioned two other community assessment projects—the first assessed social needs and the second focused on housing and public transportation needs. In short, these types of reports provided her with a starting point to refine her study in an effort to make it more useful to the residents of Airdrie.

SECONDARY DATA ANALYSES

A secondary data analysis differs from the process of reviewing existing reports in that it involves working with raw data. The data, however, have typically been collected for some other purpose than answering our needs assessment question(s). Two common types of secondary data that are used in answering needs assessment questions are census data and client and/or program data.

CENSUS DATA   Census data are periodic summaries of selected demographic characteristics, or variables, that describe a population. Census takers obtain data about variables such as, age, gender, marital status, and race. To obtain data in specific topic areas, census takers sometimes obtain data for variables like income level, education level, employment status, and presence of disabilities. Census data are extremely useful for a needs assessment that compares its sample to the target population. Census data in Airdrie, for example, showed that the city had doubled in size very quickly.

In addition to reporting how many residents lived in the city, the census data also provided a demographic profile of city residents (e.g., number people employed and unemployed, the number and ages of children living in single- and double-parent families, the length of time people had lived in the city). Thus, Paula could compare the characteristics of her 300-person sample (drawn from the city's electric company) with that of the city's total population (Over 10,000).

Census data also are useful for providing a general picture of a certain population at a certain point in time. The more data obtained during a census taking, the more detailed the description of the population. The disadvantage of census data is that they can become outdated quickly. Census surveys occur every ten years and take considerable time to compile, analyze, and distribute. In addition they give only a "general picture" of a population. Census data, for example, provide data only on the average age of residents in a community, or the percentage of childless couples living in a certain area. While these data are useful for developing an "average community profile," they do not provide us with a clear idea of individual differences or the how members of the community describe themselves.

CLIENT AND PROGRAM DATA   Two other data sources that can be used for a secondary data analysis are existing client files and program records. More and more social work programs produce informal reports that describe the services they provide. They most likely utilize data taken from client intake forms and client files. Program data typically provide information about the demographic profile of clients served and the nature of the referral problems.

Simply counting the number of individuals served by a particular program provides us with data from which to calculate how big the problem is relative to a specified time period, or for a particular client group. Programs might keep data on the number of clients turned away because they were full and/or the number of clients who were unwilling to be placed on a waiting list.

Client-related data are useful for needs assessments that focus on specific problem areas. If, for example, Paula's study focused specifically on the problems with teenage drug and alcohol abuse, she could have accessed programs serving this particular population and likely determined who the clients were, based on these recorded data. If this was so, the following questions could have been asked:

- Were the teens mostly males or females?
- How old were the teens who were receiving social services?

The disadvantages of using data from social service programs are first, that they are not always complete or consistently recorded, and second, the data apply only to clients of a single program and do not tell us about teens who received services elsewhere or who were not receiving any help at all.

INDIVIDUAL INTERVIEWS

Face-to-face interviews with key informants produce new, or original, data. Interviewing key informants is a strategy that requires us to identify, approach, and interview specific people who are considered knowledgeable about the social problem we are interested in. Key informants are leaders in their community and can include professionals, public officials, agency directors, social service clients, and select citizens, to name a few.

Our interviews can be formal, and use a structured interview schedule, in which case we could ask all six questions in Box 2.1. If we would like to obtain more detailed data, we could develop questions that help us probe for more specific and detailed answers. In Question 4 in Box 2.1, for example, Paula could have also asked her key informants to consider services in the past and present, or gaps in services.

On the other hand, when very little is known about our problem area, we can use informal unstructured interviews to permit more of a free-flowing discussion. Informal interviews involve more dialogue, in which questions we ask are generated by the key informants themselves. If, after interviewing a small number of key informants, Paula consistently hears people express concerns about crime in the city, she may develop more specific questions in order to probe this social problem.

THE USE OF KEY INFORMANTS   To help Paula define the parameters for her study she used the key informant approach to interviewing at the beginning of her needs assessment study. This strategy was advantageous because it permitted her to gather data about the needs and services that were viewed as important by city officials and representatives of social service programs. She was able to gather data about the nature of the social problems in the Airdrie community and what specific groups of people faced these problems. Because Paula talked with public officials and people directly involved in the social services, she also was able to get some indication about what concerns might become future issues.

In addition, she got a glimpse of the issues that community leaders were more likely to support or oppose. Other advantages of interviewing key informants are that it is easy to do and relatively inexpensive. Moreover, because they involve interviewing community leaders, the interviews can be a valuable strategy for gaining support from these people.

One disadvantage of the key informant approach to data collection is that the views of the people interviewed may not give an objective picture of the needs being investigated. A key informant, for example, may be biased and provide a skewed picture of the nature of the social problem and potential solution. Another drawback with key informant interviews occurs when we fail to select a good cross section of people. In Paula's study, for example, she was interested in learning about the range of social problems that the community was experiencing. If she had interviewed only professionals who worked only with delinquent youth or elderly populations, for example, then she would have run the risk of hearing more about these social problems than others.

GROUP INTERVIEWS

Conducting group interviews is a data collection method that permits us to gather the perspectives of several individuals at one time. It is more complex than individual interviews because it involves interaction between and among data sources. Three strategies for structuring group interviews are: focus groups, nominal group techniques, and public forums.

FOCUS GROUPS   Like key informant interviews, focus groups collect new, or original, data on a specific topic from a selection of individuals who are reasonably familiar with the topic. The people within the groups are not necessarily familiar with each other. Focus groups are usually semi-structured and often held in informal community settings where the group members are relaxed and comfortable in sharing their views and knowledge. If we were to hold a focus group for a needs assessment, for example, we would act as the group leader, provide some guidelines for the group process, and facilitate the dialogue for group members. We would prepare, in advance, a list of questions to ask group members and to give some direction to the discussion. Again, Paula used the six questions in Box 2.1 in her needs assessment as a guide for her focus groups.

Our main task in conducting a focus group is to facilitate discussion and to keep group members centered on the questions being asked. Because we want to capture the divergent and similar views expressed in a focus group, we have several important tasks that must be considered.

First, we not only want to ensure that group members are comfortable, we want them to have clear expectations regarding why we are talking with them. Comfort can be increased by simple gestures of providing beverages and snacks, providing comfortable seating, and so on. Clarity of the task is ensured when meaningful and well-thought-out questions are prepared in advance and we offer a clear description of what we expect from the group.

Second, we need to record what group members say. The most accurate way of recording the discussion is to have it audiotaped and later transcribed. A second option is to bring a note taker to the meeting who has the responsibility of writing down what people say.

Paula used focus groups that included community leaders, social service professionals, and selected groups of residents (e.g., elderly, parents, youth). The major advantages of focus groups are similar to those of using key informants. Because a group process is used, however, focus group interviews are perhaps even more efficient than individual interviews. The disadvantages, of course, are that we have less opportunity to explore the perspectives of individuals, and members are subject to the "groupthink" process.

NOMINAL GROUP TECHNIQUES   Nominal group techniques are useful data gathering tools for a needs assessment study because they can easily collect unbiased data from a group of people. The nominal group technique can identify problems in the development and planning of social service programs. The nominal group is comprised of individuals who can answer a particular question of interest, and the process involves members working in the presence of others but with little structured interaction. For Paula's study, for example, she wanted to select and recruit city officials, professionals, and city residents who had an opinion or knowledge about her six needs assessment questions. In doing so, she implemented the following seven steps.

1. Paula developed open-ended questions that were the focus for the group. The questions sought to generate problem dimensions such as, Question 1: What social problems or issues are area residents confronted with? This question could also focus on generating solutions, in which case she would propose Question 4: What services are needed most?
2. She selected and recruited group participants who had answers for her previously developed questions. Ideally, a nominal group has 6–9 members. If there are considerably more, the technique can be used by forming smaller groups of 6–9. Each group, or subgroup, should be seated comfortably and preferably in a circle.
3. Paula gathered the group together and gave an overview of the task. She gave each group member a sheet of paper with the questions written on it and explicit instructions that people were NOT to talk about their ideas with one another. She allowed about 15 minutes for the people to write down their responses privately.
4. Using a round-robin approach, she listed all answers generated in Step 3 on a flip chart. Since there was more than one group, each group listed their answers separately. The round robin continued until all responses were recorded. As in Step 3, this process was conducted without any discussion.
5. After all the responses were recorded on the flip charts, Paula engaged participants in some brief discussion about the responses listed. The discussion focused on clarifying what the responses meant so that everyone had a common understanding of each response.

6. Once all participants were familiar with the responses on the list, each person privately ranked the top five responses on an index card. These ranked lists were handed in and the popularity of responses was tallied on a flip chart. A second brief discussion was held to clarify any surprise rankings that occurred due to the misunderstanding of responses.

7. Paula ranked the responses so that the highest ranks reflected the social problems that were considered most important by the group members. If more specificity is desired, it is possible to rank the top responses, whereby another step of private rankings can occur.

The most obvious advantage of the nominal group technique in providing new data is that it promotes the sharing of ideas in an efficient manner. Nominal group process typically takes two to four hours, depending on the size of the group and the number of questions asked (the entire cycle is applied for each question). Because of the gamelike nature of the technique, participants can find the experience fun. When a cross section of group participants is recruited, the process can yield a comprehensive response to needs assessment questions.

PUBLIC FORUMS   Public forums, as data collection methods, have far less structure than the other two methods of conducting group interviews. Holding a public forum involves inviting the general public to discuss matters that we wish to address in our needs assessment. A public forum can be a "town hall" meeting or even a phone-in radio talk show. It simply provides a place and an opportunity for people to assemble and air their thoughts and opinions about a specific social problem. Paula invited the general citizens and leaders within Airdrie to share their views on the social needs of the Airdrie community. The discussion was guided by her six needs assessment questions but was less structured than other approaches she used so far.

The public forum approach was used at the beginning of Paula's study to "kick start" the needs assessment process. The advantage of public forums is that they offer widespread advertising of the entire process. Their main disadvantage is that they tend to draw a deliberate and select group of people who have strong opinions (in one way or another) that are not necessarily shared by the wider community.

Suppose, for example, that Paula held a public forum shortly after several lay-offs occurred within the social services. It is likely that her meeting would have been attended by many unemployed social workers who, in addition to being concerned about community needs, also had strong feelings about the loss of their jobs. When there is a strong unrest or when there is an intense political agenda in a community, public forums may exacerbate the problem.

TELEPHONE AND MAIL SURVEYS

The main goal of telephone and mail surveys is to gather opinions from numerous people in order to describe them as a group. A survey contains a list of questions compiled in an effort to examine a social problem in detail; it can be conducted by telephone or through the mail. The method chosen depends upon how many questions are asked, and how many people are sampled. If we have only a few straightforward questions and a short time in which to collect data, it may be expedient to randomly select and interview people over the telephone. On the other hand, if our questions are more comprehensive, as was the case with Paula's study, and we have more time, it may be worthwhile to send out a mailed questionnaire.

The survey approach in collecting original data was a good one to use for Paula's study because it permitted her to systematically obtain the views of Airdrie residents in a very direct way; that is, she obtained opinions about the community from the residents themselves. In addition, Paula constructed her survey questionnaire from the data she obtained from interviews with her key informants. This meant that the data she collected from the survey meshed with the data she obtained from her key informants.

There are also several disadvantages to surveys. First, surveys are more resource intensive than many other data collection methods. The costs of constructing an appropriate survey, mailing, photocopying, and hiring someone to telephone or input the data from a mailed survey can add up quickly. Second, mailed surveys have low response rates, and people do not always complete all the questions. Third, constructing a mailed survey questionnaire is a complex task. Developing a useful survey questionnaire takes a great deal of knowledge and time.

For Paula, the advantages outweighed the disadvantages and she opted to use a mailed survey. As a first step, Paula developed the mailed survey questionnaire. Because her task was to find out the community's needs, it was necessary for her to develop a survey that was directly relevant to the Airdrie community. She tackled this task by examining other existing needs assessment mailed surveys, by reviewing relevant literature, and, most importantly, by talking to her key informants within the Airdrie community.

Her mailed survey was carefully constructed so she could collect useful data about each of her questions. Her final survey was composed of seven sections: one for each of the six questions in Box 2.1 and an additional section to collect demographic data such as age, gender, marital status, employment status, income level, length of residence in Airdrie, and the neighborhood in which people lived.

In sections addressing each of the six questions respondents were asked to rate a number of statements using a predetermined measuring scale. Question Number 2, for example, aimed to find out how residents felt about living in Airdrie. Respondents were also asked to rate statements such as "I enjoy living in Airdrie" and "I feel that I am accepted by my community" on a 5-point scale, where 1 meant "strongly disagree" and 5 meant "strongly agree." To find out what services were needed most (Question 4), Paula listed a variety of social services (defined by her key informants) and asked respondents to rate the adequacy of the services. In this case, social services such as counseling for family problems, drop-in child care, and child protection services were listed. Respondents used a rating of 1 if they perceived the present level of the service to be "very inadequate" and 5 if they thought it was "very adequate." Because Paula anticipated that not all respondents would be familiar with all the social services in Airdrie, she also included an "I don't know" response category.

The major part of her mailed survey required respondents to pick a number that best reflected their response to each question. While Paula felt confident that she had covered all the critical areas necessary to fully answer her six questions, she also included an open-ended question at the end of the survey and instructed respondents to add any further comments or suggestions on the social services within Airdrie. This allowed respondents an opportunity to provide commentary on some of the questions she asked and to voice any additional thoughts, ideas, beliefs, or opinions.

Because of her concern about the potentially low number of respondents to mailed surveys, Paula adopted several strategies to increase her response rate:

- A cover letter stating the purpose of her study was sent with each mailed survey. The letter confirmed that all responses would be kept confidential and was signed by the mayor of Airdrie and another city official.
- Her questionnaire had extremely clear and simple instructions.
- A stamped, self-addressed return envelope was included in the survey.
- Incentives were provided to respondents (e.g., family pass to the City of Airdrie's swimming pool or skating arena and access to the study's results).
- A follow-up letter was sent to all respondents as a prompt to complete the survey.
- Residents were informed that the study's results would be publicized in the media.

STEP 5: ANALYZING AND DISPLAYING DATA

Whether we use existing data or collect new data, there are several options on how to proceed when it comes to analyzing and displaying them. It is important to use a variety of strategies if we hope to develop a complete picture of the social need we are evaluating. As we have seen, no one method of data collection answers all that there is to know about a particular social need. With little effort, however, it is possible to design a data collection strategy that will provide useful qualitative and/or quantitative data. In a nutshell, qualitative data take the form of words, while quantitative data take the form of numbers. Paula was working with qualitative data, for example, when she examined archival reports from Airdrie's Planning Commission and examined transcribed interviews. On the other hand, she was working with quantitative data when she computed respondents' numerical scores from her mailed survey.

QUANTITATIVE APPROACHES

Organizing and displaying data using quantitative approaches simply mean that we are concerned with amounts. Data are organized so that occurrences can be counted. Basic statistics books describe counting in terms of frequencies; that is, how frequently does an event occur? For instance:

- How many families live at or below the poverty line?
- What percentage of people over the age of 65 require special medical services?
- How many families use the foodbank in a given year?

If alcohol or drug use by teenagers was an important problem for Paula to consider, she would have counted the frequency of parents who perceive this as a problem in the community. Frequencies are usually reported as percentages, which is a rate per 100. If 45 percent of parents in Paula's sample perceived teen drug use as a problem, for example, then we would expect that 45 out of 100 parents in the total population of Airdrie would agree.

Because needs assessments often consider social problems on a larger societal level, we often find statistics reported using rates that are based on 1,000, 100,000, or more. Census data, for example, may report, that 8 per 1,000 babies are born with fetal alcohol syndrome (FES) in a certain community. These rates provide us with even more information when we have something to compare them too. Suppose earlier census data reported that the rate of babies born with FES in the same community was 4 per 1,000. This means that the rate of FES has doubled between the two census reports. By making comparisons across time, we can look to the past, examine the present, and be in a better position to project into the future.

There are many other useful comparisons that can be made based on rates. Needs assessments can be used to compare a single specific situation to an established group norm. (A norm is an amount that we expect.) We compare a norm with what we actually find. In other words, we might expect (norm) that unemployment in the city of Airdrie is at 10 percent, whereas when counted it is actually at 20 percent (what we found). What we expect is usually defined by existing standards or "cutoff" points. We can think of these as markers that set a minimum standard for most people. The poverty line, basic services provided by public welfare, and unemployment rate, are a few examples where a known "cutoff" score is set.

Comparisons can also be made across geographic boundaries. Paula, for example, examined the ratio of employed social workers to the number of citizens living in Airdrie. By reviewing existing published reports, Paula learned that there were four social workers practicing in Airdrie to serve the needs of over 10,000 people. The specific ratio of the number of social workers to the number of people was 1 to 2,608. Paula compared these data to ratios in other cities. She learned that a similar-sized city had eight social workers serving a population of 10,557. The social-worker-to-population ratio in this other city was 1 to 1,320, which was about twice as high as that of Airdrie.

When we are concerned about populations at risk, we can compare one group of people to another. Looking at the rate of alcoholism among Native Americans (NAs), for example, is more revealing when compared to the rate of alcoholism for the non-native (non-NAs) population. We can compute a ratio when comparing rates across two groups. If the rate of alcoholism among NAs is 20 per 1,000 and the rate is 2 per 1,000 for non-NAs, then the ratio of alcoholism of NAs to non-NAs is 10 to 1.

By comparing rates, we are in a better position to decide when a social problem is actually a problem. When counting problems in a needs assessment, we often report the incidence and/or the prevalence of a particular problem. Incidence is the number of instances of the problem that are counted within a specified time period. Prevalence is the number of cases of the problem in a given population. The prevalence of homelessness in a city, for example, might be reported at a rate of 1 in 100 persons as an overall figure. The incidence of homelessness in the summer months, however, may drop to 1 in 150 persons because of available seasonal employment.

Reporting quantitative data provides a picture of the problem we are assessing, and the numbers and rates can be presented numerically or graphically. Using pie charts, bar graphs, and other visual representations helps to communicate data to all audiences. Many word processing programs and basic statistical packages have graphics components that result in impressive illustrations of our data. More will be said about the presentation of data in Chapter 9.

QUALITATIVE APPROACHES

Quantitative data analyses are useful in summarizing large amounts of quantitative data. However, to capture the real "guts" of a problem we rely on qualitative data analyses. Rather than summarizing data with numbers, qualitative data analyses summarize data with words. Recall the final open-ended section in Paula's survey. By using a blank space at the end of the survey, respondents were able to add additional comments or thoughts in their own words. Because not all respondents offered comments on the same topic, the data obtained in this section of her survey were not representative of the people who responded (sample). That is, the comments did not necessarily reflect the "majority opinion" of people who completed and mailed back the survey. Nevertheless, they did add important information to how Paula looked at and interpreted the data collected in other parts of her survey.

Many Airdrie residents, for example, had views about the relationship between teen problems and the lack of supervision and recreational opportunities for the teens. Several respondents included comments that reflected this issue. The brief quotes that follow are examples of what some survey respondents said:

> In regards to some younger people, some of the concerns I have heard of, and read about, would probably be decreased if there was something for them to do.... The range of recreation activities in Airdrie is poor....

> Drug abuse is a very serious problem among 15–17 year-olds.
> We need a recreation center for young teens 14–19 years old. Supervised dances, games, etc., as well as counselors....

> The lack of entertainment facilities in Airdrie encourages teens to congregate and use drugs and alcohol as substitutes for entertainment. These teens can get into trouble for the lack of things to do.

> There is a definite need for activities and/or drop-in center for teenagers. It would keep them off the streets and out of the mall.

As can be seen, the above qualitative data offer richer information than is available through numbers alone. The respondents were voicing their views about what was needed in their community, given that they believed a drug and alcohol abuse problem existed for teens in their community. These comments hint at possible solutions for the social problems. On the one hand, Paula could have taken the comments literally and proposed a youth center in the city. On the other hand, it may be that she needed to propose an educational or awareness program for parents so that they would have gained a better understanding of the issues that youth faced.

Qualitative data are typically collected through interviews, which are recorded and later transcribed. Other forms of qualitative data collection occur through the reviewing of existing reports and client records in a social service program. A powerful form of qualitative data for a needs assessment is the case study approach. Using an example of a single·case can spark the attention of policy makers, funders, and the community to take action—when other attempts have failed.

Step 6: Disseminating and Communicating Findings

The final step in a needs assessment study is the dissemination and communication of the study's findings. It goes without saying that a needs assessment is conducted because someone—usually a program stakeholder(s)—wants to have useful data about the extent of a social problem. It is important that the five previous steps of the needs assessment be followed logically and systematically so that the results to be communicated fit with the original intention of the evaluation. The results of a needs assessment are more likely to be used if they are communicated in a straightforward and simple manner, and any written or verbal presentation of a study's findings must consider who the audience will be. In almost all cases, a report is disseminated only to the stakeholders.

SUMMARY

This chapter discussed the process and four uses of assessing needs, more commonly referred to as "needs assessment," in six major steps. A well-thought-out needs assessment has two components, which include a potential social problem(s) and a potential solution(s) to the problem(s).

EVALUABILITY ASSESSMENT

CHAPTER 1 BRIEFLY PRESENTED the concept of evaluation: the types of evaluations, why they are undertaken, who initiates them, which stakeholders benefit from them, and how the two complementry approaches to quality improvement differ in their efforts to improve the delivery of our services.

Building on Chapter 1, the previous chapter presented how evaluations are used to determine whether the social service needs of various groups of people are being met. As we saw, these types of evaluations are commonly referred to as *needs assessments*. If the social service needs of the people are not being met, then we need to establish a social service program—an evaluatable one, that is—that will meet these needs, which is the topic of this chapter.

In a nutshell, this chapter describes a simple process of how to establish a social service program that can be evaluated in a straightforward, jargon-free manner. The establishment of such a program is sometimes called *evaluability assessment*. As we will see throughout this book, a social work program that is evaluatable is much more preferable than a program that is not.

STEPS IN CREATING AN EVALUATABLE PROGRAM

Just as there are steps to follow when doing a needs assessment, there are those that also must be taken when creating an evaluatable social service program. There are eight highly interrelated steps that we need to undertake when establishing a program that will meet peoples' social needs: (1) Creating an agency, (2) Creating programs within an agency, (3) Creating a program goal, (4) Creating program objectives, (5) Creating different kinds of program objectives, (6) Creating practice objectives with clients, (7) Creating practice activities with clients, and (8) Creating maintenance objectives for a program.

Let us look at each step and see how each is logically related to the others.

STEP 1: CREATING AN AGENCY

A *social service agency* is an organization that exists to fulfill a legitimate social purpose: Hopefully the purpose was established by some form of a needs assessment as presented in the previous chapter. An agency may be established, for example:

- to protect children
- to provide vocational training for unemployed adolescents
- to deliver meals to home-bound seniors

An agency may be a public agency, funded entirely by the state and/or federal government. Or, it may be private and funded by private funds, deriving some monies from governmental sources and some from client fees, charitable bodies, private donations, fund-raising activities, and so forth.

AGENCY MISSION STATEMENTS

All agencies have mission statements that provide unique written philosophical perspectives of what they are all about and make explicit the reasons for their existence. Sometimes a mission statement is called a *philosophical statement.* Whatever it is called, it states a common vision for the organization in that it provides a point of reference for all major planning decisions. A mission statement not only provides clarity of purpose to persons within the agency, but it also helps them to gain understanding and support from those stakeholders outside the agency who are influential to the agency's success (see Chapter 1).

On a general level, an agency's mission statement establishes extremely broad parameters within which the overall goal is finally developed and refined over time. In addition, a mission statement contributes to the development of social service programs that are specifically designed to help in the achievement of the agency's overall goal. Mission statements are usually given formal approval and sanction, by legislators for public agencies and by executive boards for private ones.

Mission statements can range from one sentence to ten pages. They are as varied as the agencies they represent. Simple examples of agency mission statements are as follows:

- This agency strives to provide a variety of support services to families and children in need, while in the process of maintaining their rights, their safety, and their human dignity....
- This agency strives to promote and protect the mental health of the elderly people residing in this state by offering quality and timely programs that will deliver these services....
- The philosophy of the Receiving and Assessment Family Home Agency views both parents and workers as partners in care. This approach is consistent whether the family unit is intact or whether the child has been placed out of the home environment....
- The philosophy of this agency states that treatment services should be short-term, be intensive in nature, focus on problems in day-to-day operation of services, utilize beneficial agency and community resources, and be evaluated....
- The philosophy of this agency is to protect and promote the

physical and social well-being of this city by ensuring the development and delivery of services that protect and promote well-being, while encouraging and supporting individual, family, and community independence, self-reliance, and responsibility to the greatest degree possible....

In short, mission statements guide the conceptualization and operationalization of the programs within the agency in the hope that these programs will help the agency work toward its overall goal—the purpose of its existence. Even though mission statements are extremely important in the development of an agency's goal, we must never spend too much time developing and redeveloping them at the expense of refining our agency's overall goal.

AGENCY GOALS

As should be evident by now, an agency is established in an effort to reduce the gap between the desired state of affairs within a specific target population and what actually exists within the population; it is the disparity between an ideal "goal" and an actual "reality." In some instances, however, an agency goal may be to maintain the status quo in the face of an anticipated decline or deterioration in an existing social situation. The goal of an agency, for example, may be to avoid further increases in the costs of hospital care for poor persons whose health services are paid for under such government services as Medicaid. In all instances, a goal has two purposes that attempt to guide us toward effective and accountable practice:

- First, directed by the agency's mission statement, the agency's goal acts as a single focal point to guide the entire range of the agency's activities in a specific direction. So that it can function effectively as a guidepost, only one goal is specified for an agency.
- Second, an agency's goal functions as an umbrella under which all of its programs, program goals, program objectives, practice objectives, practice activities, and maintenance objectives within the agency are logically derived (to be discussed in Steps 2 to 8).

A program's goal is always defined at a conceptual level. Goals are not measurable and have global properties. As such, a goal is a means to an end, rather than an end in itself.

REQUIREMENTS FOR GOALS   It is essential that an agency's goal reflect the agency's mandate and be guided by its mission statement. This is achieved in forming a goal by highlighting four areas:

- The nature of the current social problem to be tackled
- The client population to be served
- The general direction of anticipated client change (desired state)
- The means by which the change is supposed to be brought about

Utilizing the above criteria that must be included in an agency's goal statement, a simple example of a goal for a family preservation agency could be the following:

Agency Goal 1:
The goal of this agency is to preserve family units where children are at-risk for out-of-home placements due to problems with physical abuse (*current social problem to be tackled and client population to be served*). The program aims to strengthen interpersonal functioning of family members (*general direction of anticipated client change*) through intensive home-based services (*the means by which the change is supposed to be brought about*).

At first glance, this agency goal can be depicted with more utility at a program-level of operation than at the case-level of operation. Goals that are vague and/or are not used for guidance, however, can quickly lead to unacceptable behaviors of the social workers (case-level operations). Suppose, for example, that the agency neglected to use the stated goal as a navigational tool. How would social work practitioners determine the suitability of clients referred to them? How would innovative interventions be assessed for fit within the agency? Likely, each individual practitioner could offer an answer to each of these important questions. However, an agency must have a common frame of reference in an effort to determine whether or not *all* services rendered by the agency are offered legitimately.

For the family preservation agency mentioned above, losing sight of its goal could cause an overwhelming diversification of its services. Without the focus of "preserving family units" and "strengthening interpersonal functioning of family members," practitioner efforts could inappropriately be diverted to community education, to self-help groups, and to other services that did not reflect the agency's overall goal or intent. A drastic variation in worker activity would surely undermine the agency's attempts to demonstrate accountability in services aimed specifically at family preservation (their reason for being).

A second example of a goal for a community-based social service agency could be written as follows:

Agency Goal 2:
The goal of this agency is to help children from low socioeconomic house- holds in Boston (*the client population to be served*) who are obtaining low grades in grade school (*nature of the current social problem to be tackled*) obtain better grades (*general direction of anticipated client change*) in grade school by providing after-school programs within their local communities (*means by which the change is supposed to be brought about*).

Let us look at a third example of an agency's goal. A child protection agency's goal could be as follows:

Agency Goal 3:
The goal of this agency is to provide temporary services (*means by which the change is supposed to be brought about*) to children who are physically and emotionally abused in Boston who are in need of protection from their parents and others (*nature of the current social problem to be tackled and client population to be served*) in order for them to return to their natural homes (*general direction of anticipated client change*).

As stated previously, all social service agencies exist for spe- cific, legitimate social purposes. The purpose may be very broad— to stop family violence in North America, or to provide quality in- home treatment services to families where a child has been placed out of the home—or relatively narrow—to increase a community's awareness of family violence or to increase the socialization of the elderly in a specific community.

As we saw in Chapter 1, an agency can be a small organization, operating from a single facility, or a nationwide endeavor comprising numerous branches at various locations. However small or large, simple or complex, an agency always functions as one entity that is governed by some sort of executive board. This board, via the input of the senior administrator, formally establishes policies and procedures for all of the programs that are guided by the agency's mission statement.

As can be seen in the three examples (i.e., preservation of families, obtaining higher grades, returning home), it should become apparent that an agency goal does not have to follow a specific format: It has to contain only the four elements mentioned above.

AGENCY OBJECTIVES

There is only one objective for an agency. This objective is to establish specific social service programs that will help the agency work toward its overall goal. This means that all programs an agency creates must be logically linked to its goal. In short, no agency should have a program in which the services it delivers, via its programs, cannot be seen to be directly connected to its goal.

In the second goal example, in relation to the community-based social service agency, the agency would be providing programs that help children to obtain better grades. It would not have meals-on-wheels programs, recreation programs, or any other programs that would not work toward the agency's overall goal, or its intended result, of grade improvement for socioeconomically disadvantaged children in Boston.

STEP 2: CREATING PROGRAMS WITHIN AN AGENCY

Whatever the current social problem, the desired future state, or the population it wishes to service, an agency sets up programs to help work toward its intended result—the goal. There are as many ways to define a social work program as there are people willing to define it, and definitions can be overly complicated and complex and use terms such as *inputs, throughputs, outputs*, and *outcomes*.

Definitions of programs can also be very simple (we support this approach). Matters are further muddied by the fact that the term *program* can be used to refer to different levels of service delivery within an agency (see Figures 3.2 and 3.3 for examples). In other words, some types of programs can be seen as subprograms of a larger one, such as the public awareness services under the nonresidential program for the women's shelter as outlined in Figure 3.3.

Putting such complexities to the side, and at the most basic level, a program can be defined according to a simple description of the services it offers. When this is done, a simple program organizational chart can also be used that shows the relationship of the programs to the agency.

The second simple method of defining a program is to use a client path flow that shows the way in which clients move into, through, and out of the program. Despite the differences between the description approach and the client path flow approach, the ultimate purpose of both is to define and represent key elements of the program's structure so that it is understandable.

AN AGENCY VERSUS A PROGRAM

What is the difference between an agency and a program? Like an agency, a program is an organization that also exists to fulfill a social purpose. There is one main difference, however; a program has a narrower, better-defined purpose than does an agency. The child protection agency mentioned earlier, for example, with its goal of protecting children, may have an investigative program: a staff of social workers whose primary function is to investigate allegations that specific children are being neglected or abused. This investigative role can be said to constitute an investigation *program* because the overall goal of the agency—to protect children—has been refined, with an investigation program (which has a narrower purpose)—to investigate child abuse/neglect allegations.

The child protection agency may also have several group homes for children in care—a group home program. It may be involved with treatment foster parents—a treatment foster care program; with public education—an educational program; or with treatment of families who are abusive—a child abuse prevention program. It may run special classes for victims of child abuse and their parents who have to appear in court—a victim-witness program. All of these programs have specialized program objectives (to be discussed later) that contribute to the overall intent or goal of the agency—to protect children.

WHEN AN AGENCY IS A PROGRAM

Sometimes an agency may itself have a narrow, well-defined purpose. The sole purpose of a counseling agency, for example, may be to serve couples who are sexually dysfunctional. In this case, the agency comprises only one program, and the terms *agency* and *program* refer to the same thing. If the clientele happens to include a high proportion of couples who are infertile, for example, it may later be decided that some staff members should specialize in infertility counseling (with a physician as a cocounselor) while other workers continue to deal with all other aspects of sexual dysfunction. In this case, there would then be two distinct sets of social work staff, each one focusing on different goals, and two separate types of clients; that is, there would be two *programs* (one geared toward infertility counseling and the other toward sexual dysfunctioning). Nevertheless, the *agency*, with its board, its senior administrator (executive director), and its administrative policies and procedures would remain.

EXAMPLES OF PROGRAMS

Figure 3.1 presents a simple organizational structure of a family service agency serving families and children. Note how the programs are rationally derived from the agency's main focus (families and children)—only at a more specific level. For example, the agency does not have a program that is geared toward other target groups such as the elderly, or the homeless.

By looking at Figure 3.1, it can be easily seen that this particular family service agency has five programs that deal with the agency's target population of family and children: a group home program for children, a family counseling program, a child adoption program, a treatment foster care program, and a family support program.

FIGURE 3.1   SIMPLIFIED ORGANIZATIONAL CHART FOR A
                       FAMILY SERVICE AGENCY

Figure 3.2 provides another example of an agency that also
deals with families and children. This agency (Richmond Family
Services) has only two programs, a behavioral adaptation treatment
program, and a receiving and assessment family home program.
The receiving and assessment family home program is further
broken down into two components, a family support component
and a receiving and assessment component. The receiving and
assessment component is further broken down into family support
services, child care services, and family home provider services.

How many programs are there in Figure 3.2? The answer is
two—however, we need to note that this agency conceptualized its
service delivery much more thoroughly than did the agency outlined in Figure 3.1. Richmond Family Services has conceptualized
the receiving and assessment component of its receiving and assessment family home program into three separate services: family
support services, child care services, and family home provider
services. In short, Figure 3.2 is much clearer in how it delivers its
services than is the agency represented in Figure 3.1. The clearer,
the better.

Another example of how programs can be organized under an
agency is presented in Figure 3.3. This agency, a women's emergency shelter, has a residential program and a nonresidential program. The residential program has crisis counseling services and
children's support services, whereas the nonresidential program
has crisis counseling services and public awareness services. This
agency distinguishes the services it provides between the women
who stay within the shelter (residential program) and those who
come and go (nonresidential program).

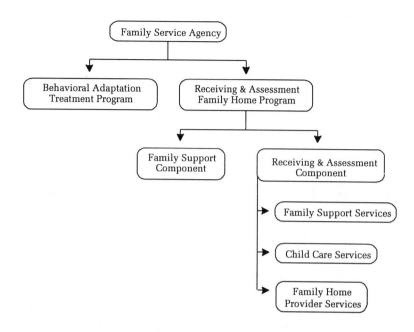

FIGURE 3.2   ORGANIZATIONAL CHART OF A FAMILY
SERVICE AGENCY (HIGHLIGHTING THE
RECEIVING AND ASSESSMENT COMPONENT)

A final example of how an agency can deliver its services is presented in Figure 3.4. As can be seen, the agency's child welfare program is broken down into three services, whereas the native child protection services is broken down into four components: an investigation component, a family service child in parental care component, a family service child in temporary alternate care component, and a permanent guardianship component.

It is unbelievable how many agencies establish programs that have nothing to do with the agency's goal whatsoever. Many times, they establish programs as funds come available for new, but unrelated programs (to the agency's goal that is), and this often coincides with the agency's need to put some of their social workers to work because the program they were working in was just shut down.

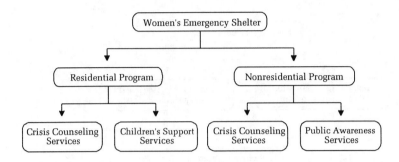

FIGURE 3.3   ORGANIZATIONAL CHART OF A WOMEN'S
                   EMERGENCY SHELTER

ORGANIZING PROGRAMS WITHIN AN AGENCY

By simply glancing at Figures 3.1 to 3.4, it can be seen that how an agency labels its programs and subprograms is totally arbitrary. For example, the agency that represents Figure 3.2 labels its subprograms as components and its sub-subprograms as services. The agency that represents Figure 3.3 simply labels its subprograms as services—not as components as was done in Figure 3.2. The main point is that an agency must structure and conceptualize its programs, components, and services in a logical way that makes the most sense to the agency's overall goal, which is guided my its mission statement and mandate.

There is no systematic approach to naming programs in the social services. Thus, social service programs can be named according to:

- FUNCTION (e.g., Adoption Program, Family Support Program)
- SETTING (e.g., Group Home Program, Residential Program)
- TARGET POPULATION (e.g., Services for the Handicapped Program)
- SOCIAL PROBLEM (e.g., Child Sexual Abuse Program; Behavioral Adaptation Treatment Program)

Program names can include acronyms such as P.E.T. (Parent Effectiveness Training), or catchy titles such as Incredible Edibles

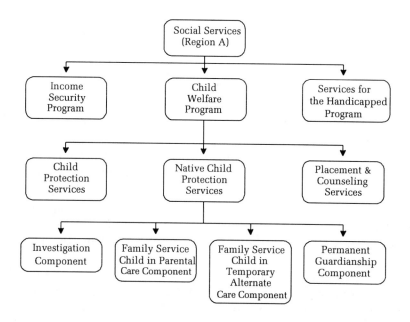

FIGURE 3.4   ORGANIZATIONAL CHART OF A STATE'S SOCIAL SERVICE DELIVERY SYSTEM (HIGHLIGHTING THE NATIVE CHILD PROTECTION SERVICES)

(a nutritional program for children). Whatever the title of a program, we always have to consider the primary purpose. To simplify communication of a program's purpose, we suggest including the target social problem (or the main client need) in the program's name. In this way, a program's name is linked to its goal and there is less confusion about what services it offers.

On the other hand, an elusive program name can lead to confusion in understanding its purpose. A Group Home Program, for example, suggests that the program aims to provide a residence for clients. In fact, all clients residing in the group home do so to fulfill a specific purpose. Depending on the goal of the program, the primary purpose could be to offer shelter and safety for teenage runaways. Or, the program might aim to the enhanced functioning of adolescents with developmental disabilities.

ORGANIZATIONAL STRUCTURES

Another important aspect of a social service agency is its struc-ture. An agency could be organized on hierarchical lines, perhaps with a board of directors at the top, followed by a senior adminis-trator (executive director), an assistant to the senior administrator, team supervisors, clinical social work staff, administrative staff, and so forth.

However, the lines of authority with respect to the educational program within the agency may be somewhat different: Perhaps, for example, a team supervisor has assumed responsibility for the educational activities of the program, and reports directly to the assistant to the senior administrator on these matters without going directly to the senior administrator—as do all the other team super-visors.

A final factor in organizational structure is clients. The people served by our hypothetical sexual abuse treatment program will be, say, sexual abuse victims and their families. The people served by the educational program may include professionals from other agencies, BSW and MSW students, the general public, and parent groups.

As the clients differ, so do the sources that refer them: Referrals for the treatment program may come from the Department of Child Welfare, physicians, lawyers, police officers, friends or family of the victims, or other treatment agencies. Requests for education more commonly come from various community or student groups or from agencies requiring training.

STEP 3: CREATING A PROGRAM GOAL

Probably the most important aspect to remember at this point is that, like an agency's goal, a program's goal must also be compat-ible with the agency's mission statement. Goals must logically flow from the mission statement, as they are announcements of expected outcomes dealing with the social problem that the program is attempting to prevent, eradicate, or ameliorate.

Like an agency's goal, a program's goal is not measurable or achievable—it simply provides a programmatic direction for the program to follow. Like an agency's goal, a program's goal must also possess four characteristics:

- It must identify a current social problem area.
- It must include a specific target population within which the problem resides.
- It must include the desired future state for this population.
- It must state how it plans to achieve the desired state.

Like an agency's goal, a program's goal reflects the fantasies of the social workers who work within the program. The workers may hope that their program will "enable adolescents with developmental disabilities who live in Boston to lead full and productive lives." More importantly, however, the program goal phrase of "full and productive lives" can mean different things to different staff members.

For example, some workers may believe that a full and productive life cannot be lived without an integration into the community. They may ,therefore, want to work toward placing these children in the ordinary school system, enrolling them in community activities, and finally returning them to their parental homes, with a view to making them self-sufficient in adult life. Other staff members may believe that a full and productive life for these children means the security of institutional teaching and care and the companionship of similar children. Still others may believe that institutional care with limited outside contact is the best compromise.

Because these various interpretations of "full and productive life" conflict, the social workers may not be able to agree upon a more exact program goal. The phrase "a full and productive life" may be the best they can do; it may satisfy all of them precisely because it is a vague phrase, empty of content, and therefore open to various interpretations.

Suppose that the workers finally agree that their program goal of Group Home X is "to enable adolescents with developmental disabilities to become self-sufficient adults." The question again arises: What is meant by "self-sufficient?" Does it mean that the children must live in the community when they are adults rather than in a supported environment? Or that they may live in a supported environment but must earn enough money from an outside source to pay for room and board? Does a sheltered workshop count as an outside source? Until it is decided exactly what "self-sufficient" means, the workers cannot know whether the children have become self-sufficient adults and, thus, whether the program has met its goal.

UNINTENDED PROGRAM RESULTS

A program's goal may lead to a number of unintended results. For example, a group home for adolescents with developmental disabilities may strive to enable residents to achieve their full potential in a safe and supportive environment. This is the intended result, or goal. Incidentally, however, the group home may produce organized resistance from neighbors—a negative unintended result. This resistance may draw the attention of the media and allow the difficulties in finding a suitable location for such homes to be highlighted in a sympathetic manner: a positive unintended result.

Meanwhile, the attitude of the community may affect residents to such an extent that they do not feel safe or supported and do not achieve their potential; that is, the home has not achieved its intended result, or goal.

PROGRAM GOALS VERSUS AGENCY GOALS

Perhaps the group home mentioned above is run by an agency that runs a number of other homes for adolescents with developmental disabilities. It is unlikely that all the children in these homes will be capable of self-sufficiency as adults; some may have reached their full potential when they have learned to feed or bathe themselves. The goal of self-sufficiency will, therefore, not be appropriate for the agency as a whole, although it might do very well for Group Home X, which serves children who function at higher levels. The agency's goal must be broader—to encompass a wider range of situations—and because it is broader, it will probably be more vague.

To begin, the agency may decide that its goal is "to enable adolescents with developmental disabilities to reach their full potential" as outlined in Figure 3.5.

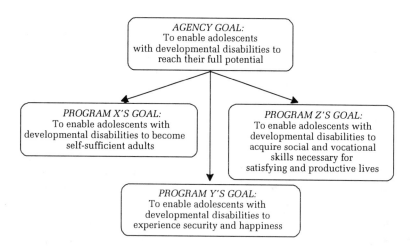

FIGURE 3.5   ORGANIZATIONAL CHART OF AN AGENCY
WITH THREE PROGRAMS

Group Home *X*, one of the programs within the agency, can
then interpret "full potential" to mean self-sufficiency and can
formulate a program goal based on this interpretation.

Group Home *Y*, another program within the agency serving
children who function at lower levels, may decide that it can
realistically do no more than provide a caring environment for the
children and emotional support for the family. It may translate this
decision into another program goal: "To enable adolescents with
developmental disabilities to experience security and happiness."

Group Home *Z*, a third program within the agency, may set as
its program goal "To enable adolescents with developmental disabilities to acquire the social and vocational skills necessary for
satisfying and productive lives."

Figure 3.5 illustrates the relationship among the goals of the
three group homes to the goal of the agency. Note how logical and
consistent the goals of the programs are with the agency's overall
goal. This example illustrates three key points about the character
of a program goal:

- First, a program goal simplifies the reason for the program to
  exist and provides direction for its workers.

- Second, program goals of different but related programs within the same agency may differ, but they must all be linked to the agency's overall goal. They must all reflect both their individual purpose and the purpose of the agency of which they are a part.
- Third, program goals are not *measurable*. Consider the individual goals of the three group homes in Figure 3.5; none of them is measurable in its present form.

Concepts such as happiness, security, self-sufficiency, and full potential mean different things to different people and cannot be measured until they have been clearly defined. Many social work goals are phrased in this way, putting forth more of a vague intent than a definite, definable, measurable purpose. Nor is this a flaw; it is simply what a goal *is*: a statement of an intended result that must be clarified before it can be measured. As we will see next, program goals are clarified by the objectives they formulate.

STEP 4: CREATING PROGRAM OBJECTIVES

A program's objectives are derived from its goal. Program objectives are nothing more than measurable indicators of the goal; they are more specific outcomes that the program wishes to achieve; they are intended results of the goal, only stated clearly and exactly, making it possible to tell to what degree those results have been achieved. All program objectives must be client-centered—they must be formulated to help a client in relation to the social problem articulated by the program goal. Since program objectives are assessed in most types of evaluation, they need to possess four qualities: They must be: (1) meaningful, (2) specific, (3) measurable, and (4) directional.

MEANINGFUL PROGRAM OBJECTIVES

A program objective is *meaningful* when it bears a sensible relationship to the longer-term result to be achieved—the program goal. If a program's goal is to promote self-sufficiency of teenage street people, for example, improving their ability to balance a monthly budget is a meaningful program objective; increasing their ability to recite the dates of the reigns of English monarchs is not, because it bears no relation to the program's goal of self-sufficiency. The point here—and a point that will be stressed over and over in this text—is that an effective social service organization must demonstrate meaningful *linkages* among an agency's overall goal (the reason for being) and its objective (the programs it creates), its programs' goals, and its programs' objectives.

As mentioned before, the overall goal of an agency must be linked to the needs of the people it intends to serve. If these meaningful linkages do not exist—and, furthermore, cannot be *seen* to exist—the organization should probably be dismantled and its funding diverted to other social service organizations that can demonstrate these linkages.

If at all possible, program objectives should be derived from the literature and specified on a meaningful and rational basis. Below is an example of how three meaningful program objectives were derived from the goal of a family preservation program.

- PROGRAM GOAL: To preserve family units where children are at-risk for out-of-home placements due to problems with physical abuse. The program aims to strengthen interpersonal functioning of family members through intensive home-based services.
- PROGRAM OBJECTIVE 1: To increase positive social supports for parents.
- PROGRAM OBJECTIVE 2: To increase problem-solving skills for family members.
- PROGRAM OBJECTIVE 3: To increase parents' use of non-corporal child management strategies.

In the above example, it should be noted that the program objectives are logically linked, in a meaningful way, to the program's goal. We have left out the time frames in which each objective is to be achieved in an effort not to confuse the reader with too much detail at this time. In addition, all program objectives should be formulated, or derived, from the existing literature.

Or to put it another way, the existing literature should provide enough information to support the creation of a program's objectives. It has been our past experience, however, that many social service organizations have program objectives that are not theoretically linked to their program goals via the literature. In addition, it is also unfortunate that many agencies have programs that are not linked to their overall goal, thus decreasing their creditability.

SPECIFIC PROGRAM OBJECTIVES

In addition to being meaningful and logically linked to the program's goal, the program objective must also be *specific*. It must have completeness and clarity in its wording. A simple way to write a specific program objective is to use the following model:

Model:
To (verb) (specific program objective) (time frame).
Example:
To increase (verb) marital satisfaction of the couple (specific program objective) after six sessions (time frame).

Three useful verbs for writing client-centered program objectives are: to increase, to decrease, and to maintain. It must be noted that all three examples of program objectives that were used above began with the words, *to increase.* These objectives would ideally have specific time frames contained within them.

MEASURABLE PROGRAM OBJECTIVES

The third quality required of a program objective is measurability. The purpose of measurement is to define the objective as accurately, completely, and succinctly as possible. A measure is usually thought of as a number: an amount of money in dollars, the length of a depression episode, or scores on simple self-administered standardized measuring instruments.

The purpose of setting a program objective is to effect change, which, if obtained, will contribute to the obtainment of the program's goal. One of the main purposes of making a measurement is to define a perceived change, in terms of either numbers or clear words. A measurement might show, for example, that the assertiveness of a woman who has been previously abused has increased by five points on a standardized measuring instrument (a program objective), or that a woman's sexual satisfaction has increased by 45 points (another program objective). If the hoped-for change cannot be perceived—that is, if it cannot be measured—there is really no point in setting a program objective. Chapter 6 presents a brief discussion of how program objectives can be measured, but, for the time being, we will turn to the fourth important quality of a program objective—directionality.

DIRECTIONAL PROGRAM OBJECTIVES

The final requirement for a program objective is that it must have a direction. All social work interventions are intended to effect some kind of change. That is, interventions are undertaken so that clients will come to have more or less of something than they had before: The level of parenting skills, aggression, racist beliefs, or whatever is to be changed, will have gone up or down. The very idea of change involves direction: Without movement in the direction of less or more, better or worse, higher or lower, no change can occur.

STEP 5: CREATING DIFFERENT KINDS OF PROGRAM OBJECTIVES

Social work programs often are designed to change either a client's knowledge, affects, or behavior. "Affects" here includes attitudes, because attitudes are rarely based on knowledge but more often spring from learned feelings about types of people or things. "Affects" also encompasses belief systems because a belief, by definition, is not knowledge, but is rather a conviction or feeling that something is true. For example, the mother of a child who has been sexually abused might believe that the child is lying and the abuse did not actually occur.

KNOWLEDGE-BASED PROGRAM OBJECTIVES

Knowledge-based program objectives are commonly found within educational programs, where their aim is to increase the client's knowledge in some specific social area. The words "to increase knowledge" are key here: They imply that the recipient of the education will have learned something. The program objective has not been achieved until it can be demonstrated (via measurement) that learning has occurred, and knowledge-based objectives should be written with this in mind.

For example, "to teach teenage mothers the stages of child development between birth and two years" is not a knowledge-based program objective. As will be discussed, teaching is an *activity* that may or may not result in learning. A better program objective would be "to increase the teenage mother's knowledge about the stages of child development between birth and two years." The hoped-for increase in knowledge can then be measured by testing her knowledge levels before and after the material is presented to her.

AFFECTIVE-BASED PROGRAM OBJECTIVES

Affective-based program objectives focus on changing either feelings about oneself or feelings about another person or thing. For example, a common affective-based program objective in social work is to raise a client's self-esteem, and attempts are often made to decrease feelings of isolation, increase marital or sexual satisfaction, and decrease depression. As well, feelings toward other people or things are important in a variety of situations. To give just a few examples, many educational programs try to change public attitudes toward minority groups, homosexuality, or gender roles.

BEHAVIORALLY BASED PROGRAM OBJECTIVES

Very often, a program objective is established to change the behavior of a person or group: to reduce drug abuse among adolescents, to increase the use of community resources by seniors, or to reduce the number of fights a married couple has in a month.

Sometimes, knowledge or affective objectives are used as a means to this end. The social worker might assume that adolescents who know more about the effects of drugs will abuse them less; that seniors who know more about available community resources will use them more often; or that married couples who have more positive feelings toward each other will fight less frequently. Sometimes these assumptions are valid; sometimes they are not. In any case, a responsible worker will verify that the desired behavior change has actually occurred.

STEP 6: CREATING PRACTICE OBJECTIVES WITH CLIENTS

A practice objective refers to the personal objective of an individual client, whether that client is a community, couple, group, individual, or institution. Practice objectives are also called *treatment objectives, individual objectives, therapeutic objectives, client objectives, client goals,* and *client target problems.*

All practice objectives formulated by the social worker and the client must be logically related to the program's objectives, which are linked to the program's goal. In other words, all practice objectives for all clients must be delineated in such a way that they are logically linked to one or more of the program's objectives.

If a social worker formulates a practice objective with a client that does not logically link to one or more of the program's objectives, the social worker may be doing some good for the client but will be harming the program because the program is eventually evaluated on whether its objectives were met. In fact, why would a program hire a social worker to do something the worker was not employed to do? At the risk of sounding redundant, a social service program is always evaluated on its program objectives. Thus, we must fully understand that it is these objectives that we must strive to attain: All of our efforts must be linked to them.

EXAMPLES OF PRACTICE OBJECTIVES

Let us put the concept of a practice objective into concrete terms. By glancing at Figure 3.5 for a moment, imagine that Bob, a resident of Group Home X, is expected to become self-sufficient in order to meet the program's goal, and to achieve his full potential in order to meet the agency's overall goal. But what are Bob's practice objectives? What social, personal, practical, and academic skills does Bob need to acquire in order to achieve self-sufficiency? Three plausible practice objectives in this case might be: to increase Bob's social contacts outside the home, to increase Bob's money management skills, and to increase Bob's language skills.

These three interrelated practice objectives for Bob demonstrate a definite link with the program's objective, which in turn is linked to the program's goal, which in turn in linked to the agency's goal. However, no one can tell, for example, whether Bob has made "more social contacts outside the home" until a "social contact" has been defined more precisely. Does saying "hello" to a fellow worker count as a social contact? It may that Bob is habitually silent at work. For a different individual, a social contact may involve going on an outing with fellow workers, or attending a recreational program at a community center.

It should be evident by now that defining a practice objective is a matter of stating what is to be changed. This provides an indication of the client's current state, or where the client is. Unfortunately, knowing this is not the same thing as knowing where one wants to go. Sometimes the destination is apparent, but in other cases it may be much less clear.

Suppose that Jane, for example, has presented job dissatisfaction as a general problem area. Enquiry has elicited that her dissatisfaction has nothing to do with the work itself, nor with the people at work, nor such job-related factors as advancement, pay, benefits, and vacations. Instead, her dissatisfaction springs from the fact that she is spending too much time at work and too little time with her children.

Various practice objectives are possible here. Perhaps Jane should try to find a different, less demanding, full-time job; or maybe she should improve her budgeting skills so that her family can manage if she works only part-time. Perhaps she should make different arrangements for her children's care, so that she feels more comfortable about their welfare. Or maybe the real problem is that she herself feels torn between pursuing a career and being a full-time mother. It may be that what she really wants is to stay home with her children, provided that she can do so without guilt, with her partner's support, and without undue financial stress.

It is apparent that Jane's underlying problem has not yet been really defined. Often, an attempt to formulate a practice objective—to specify where Jane and the practitioner want to go—will reveal that Jane is not where she thought she was; that the problem so carefully elicited by the worker is not Jane's *real* problem after all. If this is the case, additional exploration is needed to redefine the problem before trying, once again, to set the practice objective.

When the real problem has been defined, the next task is to establish a related practice objective. If possible, it should be couched in positive terms, that is, in terms of what the client should do or feel rather than in terms of what she should not. For example, if the problem is Antoinette's immaturity, and "immaturity" is operationalized to mean getting out of her seat at school without permission, then one natural practice objective is "to decrease the number of times Antoinette gets out of her seat without permission." But it may be written just as usefully, "to increase the length of time Antoinette stays in her seat during class." Many practice objectives that are aimed at decreasing a negative quality can be reformulated to increase a positive quality while still achieving the desired change.

Finally, practice objectives must be comprehensive and precise. Each one must stipulate what is to be achieved, under what conditions, to what extent, and by whom.

STEP 7: CREATING PRACTICE ACTIVITIES WITH CLIENTS

Most of this chapter has focused on the kinds of goals and objectives that social workers hope to achieve as a result of their work. The question now arises: What is that work? What do social workers *do* in order to help clients achieve higher knowledge levels, feelings, or behaviors? The answer, of course, is that they do many different things. They show films, facilitate group discussions, hold therapy sessions, teach classes, and conduct individual interviews. They attend staff meetings, do paperwork, consult with colleagues, and advocate for clients.

Clients also engage in activities: They attend therapy sessions, participate in discussions, complete homework assignments, and do a great deal of intensive, internal work.

The important point about all such activities is that they are undertaken to attain specific practice objectives that relate to one or more of the program's objectives. A social worker who teaches a class on nutrition hopes that class participants will learn certain specific facts about nutrition. If this learning is to take place, the facts to be learned must be included in the material presented. In other words, our activities must be directly related to our practice objectives. In this example, it is assumed that one of the program's objectives has to do with nutrition or we would not be teaching the nutritional material in the first place.

This may seem so self-evident as to be not worth mentioning. If no related activities are undertaken to achieve a practice objective, it is obviously foolish to expect that the objective will be achieved. Nevertheless, an amazing number of social work programs exist in which the activities performed by social workers seem to have nothing much to do with their practice objectives—or with the program's objectives.

It is critically important that a social worker who sets a practice objective should also specify what activities will be undertaken to accomplish it and what measures (if any) will determine whether it is achieved. Over the years we have seen numerous instances in which social workers say they are trying to raise their clients' self-esteem. When asked what specific activities they are doing to achieve this notable objective, they reply, "nothing specific, just supporting them when they need it." It is rather foolish to believe that merely seeing a client on a crisis basis will raise his or her self-esteem. Specific treatment interventions must be employed to raise the self-esteem of clients; it will not raise automatically.

Below are the goal and one of eight program objectives for a social service program that helps pregnant teenagers in high school. Also included is the measurement of the program objective. In addition, two practice objectives (A and B) are outlined and their corresponding measurements are given. Practice activities that are believed to achieve the two program objectives are also delineated. Notice the consistency between the concepts of the program's goal, the stated program's objective, the two practice objectives related to the program's objective, the various activities, and the two measurements.

- PROGRAM GOAL: To provide social services to pregnant teenagers in high school who have elected to keep their babies in an effort for them to become adequate mothers when they graduate from high school.

- PROGRAM OBJECTIVE: To increase the self-sufficiency of pregnant adolescents after they have their babies.
  — *Measurement of Program Objective:* Self-Sufficiency Inventory.

- PRACTICE OBJECTIVE (A): To increase parenting skills.
  — *Measurement of Practice Objective (A):* Adult-Adolescent Parenting Inventory.
  — *Practice Activities (A):* Teach specific child-rearing skills, role-model/role play effective parenting skills, teach effective child/adult communication skills, teach and model alternative discipline measures, teach age-appropriate response of children, and establish family structure (e.g., meal times, bath times, and bed times).
- PRACTICE OBJECTIVE (B): To increase the number of support systems knowledgeable to the client.
  — *Measurement of Practice Objective (B):* Instrument specially constructed for the particular city. To show how simple measuring instruments can be, Figure 3.6 presents one that was used with this practice objective. Figure 3.7 presents the correct answers.
  — *Practice Activities (B):* Review the city's information resource book with the client, provide information sheet on key resources relevant to the client, provide brochures on various agencies, escort client to needed resources (e.g., career resource center, health clinic), and go through specific and appropriate sections of the Yellow Pages with the client.

If a certain set of practice activities is successful in achieving a practice objective, we may want to repeat these activities with another client who has a similar problem. This will not be possible unless we have kept a careful record of what we did; that is, unless the activities, too, have been clearly defined. The definition of an activity usually involves a careful description of what precisely was done; when, where, how, and by whom it was done; and in what order it was done.

Such a record will enable us to know more exactly which interventions produced which results. In other words, specifying the activities to be undertaken in order to achieve a certain practice objective is another example of establishing *links*. Figure 3.8 presents

The following is a list of questions regarding resources available in the
Calgary area. Please write down as many resources as you know about
in responding to each question.

1. Where would you go for help in caring for your children?
2. Where would you go for financial assistance?
3. Where would you go for help with parenting?
4. Where would you go for medical assistance or information?
5. Where would you go for information on improving your
    education?
6. Whom would you call to help at home?
7. Where would you go for help in finding a job?
8. Where would you go to get help in finding a place to stay?
9. Who would you call if you had an immediate crisis?
10. Where would you go for assistance for food or clothing?
11. Where would you go for legal assistance?
12. Where would you go for counseling?

FIGURE 3.6   QUESTIONNAIRE ON SUPPORT
                        SYSTEMS IN CALGARY

a graphic example of how practice activities are linked to practice
objectives, which are linked to program objectives, which are linked
to the program goal.

In addition, Figure 3.9 provides a brief example of how a program
goal has derived three program objectives, and each program objective
(with literary support) has sample activities that the social workers do
to achieve the program objectives. In addition, measuring instruments
that measure the program objectives are included. Note how Figure
3.9 flows from the logic presented in Figure 3.8.

STEP 8: CREATING MAINTENANCE OBJECTIVES FOR A PROGRAM

Readers should note that in this text the term *program objectives*
is understood as being client related. That is, we view a program's
maintenance objectives (such as to provide 5,000 hours of counseling,
to admit 432 more clients by the end of the year, to enroll 35 adoles-

1. Alberta Social Services, Community Daycare/Day Home, City of Calgary Social Services, Children's Cottage

2. Alberta Social Services, church, Alberta Consumer Corporate Affairs, Alberta Student Finance Board

3. Calgary Health Services, family doctor, Parent Support Association, Calgary Association of Parents, Parent Aid, City of Calgary Social Services, Children's Hospital

4. Family doctor, hospitals, Calgary Birth Control Association, Calgary Health Services, Birthrite

5. Alberta Vocational College, Viscount Bennet School, SAIT, Mount Royal College, Canada Manpower, Alberta Social Services, Women's Career Center, Louise Dean School, University of Calgary

6. Homemaker Services (FSB), Landlord & Tenant Board, Calgary Housing Authority, Relief Society (Mormon Church), Alberta Social Services, City of Calgary Social Services

7. Alberta Social Services, Canada Manpower, Career Center, Volunteer Center, Hire-A-Student, newspapers, 12 Avenue, job boards

8. Alberta Social Services, YWCA Single Mother Program, Renfrew Recovery, Women's Emergency Shelter, Park Wood House, Discovery House, church, Avenue 15, Single Men's Hostel, JIMY Program, Alpha House, Sheriff King, McMan Youth Services, Birthrite

9. Emergency Social Services, Distress Center, Sexual Assault Center, Suicide Line (CMH), Children's Cottage, Wood's Stabilization Program, Alberta Children's Hospital, church, police/fire department

10. Interfaith Food Bank, Milk Fund, Salvation Army, church, Emergency Social Services, Alberta Social Services

11. Legal Aid, Legal Guidance, University of Calgary Legal Line, Women's Resource Center, Women's Shelter, Dial-A-Law

12. Family Service Bureau, church, Alberta Mental Health, Pastoral Institute, Sexual Assault Center, Children's Cottage, Alberta Social Services, City of Calgary Social Services, Catholic Family Services, Parents Anonymous, Distress Center

Note: Clients may respond to the questionnaire with answers not listed above but which may be entirely appropriate to their own unique situations and thus be evaluated as correct.

FIGURE 3.7   ANSWERS TO QUESTIONNAIRE ON SUPPORT
SYSTEMS IN CALGARY (FIGURE 3.6)

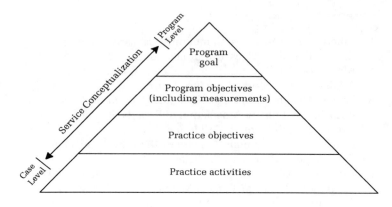

FIGURE 3.8   A PROGRAM LOGIC MODEL FOR
                        CONCEPTUALIZING TREATMENT SERVICES

cents in a certain program by a certain time) as necessary in order for
that program to survive, but hardly as criteria by which to evaluate
whether the program is delivering quality services to its clients.

If a program is to survive, it must set maintenance objectives.
These objectives are formulated in an effort to keep the program
financially viable and involves such maintenance objectives as "to
increase private donations by 25 percent in 1998," "to recruit 25
volunteers in 1998," "to increase the number of billable hours by 25
percent in 1998," "to have three individuals complete the internship
program by July 1, 1998," and "to recruit and utilize four volunteers
in covering the telephone lines."

Maintenance objectives that deal with training staff, recruiting
clients, acquiring improved equipment, or restructuring the organization are all maintenance objectives. Thus, program objectives are
constructed for the client's benefit, whereas maintenance objectives
are constructed for the program's benefit. We should, however, be
clear about how these two purposes relate to each other. Maintenance
objectives, although necessary to the program's continued existence,
are not why the program is being funded. A program is not funded
merely to exist and perpetuate itself; it is funded to deliver a social
service. Maintenance objectives are to programs what food is to human beings: We need to eat, we may even get great pleasure from
eating, but in the final analysis we do not live to eat—we eat to live.

FAMILY PRESERVATION PROGRAM

Program Goal and Philosophy

To preserve family units where children are at-risk for out-of-home placement due to problems with physical abuse (goal). The program aims to strengthen interpersonal functioning of family members through intensive home-based services (philosophy).

Program Objectives

1. *To increase positive social support for parents.*
   - *Literary Support:* A lack of positive social support has been repeatedly linked to higher risk for child abuse. Studies indicate that parents with greater social support and less stress report more pleasure in their parenting roles.
      - *Sample of Activities:* Refer to support groups; evaluate criteria for positive support; introduce to community services; reconnect clients with friends and family.
      - *Measuring Instruments:* Client log; *Provision of Social Relations* (Turner, Frankel, & Levin, 1987).

2. *To increase problem-solving skills for family members.*
   - *Literary Support:* Problem solving is a tool for breaking difficult dilemmas into manageable pieces. Enhancing individuals' skills in systematically addressing problems increases the likelihood that they will successfully tack new problems as they arise. Increasing problem-solving skills for parents and children equips family members to handle current problems, anticipate and prevent future ones, and advance their social functioning.
      - *Sample of Activities:* Teach specific steps to problem solving; role-play problem-solving scenarios; supportive counseling.
      - *Measuring Instrument: The Problem-Solving Inventory* (Heppner, 1987).

3. *To increase parents' use of noncorporal child management strategies.*
   - *Literary Support:* Research studies suggest that deficiency in parenting skills is associated with higher recurrence of abuse. Many parents who abuse their children have a limited repertoire of ways to discipline their children.
      - *Sample of Activities:* Teach noncorporal discipline strategies; inform parents about the criminal implications of child abuse; assess parenting strengths; provide reading material about behavior management.
      - *Measuring Instruments:* Goal Attainment Scaling; Checklist of Discipline Strategies.

FIGURE 3.9   PROGRAM-LEVEL SERVICE CONCEPTUALIZATION

SUMMARY

This chapter discussed what is meant by an agency, a program, a program goal and objective, a practice objective, a measurement, and an activity. Most importantly, it discussed the linkages that must exist among these elements.

OUTCOME EVALUATION

A PROGRAM OUTCOME EVALUATION does nothing more than evaluate a program's objectives. As we know from the previous chapter, program outcomes are what we expect clients to achieve by the time they leave a social service program. In most cases, we expect some positive change for the recipients of our services. When clients show improvement we can feel optimistic that the program has had a positive impact on their lives.

A critical aspect of program outcome evaluation is that we must have a clear sense of what expected changes (the program's outcomes) we hope to see; as we know, these changes are not freely decided upon. As we have seen in Chapter 3, program objectives are developed by giving consideration to the views of stakeholders, as well as to the knowledge gained from the existing literature, practice wisdom, and the current political climate. When program objectives are developed using the strategies proposed in the previous chapter, they have a solid foundation on which to rest and serve to guide day-to-day program activities. Thus, by evaluating a program's objectives, we are, in effect, testing hypotheses about how we think clients will change after a period of time in our program. We would hope that clients participating in the family preservation program (introduced in Chapter 3), for example, will show favorable improvement on the program's objectives. This chapter uses the family preservation program as an example of how to develop a simple and straightforward program outcome evaluation.

In a nutshell, the program outcomes we eventually evaluate are nothing more than the operationalization of our program objectives. If we have not succinctly stated a program's objectives, however, any efforts at outcome evaluation are futile, at best. This fact places some social service programs in a bind because of the difficulty they face in defining concepts (or social problems) such as homelessness, self-esteem, child neglect, child abuse, and violence. Most of these concepts are multi-faceted and cannot be solved by focusing on any one particular simple program objective (e.g., behavior, knowledge, or affect). Thus, we must be modest about our abilities as helping professionals and feel comfortable with the fact that we can assess only one small component of a complex social problem through the efforts of a single social service program. Let us now turn our attention to the purpose of doing an outcome evaluation.

PURPOSE OF PROGRAM OUTCOME EVALUATION

The main purpose of a program outcome evaluation is to demonstrate the nature of change, if any, for our clients after they have received our services—that is, after they have left the program. Given the complexity of many social problems that social service programs tackle, we must think about program outcome evaluation as an integral part of the initial conceptualization and final operationalization of a program. Suppose, for example, we wanted to evaluate one program objective—to increase parents' knowledge about parenting skills—for parents who participate in a family preservation program (the Program). If our Program serves 10 parents and runs for 10 weeks, we gain a limited amount of knowledge by evaluating one round of the Program's objective (to increase parents' knowledge about parenting skills). If we evaluate this single program objective each time and monitor the results over a two-year period, however, we will have much more confidence in the Program's results.

There are many reasons for wanting to monitor and evaluate a program's objectives. One reason is to give concrete feedback to a program's stakeholders, including clients. As we know, a program's goal and its related objectives are dynamic and change over time. These changes are influenced by the political climate, organizational restructuring, economic conditions, clinical trends, staff turnover, and administrative preferences. In addition, sometimes a program's goal and objectives are changed or modified because of the results from a program evaluation.

Another reason for doing a program outcome evaluation is that we can demonstrate accountability in terms of showing whether or not a social service program is achieving its promised program objectives. In this spirit, a program outcome evaluation plan serves as a program map—it is a tool for telling us where we are headed and the route we plan to take to arrive at our destination. This focus helps to keep program administrators and workers in sync with the program's mandate (which is reflected in the program's goal). If an outcome evaluation is positive, we then have more justification to support the program.

On the other hand, if the evaluation of a program's objectives turns out to be poor, we can investigate the reasons why this is so. In either case, we are working with data in which to make informed case and program decisions. Because we want our clients to be successful in achieving our program's objective(s), we select activities that we believe have the greatest chance of creating positive client change. Selecting activities in this way increases the likelihood that a program's objectives, the practice objectives, and the practice activities have a strong and logical link (see Figure 3.8).

Social service programs are designed to tackle many complex social problems such as child abuse, poverty, depression, mental illness, and discrimination. As we saw in Chapter 3, programs must develop realistic program objectives, given what is known about a social problem, the resources available, and the time available to clients. Unfortunately, we attempt to do more than is realistically possible. Evaluating a program's objectives gives us data from which to decide what can be realistically accomplished. By selecting a few key program objectives, for example, we can realistically place limits on what workers can actually accomplish. It also places limits on the nature of practice activities that workers might engage in. Suppose, for example, the family preservation program begins to receive referrals of childless couples who are experiencing violence in their relationships. Rather, than try to alter the Program to meet clients whose problems and needs do not fit, the Program can educate its referral sources about the type of services it offers and the nature of the clientele it serves.

A program outcome evaluation is always designed for a specific social service program. Thus, the results tell us about specific program objectives and not general social indicators. A four-week unemployment program showing that 75 percent of its clients found employment after being taught how to search for jobs cannot make any claims about impacting the general unemployment rate. The results are *specific* to one *specific* group of clients, experiencing the *specific* conditions of one *specific* program over a *specific* time frame at a *specific* time.

USES OF PROGRAM OUTCOME EVALUATION

Given that a program outcome evaluation focuses on the program's objectives when clients exit a program, its uses may seem, at first blush, to be quite limited. The outcomes of a program's objectives, however, are pivotal points at which clients leave a program and begin life anew—equipped with new knowledge, skills, affects, or behaviors related to a specific social problem. Therefore, evaluating the outcomes of a program's objectives gives us important information that can be used in three ways. An outcome evaluation can: (1) improve program services to clients, (2) generate knowledge for the profession, and (3) estimate costs.

IMPROVING PROGRAM SERVICES TO CLIENTS

A primary use of any program outcome evaluation is to improve a program's services that it delivers to clients. As we know, a program outcome evaluation evaluates a program's objectives. Thus, data collected in an outcome evaluation tells us things like how many clients achieved a program objective(s) and how well the objective(s) was achieved. Suppose, for example, a rural child abuse prevention program has as one of its program's objectives:

Program Objective:
To increase parents' awareness of crisis services available to them.

At the end of our program, however, we learn that, for 80 percent of our parents, their awareness level of the available crisis services remained the same. Looking into the matter further, we find that there is only one crisis service available to parents living in the rural area and the majority of parents knew about this service before they became clients of the child abuse prevention program. In other instances, our program objectives may expect too much, given the amount of time clients are exposed to the program.

Ideally, a program outcome evaluation should have a major impact on concrete program decisions. Realistically, however, the data from a program outcome evaluation have few major direction-changing decisions. It is more likely that its results will assist us in resolving some of our doubts and confusion about a program or will support facts that we already know. The results contribute independent information to the decision-making process rather than carrying all the weight of a decision. The findings assist us by reducing uncertainty, speeding things up, and getting things started.

When outcome data (program objectives) are routinely collected, results can be reviewed and compared at regular intervals. By reviewing outcome data, we improve on our ability to identify problem areas and any trends occurring over time. Such analyses assist us in pinpointing areas of the program that need further attention.

GENERATING KNOWLEDGE FOR THE PROFESSION

Evaluating a program's objectives can also lead us to gain new insight and knowledge about a social problem. As we saw in Chapter 3, program objectives are derived, in part, from what we know about a social problem (based on the literature and previous research studies). Thus, when we evaluate a program's objectives, we are in effect testing hypotheses—one hypothesis for each program objective. We make an assumption that clients who receive a program's services will show a positive change on each program objective more so than if they did not receive the services. How well we are able to test each hypothesis (one for each program objective) depends on the research design used (see Chapter 8).

If we simply compare pretest and posttest data, for example, we can say only that client change occurred over the time the program was offered, but we cannot be certain that the program caused the observed changes. On the other hand, if we use an experimental design and are able to randomly assign clients to a treatment and a control group, we will arrive at a more conclusive answer. The results obtained from a program evaluation provide supporting pieces of "effectiveness," rather than evidence of any "absolute truths." Much more will be said about this in Chapter 8.

ESTIMATING COSTS

Administrators of social service programs are concerned with the costs associated in producing their programs' objectives. While improving human lives and social conditions is a priority of all social service programs, we are expected to accomplish a program's objectives in an efficient manner. A social service program is cost-effective if it is able to achieve its specified program objectives in relation to it costs. A program is considered cost-efficient when it is able to achieve its program objectives at lower cost, compared to another program striving for the same program objectives.

A "probation program," for example, costs less than a "jail program" simply because the probation program is not required to have 24-hour supervision, an institutional facility, and so on. If the probation program is successful in preventing future criminal behavior, the savings are even higher. Costs associated with prevention, however, are difficult to estimate because we cannot know for certain whether the absent problem was a result of the program.

The simplest way to calculate the cost of a program is to first determine the total amount of monies spent on program operations. These expenditures include costs associated with personnel (e.g., salaries, benefits, training), facilities (e.g., office space, computers, telephone, photocopying), clients (e.g., petty cash, special services, food), and other needs of the program. Once the overall costs have been determined, we simply divide this amount by the total number of clients served for that fiscal period. The result will be the "outside" cost of how much the program spent per client. For more detailed information on program effectiveness, we need to pay attention to program structure and process, which are covered in Chapter 5. The figures we end up with for these calculations fluctuate depending on what we have included in program costs and how we have counted clients.

Neither of these tasks is as straightforward as it may seem. Do we include overtime, secretarial support, and advertising in our program costs, for example? In the case of counting clients, do we include repeat clients, or clients who drop out of the program after the first day? Do we factor in clients who call the program for information but never actually participate? The way a social service program is conceptualized has a considerable influence on the way data are collected and analyzed in any evaluation plan.

STEPS IN PROGRAM OUTCOME EVALUATION

In Chapter 3, we discussed how to conceptualize a program by defining its goal and stating its related objectives. A program outcome evaluation plan is unique to the context of the program for which it was designed. Using the family preservation program as an example, there are six major steps in conducting an outcome evaluation: (1) operationalizing program objectives, (2) selecting the measurements and stating the outcomes, (3) designing a monitoring system, (4) analyzing and displaying data, (5) developing a feedback system, and (6) disseminating and communicating results.

STEP 1: OPERATIONALIZING PROGRAM OBJECTIVES

An outcome evaluation is a major collaborative effort. It is most successful when staff are included in its design and implementation. In programs where an "outcome evaluation mentality" does not exist, staff should be included in their conceptualization. Eventually, as programs evolve to integrate evaluation activities with practice activities, planning for an outcome evaluation becomes an integral part of day-to-day program activities. If a program has clearly defined its goal and program-related objectives, the first step in an outcome evaluation is nearly done. Theoretically, a program's objectives should be tied to theory. Thus, an outcome evaluation, in effect, is theory-driven.

By focusing on a program's objectives, we can be sure that we will not unnecessarily collect data on variables we do not want to know about. It is very tempting, for example, for program administrators—and workers alike—to make a last-minute decision to include an "interesting question" on an intake form or some other data recording instrument. However, data are expensive to collect and analyze. Thus, all data collected should be directly related to a program's objectives. Resources spent on collecting "extra" data detract from the quality of the data collected to monitor a program's objectives. In other words, straying from a program's data collection plan seriously compromises the results of a carefully designed outcome evaluation plan.

Operationalizing a program's objectives is a critical task because it defines how we understand our overall program in concrete terms. In Chapter 6, we will discuss the various ways in which we can measure a program's objectives. For now, we need to know only that we can measure them in several ways. As we saw above, one of the program objectives in the family preservation program is "to increase problem-solving skills of family members." We need to determine specifically how program staff define "problem-solving skills of family members." Is problem solving the skill whereby family members apply prescribed steps in the problem solving process? Is it the number of problems they successfully solve in a given day? Is it problem solving in a general sense or problem solving that is specific to family conflict?

Clearly, there are a many ways to operationalize problem solving. To ensure that the program objective remains linked with the broader expectation of the program, we can look for direction at the program's goal. As a guide, the program goal is more helpful in telling us what problem-solving is not, rather than what it is.

While the idea of operationalizing a social service program's objectives is relatively straightforward, we must be aware that there are many factors influencing the task. Evaluation of a program's objectives is more often than not an uphill battle. This is because major stakeholders want (and often demand) concrete objective results. Given the difficulties faced with measuring change in a client's self-esteem, for example, programs often opt to monitor variables such as the number of clients served in a given year and the number of hours of direct-service contact between social workers and clients. While these performance data are important to decision making around client services and worker supervision, they seriously misguide the direction of a program. If, in fact, performance measures are used to define program outcomes, then social workers focus on maximizing direct service time without necessarily giving thought to how such time is spent or what it will accomplish.

Even more serious, by focusing on these types of outcomes, a program is at-risk for developing an unhealthy culture among its workers. If workers in the family preservation program were to focus on increasing the number of direct service hours spent with clients, for example, then we might easily become misled into thinking that the social worker who spends the greatest number of hours in direct service hours with clients is in fact the "best" social worker. It may be, however, that this practitioner's work does not benefit clients at all.

Focusing on these operational statistics has an important role for administrative decision making and should be included in process evaluations (Chapter 5). However, when these types of objectives are included as part of an outcome evaluation, they can undermine staff morale because social workers are forced to define their work by meaningless outcome measures.

STEP 2:   SELECTING THE MEASUREMENTS
AND STATING THE OUTCOMES

Selecting the best measurements for a program's objectives is a critical part of an outcome evaluation and requires a great deal of forethought. As we will see in later chapters, data can be collected using data collection methods such as standardized self-report measuring instruments, self-report questionnaires, and self-anchored scales.

To measure Program Objective 2 in our family preservation program, for example, we could use a standardized measuring instrument that has high validity and reliability:

Program Objective 2 (from Figure 3.9):
To increase problem-solving skills for family members.

If no such instrument was available, or using a questionnaire was not feasible, we might ask clients a few direct questions about their problem-solving skills. We might ask clients to talk about a problem solving example in the past day and count the number of steps to problem solving that were applied. We could also rely on the individual client's own perspective and ask, "Since completing the program have your skills at problem solving improved?" We could ask the client to respond "yes" or "no," or have the client rate the degree of improvement on five-point scale, where "1" means problem-solving skills are worse, "3" means they are about the same, and "5" means they have improved.

There are many different ways to measure outcomes, ranging from simple to complex. Chapter 6 presents the importance of validity and reliability in choosing measuring instruments. At the very least, we can put our efforts into making sure that the measurements of our program objectives have face validity. We want each question (in addition to the whole questionnaire) to:

- directly relate to the program objective being measured,
- be part of a group of questions that together directly assess the program objective, and
- provide descriptive data that will be useful in the analysis of our findings.

Once we have determined what measuring instrument(s) is going to be used to measure each program objective and who will provide the data (data source), we need to pretest or pilot test the instrument(s). A pilot test helps to ascertain whether in fact the instrument produces the desired data, as well as whether any obstacles got in the way, such as when instructions are not clear or too many questions are asked at one time.

Therefore, we want to pilot test all instruments at all phases of an outcome evaluation, including pretest, in-program, posttest, and follow-up. Because we are interested in collecting data *about* (and not *from*) the data collection instrument (and not the content of our questions), we want to observe how clients react to completing it. To gain more information about the clients' understanding of questions, we might ask them to verbalize their thinking as they answer a question or ask them to comment on the process of providing the data.

When a self-report measuring instrument is used to measure a program objective, we need to check the accuracy of the data it generates by using multiple data sources in the pilot study. In using self-report data, for example, we might ask clients for their permission to interview a family member or another person familiar with the problem. Since we are only pilot testing the self-report instrument, we might ask the opinion of the social worker currently working with the client. This pilot testing activity gives us greater confidence as to whether we can rely on only client self-report data that will be collected later on in the program outcome evaluation.

If we are having difficulty choosing between two closely related measuring instruments, or are having difficulty with the wording of a difficult question, we could ask clients to respond to two options and ask which one they prefer, and why. We need to give extra attention to clients who do not complete measuring instruments or refuse to respond to certain questions. In these cases, we need to explore the reasons why a certain type of client did not answer, and we must do so in a manner that is sensitive to the client's needs.

After a measuring instrument that is used to measure a program objective has been selected and pretested, it is essential to establish clear procedures for scoring it. Scoring instructions accompany most standardized measuring instruments. Thus, we need to decide only who will be responsible for carrying out the scoring task.

When a program develops it own nonstandardized measuring instrument, it is necessary to agree upon a systematic set of procedures for administering and scoring the instrument. Suppose, for example, that to measure Program Objective 2 in the family preservation program mentioned above, we ask clients to talk out loud about a problem they encountered in the past week and to tell us the steps they took in solving the problem. Given that client responses will vary, we would need a consistent way to determine what steps were taken. First, we must agree, as a program, on what the steps of problem solving are. Second, we need to examine the possible range of responses provided by clients. We might use several raters in the pilot test to establish a protocol for scoring and, later, use the established procedures to train the people who collect the data.

Measurement is a critical aspect of all types of evaluations and should not be taken lightly. Where possible, we need to look for means and methods to corroborate our data-generated results and strengthen the credibility of our results. Without at least minimal pretesting of a measurement instrument, we cannot be confident about its ability to provide accurate data.

Step 3: Designing a Monitoring System

There are many procedural matters that must be thought through in carrying out a program outcome evaluation, and the evaluation is more likely to go smoothly when these matters are considered in advance. Practical steps are dictated by the need to minimize cost and maximize the number of clients included in the evaluation.

Time and resources are important considerations for developing an outcome evaluation design. As we saw in Chapter 1, the monitoring approach to evaluation incorporates evaluation activities and tasks into ongoing client service delivery. Thus, we must be careful not to overburden the workers, such that direct client service delivery is compromised. To gather valid and reliable data, we must consider type and amount of changes we expect from social workers.

How we design our evaluation can impact when social workers meet with their clients. It may also change the nature of worker-client interaction in a first meeting, as is the case when standardized measuring instruments are administered. Evaluation activity almost always affects the way social workers record client data. Because these evaluation activities directly impact a social worker's behavior, they have important implications for how clients are served and how evaluation data are collected.

Deciding the Number of Clients to Include (Unit of Analysis)

In general, we want to collect outcome data for as many clients as possible in an outcome evaluation. For programs with a few clients, such as a single group home program, or a private social worker working independently, 100 percent coverage of clients served is more likely. For programs with many clients, such as child protection services, or a major family service agency, we can use basic sampling techniques to develop a representative sample of all clients receiving services. The major issue affecting sample size, however, is whether or not program resources exist to collect data from all clients in the program. If it is not feasible to do so—an independent private social worker cannot afford to include 30 minutes of testing for each client, or a family service agency does not want to give up valuable "client time" for evaluation activities—then, sampling is an option.

The number of clients needed for an outcome evaluation is affected by the number of subgroups that may be included in the evaluation. Suppose for example, the family preservation program wants to compare the levels of problem-solving skills (Program Objective 2) for single- and double-parent families. Ideally, we want to have roughly equivalent groups so that we do not end up comparing, say, 120 single parents with 240 double parents. Clearly, the double parent families are better represented in this comparison. Ideally, we should aim to have a minimum of 30 clients for each subgroup included in our analyses. The more subgroups we include (say we are also interested in the age of parents, whether substance abuse is a factor or what services the family has used previously) the more clients we need.

When there are not enough resources to support data collection from all clients, the task can be lightened by randomly selecting clients for inclusion in the evaluation. Random selection can occur so long as the program aims to have a reasonable number of clients at critical points within the data analysis, such as when the program's annual or semi-annual report are due. The idea behind random sampling is that each client has an equal chance of being included in the evaluation. In theory, this is a simple notion. In practice, however, there are many obstacles to consider.

The first matter to consider is deciding the total client population served by the program. In the family preservation program, for example, it may be that parents periodically phone the program for crisis support and speak to a social worker on the telephone for a brief period; or at times, an inappropriate referral is made and program time is used to reroute the client to a better matched service. While these clients may receive some assistance from the family preservation program, it would be unreasonable and even unimaginable to try and collect data related to the program's objectives. Rather, the family preservation program has as its primary client group families who are referred and accepted to the program to participate in the 12-week intervention.

Since clients of the family preservation program are referred on an ongoing basis, it is possible for random selection to occur by including every second or third client referred or by flipping a coin ("heads" the family is included, "tails" they are not) each time a client comes to the program, with a predetermined maximum number. If we are particularly interested in how outcomes relate to specific client groups (e.g., single- and double-parent families), we can use a stratified sampling strategy. The critical aspect of random selection is that the decision to include clients is made without bias. That is, a program administrator does not select families because they appear to be cooperative, or social workers do not exclude families because they are concerned that the families might not respond positively toward the program.

The philosophy behind monitoring evaluation is that evaluation is part and parcel of good practice. Just as we allow clients the right to self-determinism—to say whether or not a particular intervention fits for them—we must also be willing to give clients the option to participate in evaluation activity. When clients decline to answer questions or fill out questionnaires, then we are faced with the problem of missing data. That is, we will have some unknowns in our final client sample. The less missing data we have, the more confident we will be that our evaluation results are reflective of all clients served within our program.

Another matter to decide in sampling is whether we want to collect data from the *same* clients throughout the entire evaluation (a cohort analysis) or whether we want to collect data from a *different* set of clients at program intake and exit (a cross-sectional analysis). A cohort analysis permits us to address questions of change over time for a single group of clients. We could then compare, for example, the percentage of clients who showed an improvement in their problem-solving skills, and the amount of change.

A cross-sectional analysis would give us a slightly different set of data. In this case, we could determine the percentage of improvement in the average score for clients at intake (Time 1) and at termination (Time 2). We could not indicate how many clients' problem-solving skills got better or worse, however.

The advantage of using the same clients throughout the entire evaluation is that it reduces the difficulties associated with comparing two different groups of clients. The drawback of including only one set of clients in the evaluation is that they may, in effect, receive special treatment as a result of their inclusion, which will bias the representativeness of the results to the entire program.

DECIDING WHEN DATA WILL BE COLLECTED

When the data are collected directly relates to the question asked in outcome evaluation. An outcome evaluation indicates *whether* the program is working, but it says nothing about *how* it is working (or failing to work). Nor is there any mention of efficiency—that is, the time and dollar cost of client success. After all, if a program achieves what it is supposed to achieve by the attainment of its program objectives, why does it matter how it achieves it? If the program is to be replicated or improved, it *does* matter, and efficiency assessments and process analysis (Chapter 5) can answer such questions.

Questions related to outcome generally fall into four major categories, which have a direct link to the type of evaluation design used (to be discussed in Chapter 8). First, the evaluator wants to know to what degree the program is achieving its objectives. Does participation in the family preservation program, for example, increase positive social support for parents (Program Objective 1 in Figure 3.9), and by how much? This question requires that we collect data at (or near) the beginning of the program and at (or near) the end of the program in order to detect how much *change* has occurred. As discussed earlier, we need to make a decision as to whether data will be collected for all incoming clients. Unless, the data are in some way used to plan and implement a treatment intervention, data collection from all clients might be excessive, and a sampling strategy can be used.

Second, we want to know whether people who have been through the family preservation program have more positive social supports than similar people who have not been through the program. This question suggests that we collect data not only from clients in the program but also from clients who did not participate in the program. These could be clients who were turned away or, perhaps, are on a waiting list for program services. The aim of this question is to directly *compare* outcomes for clients receiving program services with those who do not.

Third, there is the question of *causality*. Is there any evidence that services provided by the family preservation program *caused* the increase in positive social supports? This question is more sophisticated than the first two and requires the use of explanatory research designs described in Chapter 8.

Fourth, we might be interested to assess the *longevity* of changes made by clients. In this case, we want to collect data from clients not only at program exit, but also at some predetermined points afterward. Many clients who have exited from human service programs return to their previous social environments, which were at least partially responsible for their problems in the first place. Often, clients' gains are not maintained, and equally often, programs have no follow-up procedures to find out if they in fact have been maintained. Ideally, follow-up data are collected at intervals, such as 3, 6, or 12 months after clients exit a program. The time span should allow for enough time to pass in order to comfortably say that the program effects were not simply temporary.

The challenge of collecting client follow-up data is that the task is not always easy. Sometimes it is very difficult to locate clients after they leave a program. Programs working with economically disadvantaged clients may have an especially difficult time because clients may not have telephones. Clients who are transient, clients with mental illness, clients with criminal backgrounds, and clients who are homeless are hard to track. The difficulties associated with locating clients are very expensive and time consuming. Because of the additional costs, every effort should be made to collect posttest data just prior to clients' leaving the program.

Outcome data imply that we are interested in how clients change in terms of relevant program objectives at the end of our services. This assumption requires that a clear program end does in fact exist. In some cases, services to clients with on-going difficulties may extend beyond those of the typical program. Suppose, for a moment, that a family within our family preservation program receives a 2-week extension of services because the family needs additional assistance for one reason or another.

When brief extensions are granted, the end of the program is also extended. If, however, longer-term extensions are given, such that the client essentially repeats the program, then the *true* program end technically is decided by the predefined program service time. The downside of looking at things this way is that the client may not show positive improvement at the predefined end of the program. While this is unfortunate for our evaluation results, it is true. Frankly, we are in a better position to learn how to improve client service delivery if we work from objective data.

A related problem with collecting follow-up data is that clients may be receiving services from other social service programs during the follow-up period. How will we know if treatment effects are maintained as a result of our work with clients, or if the other current social service is somehow helping clients to do well? While there are no perfect solutions to such a problem, we can simply ask clients what additional social services they are involved with, if any. These data can be used to compare clients who are receiving additional social services to those who are not.

So far, we have been discussing data collection from the vantage point of program-level evaluation. As we will see in Chapter 7, it is also possible to use aggregated case level data to evaluate a program's outcomes. When case level data are used, there are usually many more data collection points. Just how many is determined by the worker and the client in designing an individual monitoring system for their unique practice objectives.

DECIDING HOW DATA WILL BE COLLECTED

We can collect outcome data from clients by telephone, mail, or in person. Clearly, in-person costs are higher than if we collect data during our last contact with clients before they exit the program, or if we contact clients by telephone (provided clients have phones). Ideally, we want to collect data from all clients who are represented in our program objectives. In our example, Program Objective 2 within our family preservation program example, focuses on problem-solving skills of all family members.

This raises the question of whether we should collect data from children, as well as the parent(s). We must decide how feasible it is to use more than one data source. If time and resources limit us to one data source, then we must pick the one we think is most representative, or one that will provide the most meaningful data in relation to the program objective.

Who is going to be responsible for collecting data is a critical question. When data are collected at intake, workers usually will gather the facts from clients as part of the assessment process. When social workers collect data at program exit, there is great risk of biasing results, which can discredit the outcome evaluation. Because social workers and clients come to know each other well, the helping relationship can influence how clients respond to measuring instruments. Furthermore, having social workers evaluate their own performance is not generally accepted as a way to provide accurate data. Another reason for not using social workers to collect outcome data is that the additional task is likely to overload them. As clients exit a program, new clients are admitted. It becomes unwieldily for a single social worker to juggle a new admission, a termination, a clinical follow-up, and an evaluation follow-up in addition to his or her ongoing caseload.

Quality data collection requires several explicit procedures that need to be laid out and strictly followed. Minimal training is needed for consistent data collection. It is rather inefficient to train all social workers within a single program to collect data (in addition to the disadvantages already stated). Thus, it is advisable to assign data collection tasks to a small number of workers who are properly trained in the data collection effort. These individuals do not necessarily have to have any background in evaluation procedures; they simply need to have good interviewing skills and be able to following basic standardized instructions.

STEP 4: ANALYZING AND DISPLAYING DATA

It is possible that, by the time clients have answered questions on a program intake form and completed any standardized measuring instruments used by a program, they may have produced 50 or more separate pieces of data. From marital status, to service history, to the level of a social problem—we must decide how each unit of data will be presented and what the possibilities for analyses are. With outcome data, our data analyses tasks focus on the output of the program; that is, what is the condition (or situation) for clients at the time they exit the program and beyond? We may use demographic data on our intake form to present outcome data, according to subgroups, that reveal interesting results.

Suppose, for example, that overall family progress on problem-solving skills (Program Objective 2) for the family preservation program was rather mediocre. But with further analyses, we are able to show that families with toddlers had great improvement, compared to families with teens, where almost no improvement was observed. The additional information that can be gained from analyzing data in subgroups gives important detail for program decision makers. It also helps to pinpoint a program's strengths and weakness, rather than simply looking at a program's results as a whole.

While social workers may have some interest in analyzing client data on a question-by-question basis, outcome data are most useful when data can be aggregated and summarized to provide an overview on client outcomes. We must, therefore, decide how to aggregate responses to individual questions. When a standardized measuring instrument is used, the procedures for scoring and summarizing data derived from it are usually provided with the instrument.

Suppose we used a simple standardized measuring instrument to measure problem-solving skill, where a score of zero is considered "very low problem-solving skill" and a score of 100 is considered "very high problem-solving skill." If we measured clients at program intake (pretest data) and program exit (posttest data), we might report the average score for all clients at intake (e.g., 40) and the average score at program exit (e.g., 80), thereby reporting an "average" increase in problem-solving skill of 40 points.

We can report additional information when normative data are available with standardized measuring instruments. For example, if our measuring instrument reported that when tested on a clinical population, the mean score was 50, and when tested on a nonclinical population, the mean score was 70, we could use these data to compare our client scores to these normative data. Normative data are particularly helpful for interpreting client data when measurement occurred only at program exit.

Because many stakeholders desire concrete and objective results, it is also worthwhile to consider reporting outcome data according to preset expectations. We may have worded Program Objective 2, for example, as follows: "Seventy-five percent of families will show improvement in their problem-solving skills." We should only measure outcomes in this way if we have a sound rationale for estimating success. Estimates may be derived from previous evaluation data, research studies, or general expectations of a given population. Estimates may focus on the amount of "average improvement" rather than the number of clients expected to show success. Including such estimates serves to educate stakeholders who might not be as well-informed about a client population or a social problem.

It is important that stakeholders understand that 100 percent success in deterring runaways, family violence, drug addiction, child prostitution, crime, and welfare fraud is an unrealistic expectation for any social service program. In some cases, we may not expect a better than 50–50 chance of seeing improvement for clients. If this is the case, then outcome results should be interpreted in this context.

In addition to comparing outcome data to normative scores and to preset expectations, we may also choose to present outcome data over time. It is possible, for example, to report client outcomes from one year to the next in order to show program trends. If outcome data from similar programs exist, it also is possible to compare the results of one program with another.

For the most part, analysis of outcome data is done by summarizing key outcome measures and reporting either the amount of change or the number of clients achieving a certain level of change. In either case, it is helpful to report these data using actual numbers and percentages. The numbers provide stakeholders with a realistic view of how many clients are included in each analysis, while percentages offer an easy way of comparing data across categories. We can also use basic graphing techniques and statistics to gain further insight into our data analysis.

STEP 5: DEVELOPING A FEEDBACK SYSTEM

Outcome evaluation can produce useful and telling data about what is happening for clients after they receive program services. The results are most useful when they are routinely shared with key stakeholders. In most cases, the emphasis on outcome data is for the benefit of the stakeholders who are external to the program.

Funders and policy makers learn about program outcomes through annual reports or, perhaps, new proposals. Program outcomes may be disseminated more broadly as well. The local newspaper may be interested in doing a feature article on the services a program offers. In addition to providing anecdotes and general descriptions of a social problem, program administrators have the option of reporting outcome data, thereby increasing public awareness.

When it comes to program-level evaluation, developing a feedback system for internal stakeholders such as program administrators and social workers is absolutely essential. Making outcome data available to them on a regular basis helps to keep them focused on the program's goal. Discussing outcome data can also stimulate important questions such as, Why are our clients doing so well? or so poorly? Are our program outcomes realistic? Are there any aspects of client outcomes that are being ignored? When program personnel have an opportunity to respond to concrete data, discussions become more purposeful and focused.

STEP 6: DISSEMINATING AND COMMUNICATING RESULTS

Disseminating and communicating results need be taken seriously if we want to see our outcome evaluation used. As we have seen, the findings that emerge from an outcome evaluation give us objective data from which to make decisions about how clients make changes. Such results can affect program operations, funding, and even what we believe about our clients and the expectations we have of our programs. The likelihood of having evaluation results used is increased when results are presented in a straightforward manner.

It is useful to think about the obstacles that get in the way of putting evaluation results into practice. One obstacle occurs when we fail to remember the law of parsimony when presenting the final report. As mentioned in the last chapter, a report should be straightforward, clear, and concise. It should be designed for the intended audience (stakeholder group). Note, however, that a program might have several versions of the same evaluation report—one version for each type of stakeholder. A report may be presented to the program's funders, while a pamphlet on the same information (presented differently) may be available for clients.

Another obstacle to using the findings of an outcome evaluation is created when the results contradict strong predetermined beliefs. It is fair to say, for example, that most social workers believe that their efforts are helpful to clients. We design programs with the hope and promise of improving human lives and social conditions. Thus, when our outcomes show that no, or little, client change has oc-curred, or that a client problem has worsened, it is easy to become defensive and to question the integrity of the evaluation methods.

Given that evaluation research methods are fraught with threats to internal and external validity, it is tempting to raise such concerns and then continue practicing as we always have. In other instances, the public may hold strong convictions about a particular social problem. An evaluation of a prison program, for example, may show that the program is unsuccessful in preventing prisoners from com-mitting further crimes once released. Yet, the general public may have a strong opinion that people who commit crimes should be punished by being sent to prison. In such a case, the evaluation results will have little influence on program changes.

Whatever the form of reporting and disseminating our evaluation findings, confidentiality is of utmost importance. Confidentiality is most easily established when data are reported in aggregate forms. By summarizing data by groups, we avoid singling out any one client.

SUMMARY

Outcome evaluations are practical endeavors. We want to know whether client changes have occurred as a result of our intervention efforts. Thus, our evaluation plan is designed to give us valid and reliable data that can be used for decision making. To arrive at the best plan to answer our questions, we must consider how much time and money are available, what research design is feasible, and what biases exist.

Program outcome assessment is an evaluation that determines to what degree the program is meeting its overall program objectives. In our profession, this usually means the degree to which our inter-ventions are effective. A program in which a high proportion of clients achieve their individual practice objectives (sometimes referred to as treatment objectives, or client objectives), for example, can be considered a successful program. If the majority of clients terminate unilaterally without reaching their practice objectives, the program can be considered less than successful.

PROCESS EVALUATION

THE PREVIOUS CHAPTER briefly discussed outcome evaluations—evaluations that answer questions about the nature and degree of how clients change when they terminate from social service programs. As we know from the last chapter, an evaluation of a program's client outcomes determines how clients fared on the program's objectives. The primary focus of an outcome evaluation, therefore, is on the end result of a program's intervention(s).

In contrast to an outcome evaluation, a process evaluation—the topic of this chapter—focuses on the program's approach to client service delivery in addition to how it manages its day-to-day operations. Thus, a process evaluation is not interested in the end result of a program. In short, a process evaluation examines how a program's services are delivered to clients and what administrative mechanisms exist within the program to support these services.

There is a direct connection between a process evaluation and an outcome evaluation, however. A process evaluation can be done if a program performs poorly on an outcome evaluation. In this case, we would be interested in finding out the reasons why the program had a poor outcome evaluation. Ideally, a process evaluation occurs before, or at the same time, as an outcome evaluation. When new social service programs are being implemented, for example, it makes sense to check whether the program was implemented in the way it was intended before evaluating its outcomes. Therefore, by evaluating the program's processes and outcomes, we are in a better position to suggest what specific processes lead to what specific successful client outcomes.

Program processes refer specifically to the activities and characteristics that describe how a program operates. In general, there are two major categories of processes—the client service delivery system within the program and the program's administrative support systems that sustain client service delivery. Client service delivery is composed of what workers do (e.g., interventions, activities) and what clients bring to the program (e.g., client profile, client satisfaction). On the other hand, administrative support systems comprise the administrative activities that exist to support the program's client service delivery system.

Suppose, for example, we want to conduct a process evaluation of a family preservation program. Instead of focusing our evaluation efforts on client outcomes, as is done in an outcome evaluation, we turn our attention to the program's day-to-day operations. Program Objective Two in the family preservation program (discussed in Chapter 3), for example, aims "to increase problem-solving skills of family members." In a process evaluation, we could ask:

- What *treatment interventions* do workers and clients engage in to increase family members' problem-solving skills?
- How much time do workers spend with family members on problem-solving interventions?

PURPOSES OF PROCESS EVALUATIONS

In a nutshell, a process evaluation aims to monitor a social service program in an effort to assess the services it provides to its clients, including how satisfied key stakeholder groups are with the program's services. If we know exactly what type of services are offered, how these services are being delivered, and how satisfied stakeholder groups are (especially clients) with the services, then we are in a better position to decide whether the program is, in fact, the best vehicle to help clients.

Like all types of evaluations presented in this book, a process evaluation is simple to understand but difficult to carry out. Recall from Chapter 3 the challenges involved in developing a program's goal and its related objectives (e.g., agreement had to be reached on what client outcomes the program would strive for, objectives had to be prioritized). There are similar problems in doing a process evaluation. To evaluate a program's approach to client service delivery, for example, program staff need to establish a common "program language." Do workers and/or administrators, for example, mean the same thing when they refer to "counseling" versus "therapy?" Are these activities (remember, these are not program objectives) the same or different? How would we distinguish between the two?

Using a consistent language to describe how a social service program delivers its services requires a level of precision that is difficult to achieve. This is particularly true when workers come from different disciplines, have different levels of training, or have different theoretical orientations. Many social service programs do not have a well-consolidated and well-thought-out treatment intervention approach. Thus, creating an intervention approach can be the first task of a process evaluation.

A process evaluation can fine-tune the services that a program delivers to its clients. In this spirit, a process evaluation is a critical component of delivering good social work services. In the same way that we ask clients to monitor their progress using practice objectives (Chapter 3), workers must be willing to monitor their interventions and activities to assess whether they are helping their clients in the best way possible. It is also the responsibility of administrators to maintain a healthy work environment.

By defining, recording, monitoring, and analyzing a program's operations, we will gain a better understanding of what types of interventions (and associated activities) lead to what type of client outcomes (positive and negative). We can also gather data to assess whether the program's current administrative operations are adequately supporting the workers as they help clients. We can, for example, monitor the frequency of worker-client contact, the amount of supervision the workers receive, and the number of training sessions the workers attended over the last year or so.

Clearly, there are many dimensions to conducting process evaluations. In general, however, they have three main purposes: (1) to improve a program's operations, (2) to generate knowledge for our profession, and (3) to estimate cost efficiency.

To Improve a Program's Operations

In general, data collected in a process evaluation are primarily used to inform decisions pertaining to the further development of the program's services. Even when a social service program is adequately conceptualized before it actually opens its doors for the first time, the day-to-day implementation of the program does not always go as smoothly as initially planned. There are many practical, legal, political, and ethical obstacles that prevent programs from being implemented as theoretically planned. More often than not, these obstacles are not realized until the program gets underway. A family preservation program, for example, unexpectedly may find that the building in which it is located is locked on weekends, or that its funding source places last-minute demands on the workers' caseload size.

A process evaluation is sometimes referred to as a *formative evaluation:* the gathering of relevant data for the continuous ongoing feedback and improvement of the client-related services a program offers. As will be seen shortly, a process evaluation provides us with important feedback about the two levels of program processes already discussed—its client service delivery system and its administrative supports.

We recommend that all process evaluations occur at a stage in which new programs start to focus their efforts on developing well-thought-out client service delivery systems. After a well-conceptualized client service delivery approach is established (a process that can take up to two years), a process evaluation can shift its emphasis to the program's administrative operations. The reason for beginning with direct client service delivery is that all worker supervision, training, and other administrative support, should ultimately exist to support the workers' direct services to their clients. Unless we are clear about what the nature of the program's client service delivery approach is, our beginning attempts to design and implement supporting systems to help workers will be futile.

TO GENERATE KNOWLEDGE FOR OUR PROFESSION

Chapter 4 discussed how outcome evaluations help us to learn more about how clients demonstrate change (if any) when they go through a program. In comparison, process evaluations give us insight into what specific treatment interventions and associated activities lead to these client changes (if any). Our profession has often referred to the client service delivery component of a social service program as a "black box." This somewhat negative label reflects the notion that clients enter and exit a program with no clear idea as to what actually took place (the "black box") while they were in the program. As we know, process evaluations include the monitoring of our treatment interventions and activities. Thus, they have much to offer us in relation to telling us what is really in the "black box."

First, to monitor interventions and activities implies that we have labels and definitions for what we do with our clients. This, in turn, increases communication and reduces the need to reinvent labels for basic intervention approaches (e.g., educational, therapeutic, supportive) and activities (e.g., active listening, confrontation).

Second, by monitoring what works (and what does not) with clients, we can avoid wasting time on treatment interventions and/or activities that do not work.

Third, we can begin to respond to long-standing questions that are ingrained in our profession but have not been adequately answered, such as:

- Are our interventions more effective in an office or community setting?
- Is 50 minutes the optimal time for a counseling session?
- What are the results of helping clients to cope with poverty versus helping them to challenge the system?

Fourth, if process evaluations are conducted across several social service programs, we can compare different client service delivery systems in terms of their differences and similarities. This information will help us to know *what* interventions work best for *whom*.

TO ESTIMATE COST EFFICIENCY

The data collected for a process evaluation can be used to more precisely calculate the cost of delivering a specific social service program to a specific client population. Chapter 4 presented how outcome evaluations can be used to estimate the cost-effectiveness of social service programs: Does the program accomplish its objectives within budget? On the other hand, a process evaluation permits us to ask more detailed questions that deal with a program's efficiency. By monitoring the amount of time clients spend receiving individual and group interventions, and by keeping track of client outcomes, for example, we will be able to determine which interventions (e.g., group or individual) are more efficient—which ones cost less but produce similar client outcomes, or results.

STEPS IN A PROCESS EVALUATION

The major aim of a process evaluation is to determine whether a program is operating as it was intended. In this chapter, we discuss six steps to conducting a process evaluation: (1) deciding what questions to ask, (2) developing data collection instruments, (3) developing a data collection monitoring system, (4) scoring and analyzing data, (5) developing a feedback system, and (6) disseminating and communicating results.

STEP 1: DECIDING WHAT QUESTIONS TO ASK

We have already discussed that a process evaluation can focus on two important dimensions of a program—its client service delivery system and its administrative operations. As such, it is important to develop clear questions for a process evaluation. In Step 1, we discuss eight major questions that can be asked when doing a process evaluation: (1) what is the program's background? (2) what is the program's client profile? (3) what is the program's staff profile? (4) what is the amount of service provided to clients? (5) what are the program's interventions and activities? (6) what administrative supports are in place to support the program's client service delivery system? (7) how satisfied are the program's stakeholders? and (8) how efficient is the program?

WHAT IS THE PROGRAM'S BACKGROUND?

Developing a program goal and objectives, via the process delineated in Chapter 3, is part of the answer to this simple question. By defining a program's goal, we articulate who will be served, what social problem will be tackled, what change is to be accomplished, and how we intend to create this change. This information provides a description of the program in a straightforward way whereby we can easily grasp its scope and boundaries.

Other background questions that we can ask are, What is the program's history? How did the program get started? and What is the program's philosophy? The answers to these types of questions provide us with the program's *context*—that is, the circumstances surrounding the program that help us to interpret data derived from the process evaluation.

A pro-life social service program, for example, will have a different theoretical approach to working with pregnant teens than a pro-choice program, yet both programs work with the same client population and tackle the same social problem. Furthermore, the two programs may have similar goals—to prevent teenage pregnancy.

Remember that social service programs often are initiated in response to political agendas, recommendations from needs assessments, and simply on ad hoc bases when additional social service funds are available near the end of the fiscal year. Questions having to do with the program's history and philosophy provide us with information about the program's background in addition to its political and social environment in which it operates. A program's history can be critical to fully understanding its day-to-day operations and helps us to work within its current political and social context. A program's philosophy can tell us how the major beliefs and values of the program's administrators (and workers) influenced the program's operations.

WHAT IS THE PROGRAM'S CLIENT PROFILE?

Knowing who is directly served by a program has implications for how the processes within it are monitored. Clients are one stakeholder group as identified in Chapter 1. Remember that clients can be individuals, families, groups, communities, and organizations. Regardless of whether "the client" is defined as, "a family with a child at-risk for placement," or "a placement program" that accommodates these children, a clear picture (or profile) of whom the program serves (the client) is necessary.

If the clients are families, for example, we need to know their sociodemographic characteristics. Gathering relevant client data such as age, gender, income, education, race, socioeconomic status, and other relevant demographic characteristics gives us a general idea of whom we are trying to serve. We also want to know where our clients come from. In other words, how are clients referred to the program? Are clients self-referred? Do they come primarily from one geographic area? How did they learn about the program?

If the client *is* a program, we will ask different questions, such as, Where is the program located? Who are its funding sources? What are the program's boundaries? How many staff are employed? What is the program's main intervention approach?

WHAT IS THE PROGRAM'S STAFF PROFILE?

Social service programs are staffed by individuals (workers and volunteers) with diverse backgrounds. Educational backgrounds and employment experiences can easily be used to describe the qualifications of workers. By monitoring worker qualifications, we can gain insight into establishing minimum-level qualifications for job advertisements. Are MSWs substantially better than BSWs in providing family preservation services, for example? Presumably, those with additional years of education have more to offer. If this is the case, what are the differentiating characteristics between the two levels of education? Sociodemographic data such as age, gender, and marital status are typical features used to describe program workers (or volunteers). Other meaningful descriptors for workers include salaries, benefits, and job descriptions.

There may be other staff characteristics that are important to a specific social service program. If we believed, for example, that being a parent is a necessary qualification for workers who help children in a foster care program, we might collect data that reflect this interest. Developing profiles for workers and volunteers alike provides data by which to make decisions about further recruiting and hiring. By monitoring key characteristics of social workers, for example, we might gain some insights as to the type of individuals that are best matched for employment within the program.

WHAT IS THE AMOUNT OF SERVICE PROVIDED TO CLIENTS?

Just because a social service program may be designed to serve clients for one hour per week for six weeks does not mean that it happens this way. Some clients leave the program much earlier than expected and some stay much longer than anticipated. It is basic to record client start and termination dates in order to determine how long clients received services.

When programs do not have clear-cut intake and termination dates (e.g., an outreach program for youth living on the street) or when these dates are not particularly meaningful (e.g., a long-term group home for adults with developmental disabilities), it may be necessary to collect data that are more useful. For instance, how long are street workers able to engage youth living on the street in a conversation about their safety? How many youth voluntarily seek outreach workers for advice? For adults with developmental disabilities who are living in a long-term group home, we might record the onset and completion of a particular treatment intervention.

Deciding when services begin and end is not as straightforward as it might seem. For instance, support services are sometimes provided to clients who are awaiting formal entry into a program, or follow-up services are offered to clients after a program's services have officially ended. Duration of service can be measured in minutes, hours, days, weeks, months, or years and provides us with data about how long a client is considered a client.

We might also want to know the intensity of the services provided to clients. This can be monitored by recording the amount of time a worker spends with, or on behalf of, a client. Worker time, for example, can be divided into face-to-face contact, telephone contact, report writing, advocacy, supervision and consultation, and so on. If we divide the amount of time spent in each one of these categories by the total time spent receiving services for one client, we can calculate the proportion of time spent in each category for that client. These simple calculations can produce the following data: Overall worker time for Client A was 40 percent face-to-face contact, 25 percent telephone contact, 25 percent report writing, 5 percent advocacy, and 5 percent supervision and consultation.

These data can be used to formulate an estimate that can assist workers in gauging the timing of their interventions. We might determine, for example, that workers in a family preservation program spend an average of 60 percent of their time in direct client contact. The other 40 percent is spent in meetings, writing up paperwork, participating in staff meetings, and so on. If a few workers have particularly difficult families, it might be reflected in their reported hours. Perhaps their face-to-face hours are low for a family, say around 20 percent, because the families miss many appointments. It is also possible that their face-to-face hours are high, say 75 percent, because the families had a series of crises. These data alone can be useful when deciding whether to continue or change services being offered to any one family.

WHAT ARE THE PROGRAM'S INTERVENTIONS AND ACTIVITIES?

This question gets at the heart of a program's treatment intervention strategy (and associated worker activities). It asks, What approach do workers use (the intervention), and how do they do it (the activity)? Of all process evaluation questions, this one in particular can pose a threat to workers and administrators alike because it requires them to articulate the nature of the program's interventions and workers' activities related to these interventions in terms that others can understand. Social workers who rely on professional jargon for efficient communication in the office should learn to explain what they do in lay terms so that nonprofessionals (especially clients) can understand what to expect from the program's services.

It is our position in this book that a worker should not be specifically evaluated on his or her client success rate. In other words, it would be a misuse of a process evaluation to take data about one worker's client success rate and compare this rate with another worker's rate, or any other standard. Obviously, this type of analysis would influence the worker to record favorable data—whether accurate or not. Rather, monitoring of client success rates ought to be done in the spirit of program development, appealing to the curiosities of workers in learning about their day-to-day efforts.

WHAT ADMINISTRATIVE SUPPORTS ARE IN PLACE TO SUPPORT CLIENT SERVICE DELIVERY?

Administrative supports include the "fixed" conditions of employment, as well as the administrative operations that are designed to support workers in carrying out the program's clients service delivery approach. Fixed conditions of employment describe things that remain relatively stable over time. Examples include location of intervention (e.g., office, client's home, community), staff-worker ratio, support staff, available petty cash, use of pagers, hours of service delivery, and so on. Administrative operations, on the other hand, may change depending on current program stresses and include things such as worker training, supervision schedules, and program development meetings.

The most important thing to remember about a program's administrative supports is that they exist to *support* workers in carrying out their functions with clients. Workers who are paid poorly, carry pagers 24 hours per day, have high caseloads, and consistently work overtime on weekends will likely respond to clients' needs and problems less effectively than will those who work under more favorable conditions.

Administrative supports should exist by design. That is, they ought to promote workers in offering sound client service delivery. What is most important to remember is that the approach to administrative support is not written in stone. As with all other aspects of a social service program, it remains flexible and open to review and revision.

A dramatic example of a how an administrative decision leads to change in client service delivery occurred when administrators of a group home program for delinquent youth questioned "group care" as the setting for client service delivery. The program's administrators questioned how living in a group home helps delinquent youth to improve on the program's objectives.

After collecting data about the effects of group living, the administrators determined that their program's objectives could be achieved using a less intrusive (and less expensive) setting for service delivery—providing interventions to youth while they continued living with their families.

In another example, an administrator of an outreach program for street youth noticed that the program's workers were consistently working over-time. By reviewing data collected on the amount of time workers spent "on the street" versus at the "store-front" office and by talking to the workers directly, the administrator learned that workers were feeling overwhelmed by the increasing number of youth moving to the streets.

Workers were spending more time on the streets in an attempt to help as many youth as possible. Workers, however, felt that they were being reactive to the problems faced by youth on the street because they did not have time to reflect on their work in relation to the program's goal and objectives or have time to plan their activities. With these data, the program administrator decided to conduct weekly meetings to help workers overcome feelings of being overwhelmed and to develop a plan to handle the increase in the number of clients.

HOW SATISFIED ARE THE PROGRAM'S STAKEHOLDERS?

Stakeholder satisfaction is a key part of a process evaluation because satisfaction questions ask stakeholders to comment on the program's services. Using a client satisfaction survey when clients exit a program is a common method of collecting satisfaction data. In a family support program, for example, clients were asked for their opinions about the interactions they had with their family support workers, the interventions they received, and the social service program in general. Figure 5.1 presents a list of client satisfaction questions given to parents and children after they received services (at termination) from the program.

The data collected from the questions in Figure 5.1 can be in the

---

How satisfied are you...

1. that the worker wanted what was best for you?
2. that the worker was pleasant to be around?
3. that you learned important skills to help your family get along better?
4. that the worker was fair and did not take sides?
5. with the amount of communication you had with the worker?
6. that you had a chance to ask questions and talk about your own ideas?
7. that the worker helped to improve your parent-child relationship?

FIGURE 5.1   FAMILY SATISFACTION QUESTIONNAIRE

form of words or numbers. Clients' verbal responses could be recorded for each question using an open-ended interview format. On the other hand, clients could be asked to respond to each question by giving a numerical rating on a 5-point category partition scale, for example. In this case, the rating scale would range from a response of 1, meaning "not at all satisfied" to 5, meaning "very satisfied."

Client responses to the seven questions in Figure 5.1 can easily provide a general impression about how they viewed the program's services. Because questions were asked from parents and children alike, it was possible to compare parents' and children's views of the services provided. Suppose, for example, that the satisfaction data showed that parents reported higher satisfaction rates than their children. This finding alone could be used to reflect on how treatment interventions were delivered to the parents versus their children.

Client satisfaction data can also be collected from other key stakeholder groups. Suppose the family support program operated under a child protection mandate. This would mean that each family coming into the program had an assigned child protection worker. Figure 5.2 on the following page shows the satisfaction questions asked of this group. Because client satisfaction involves the opinions of people "outside" the program, data collection has special considerations with respect to who collects them.

How satisfied are you...

1. with the amount of cooperation you received from the worker in his or her interactions with your department?
2. that the program connected the family with appropriate resources?
3. that the program was effective in helping the family get along better?
4. that the program helped to improve communication between the parent(s) and your department?
5. that the program helped to improve parent-child relationships?

FIGURE 5.2   CHILD PROTECTION WORKER SATISFACTION QUESTIONNAIRE

HOW EFFICIENT IS THE PROGRAM?

Estimating a program's efficiency is an important purpose of a process evaluation. This question focuses on the amount of resources expended in an effort to help clients achieve a desired program objective. Because a process evaluation looks at the specific components of a program, it is possible to estimate costs with more precision than is possible in a traditional outcome evaluation, as presented in Chapter 4.

Given the many questions that we can ask in a process evaluation, it is necessary to determine what questions have priority. Deciding which questions are the most important ones to be answered is influenced by the demands of different stakeholder groups, trends in programing, and plans for program development.

STEP 2: DEVELOPING DATA COLLECTION INSTRUMENTS

It is important to collect data for all eight question categories briefly discussed in Step 1 if we hope to carry out a comprehensive process evaluation. This might seem an unwieldy task, but data for several of the question categories usually already exist. Questions about *program background*, for example, can be answered by reviewing minutes of program meetings, memos, and documents that describe the phases of the program's development. If written documentation does not exist, however, we can interview the people who created the program. *Staff profiles* can be gleaned from workers' resumes. A *program's approach to providing administrative support* can be documented in an afternoon by the program's senior administrator. Ongoing recording of training sessions, meeting times, worker hours, and so on can be used to assess whether administrative supports are being carried out as designed. Finally, data relating to the *program's efficiency* are available from the program's budget.

Data for the program's client service delivery approach should be routinely collected. To do so, it is necessary to develop useful data collection instruments. Useful instruments possess three qualities. They (1) are easy to use, (2) fit with the flow of a program's operations, and (3) are designed with user input.

EASE OF USE

Data collection instruments should help workers to do their jobs better—not tie up their time with extensive paperwork. Instruments that are easy to use are created to minimize the amount of writing that workers are expected to do and the amount of time it takes to complete them. In some cases, data collection instruments have already been constructed (and tested) by other social service programs. The National Center of Family Based Services, for example, has developed an intervention and activity checklist for generic family preservation programs. The checklist contains various interventions and activities in which workers are instructed to check appropriate columns that identify which family members (i.e., child[ren] at-risk, primary caretaker, other adult) were involved in the intervention and related activities.

Where data collection instruments do not exist, workers may agree to use an open-ended format for a limited period of time. Workers' responses can then be reviewed and categorized to create a checklist that reflects the uniqueness of their program. The advantage of using an open-ended checklist versus a prescribed one is that the listed intervention may be more meaningful to the workers.

Suppose, for example, we asked the workers within a drug and alcohol counseling program for youth to record the major interventions (and associated activities) they used with their clients. After reviewing their written notes, we list the following activities that were recorded by the workers themselves: gave positive feedback, rewarded youth for reduced alcohol consumption, discussed positive aspects of the youth's life, cheered youth on, and celebrated youth's new job. These descriptors all appear to be serving a common function—praise, or noting clients' strengths. Thus, we could develop a checklist item called "praise." The checklist approach loses important detail such as the workers' styles or the clients' situations, but when data are summarized, a general picture of the workers' major activities soon emerges.

Another critical data collection instrument that exists in almost all social service programs is the client intake form, which typically asks questions in the areas of client characteristics, reasons for referral, and service history, to name a few. The data collected on the client intake form should be useful for case-level (Chapter 7) and program-level (Chapter 8) evaluations. Put another way, data that are not used (i.e., not summarized or reviewed) should not be collected.

APPROPRIATENESS TO THE FLOW OF A PROGRAM'S OPERATIONS

Data collection instruments should be designed to fit within the context of the social service program, to facilitate the program's day-to-day operations, and to provide data that will ultimately be helpful in improving client service delivery. As mentioned previously, data that are routinely collected from clients, or at least relate to them, ought to have both case- and program-level utility. For instance, if the client intake form requires the worker to check the referral problem(s), these data can be used at the case level to discuss the checked items, or presenting problems, with the client and to plan a suitable intervention(s). These data can also be summarized across clients to determine the most common reason for referral to the program.

Client case records can be designed to incorporate strategies for recording the amount of time workers spend with their clients and the nature of the workers' intervention strategies. Space should also be made available for workers' comments and impressions. While we do have some suggestions for formatting client data recording instruments, there is no one ideal design. Just as treatment interventions can be personalized by the workers within a program, so can data collection instruments.

When designed within the context of the program, these instruments can serve several important functions. First, they offer a record of case-level intervention that can be used to review individual client progress. Second, components of the data collection instruments can be aggregated to produce a "program summary." Third, the instruments can be used as the basis for supervisory meetings. They can also facilitate case reviews as they convey the major client problems, treatment interventions, and worker activities in a concise manner.

DESIGN WITH USER INPUT

It should be clear by now that the major users of data collection instruments are the line-level workers who are employed by the program. Workers often are responsible for gathering the necessary data from clients and others. Therefore, their involvement in the development and testing of the data collection instruments is critical. Workers who see the relevance of recording data will likely record more accurate data than workers who do not.

In some instances, the nature of the data collected requires some retraining of staff. Staff at a group home for children with behavior problems, for example, were asked to record the interventions and activities they used with children residing at the group home. The majority of staff, however, were initially trained to record observations about the children's behavior, rather than their own. In other words, they were never trained to record the interventions and activities that they engaged in with clients.

STEP 3: DEVELOPING A DATA COLLECTION MONITORING SYSTEM

The monitoring system for a process evaluation relates closely to the program's supervision practices. This is because program process data are integral to delivering client services. Data about a program's background, client profile, and staff characteristics can, more or less, be collected at one time period. These data can be summarized and stored for easy access. Program changes such as staff turnover, hours of operation, or caseload size, can be duly noted as they occur.

In contrast, process data that are routinely collected should be monitored and checked for reliability and validity (Chapter 6). Time and resources are a consideration for developing a monitoring system. When paperwork becomes excessively backlogged, it may be that there is simply too much data to collect, data collection instruments are cumbersome to use, or staff are not invested in the evaluation process. Considerations for developing a monitoring system for a process evaluation include: (1) the number of cases to include in the evaluation, (2) when to collect the data, and (3) how to collect the data.

NUMBER OF CASES TO INCLUDE (UNIT OF ANALYSIS)

In an outcome evaluation, we have to decide whether to include all clients served by the program or only a percentage of them. In a process evaluation, we need to make a similar decision. However, what constitutes "a case" can change depending upon the questions we ask. If we ask a question about the program's history, for example, the program is our unit of analysis and we have only to decide how many people will be interviewed or how many documents will be reviewed to get a sufficient answer to our history question.

When questions are aimed at individual clients, we can use the same sampling practices that we discussed for outcome evaluation. Data that are used for case-level activities should be collected from all clients. Intake and assessment data are often used to plan client treatment interventions. Indeed, these data also serve important purposes, such as comparing groups of clients, in an outcome evaluation (Chapter 4).

Often times, client intake forms are far too lengthy and detailed. Thus, a program may consider developing two intake forms, a short form and a long form. The short instrument could include only those data that workers deem relevant to their case-level work. In a sex offender program, for example, we might use a short data collection instrument at client intake to gather data such as age of client, family composition, referral problems, service history, employment status, and so on.

In addition to these questions, a longer form could collect data that enriched our understanding of the client population served by the program. For example, what services would the client have used if the sex offender program were not available? What is the length of employment at the client's current job? What community services is the client actively involved in? and so on.

If two data collection instruments are available (one short and one long), deciding which one to use is a matter for random sampling. Workers could use the long one with every second or third client. To maintain a true sense of "randomness," however, the assignment of a specific data collection instrument to a specific client should occur as close as possible to the actual intake meeting.

The use of a short-long instrument can also apply to collecting data about a worker's activities. Data collection is always a balance between breadth (how many cases to include) and depth (what and how many questions to ask).

Whether the unit of analysis is the client, the worker, the administrator, or the program, our aim is to get a representative sample. For smaller social service programs, the number of administrators and workers may be low, in which case everyone can be included. In larger programs, such as public assistance programs, we might use random sampling procedures that will ensure that all constituents are represented in our evaluation. When outcome and process evaluations happen concurrently, we should consider developing sampling strategies that are compatible with both types of evaluations.

Data that are not used for the benefit of a case-level evaluation may not need to be collected for all clients. Client satisfaction questionnaires, for example, are usually collected at the end of the program and are displayed only in an aggregate form (to ensure confidentiality). Because client satisfaction data aim to capture the clients' feelings about the services they received, the questionnaires should be administered by someone other than the worker who provided the services to the client. However, having a neutral individual (e.g., another worker, a program assistant, a supervisor) administer the client satisfaction questionnaire can be a costly endeavor.

Recall that in the family support program example, client satisfaction questionnaires were given to the parents and their children (see Figures 5.1 and 5.2). While the questionnaires were not very long, they were completed in the clients' homes and thus involved travel costs. If a program's staff decide that client satisfaction data is a major priority, then creative strategies could be developed to collect relevant, valid, and reliable client satisfaction data. It may be possible, for example, to obtain these data over the telephone rather than in-person.

A simple solution is to randomly select clients to participate in our client satisfaction survey. As long as an adequate number of clients are truly randomly selected, then we can generalize our results to all of the clients within the program who did not participate in our survey. Ideally, our client random selection process should occur at the time clients leave the program (terminate).

WHEN TO COLLECT THE DATA

Earlier we discussed the uses of short and long data collection instruments to collect client-relevant data. If we decide that numerous data are to be collected from every client, we may choose to administer the short data collection instrument at one time period and administer the longer one at a different time period. Workers could decide what data will be collected at the intake interview (the shorter instrument), and what data can be collected later on (the longer instrument).

It may be that the intake procedures ask harmless questions such as age, gender, employment status, and so on. After the worker has developed a rapport with the client, it may be more appropriate to ask questions of a more sensitive nature (e.g., service history, family income, family problems, family history). We should not make the mistake of collecting all data on all client characteristics at an intake interview. Many client characteristics are fixed, or constant (e.g., race, gender, service history, problem history). Thus, we can ask these questions at any time while clients are receiving services.

In a process evaluation, we can collect data that focus on the workers' treatment interventions and activities, and the time they spend with their clients. Here we need to decide whether they need to record all of their activities with all of their clients. Because there are important case-level (and sometimes legal) implications for recording worker-client activity for each case, we recommend YES! In addition, we have already recommended that the data on the worker activity instrument be used for supervisory meetings. Ideally case records should capture the nature of the worker's intervention, the rationale for the worker's actions, and changes in the client's knowledge, behavior, feelings, or circumstances that result from the workers' efforts (i.e., progress on client practice objectives).

Program administrators have the responsibility to review client records to determine what data are missing from them. The feedback from this review can, once again, be included in supervisory meetings. These reviews can be made easy by including a "program audit sheet" on the cover of each client file. This sheet lists all of the data that need to be recorded and the dates by which they are due. Workers can easily check each item when the data are collected.

If program administrators find there is a heavy backlog of paperwork, it may be that workers are being expected to do too much, or that the data collection instruments need to be shortened and/or simplified. Furthermore, we want to leave room for workers to record creative treatment interventions and/or ideas that can be later considered for the further refinement of the program.

HOW TO COLLECT THE DATA

Recording workers' activities is primarily a paperwork exercise. It is time-consuming, for example, to videotape and systematically rate worker-client interactions. Because data on line-level workers' activities are often collected by the workers themselves, the reliability of the data they collect can come into question. Where supervision practices include the observation of the workers' interventions and activities with clients, it is possible to assess the reliability of workers' self-reports. For example, if supervisors were to observe family support workers interacting with their families, they could also complete the therapeutic intervention checklist (discussed earlier) and compare the results with the ratings that workers give themselves.

Through this simple procedure, inter-rater reliability scores can be calculated, which provides us the extent of agreement between the workers' perceptions and the supervisors' perceptions.

For client satisfaction data, "social desirability" can become an issue. If a worker who is assigned to a client administers the client satisfaction questionnaire (Figure 5.1) at the end of the program, the resulting data, generated by the client, will be suspect, even if the questionnaire is carried out in the most objective fashion. Clients are less likely to rate workers honestly if the workers are present when clients complete the instrument. This problem is exacerbated when workers actually read out the questions for clients to answer. In this instance, it is useful to have a neutral person (someone not personally known to the client) read the questions to the clients.

Before clients answer satisfaction questions, it should be explained to them that their responses are confidential and that their assigned worker will not be privy to their responses. They should be told that their responses will be added to a pool of other clients' responses and reported in aggregate form. A sample of a previous report that illustrates an example of aggregated data could be shown to clients.

How data are collected directly influences the value of information that results from the data. Data that are collected in a haphazard and inconsistent way will be difficult to summarize. In addition, they will produce inaccurate information.

For example, in the pilot testing of data collection instruments regarding the amount of time workers spent with their clients, workers were diligent about recording their time in the first two weeks of a six-week intervention program. After the initial two-week period, however, workers recorded data more and more sporadically.

The resulting picture produced by the "incomplete" data was that the program appeared to offer the bulk of its intervention in the first two weeks of the program. A graph of these data would visually display this trend. Suppose such a graph was shown to the program's workers. With little discussion, the workers would likely comment on the inaccuracy of the data.

Moreover, the workers may share their beliefs about what the pattern of the remaining four weeks of intervention look like (in the absence of any recorded data). Rather than speculate on the "possible" patterns, the "hard" data could be used to encourage workers to be more diligent in their data recording practices. Discussion could also center around what additional supports workers may need (if any) to complete their paperwork.

The bottom line is simple: Doing paperwork is not a favorite activity of line-level social workers. When the paperwork that workers complete is not used for feedback purposes, they can become even more resistant to doing it. Thus, it is important that we acknowledge data-recording efforts by providing regular summaries of the data *they* collected. For programs that are equipped with computer equipment and a management database system, it is possible for workers to enter their data directly into the computer. This luxury saves precious time.

STEP 4: SCORING AND ANALYZING DATA

The procedures for collecting and summarizing process data should be easy to perform, and once the data are analyzed, they should be easy to interpret. As mentioned, if a backlog occurs in the summarization of data, it is likely that the program is collecting too much data and will need to cut back on the amount collected and/or reexamine its data collection needs.

Thinking through the steps of scoring and analyzing data can help us decide if we have collected too much or too little data. Consider a family support worker who sees a family four times per week for 10 weeks. If the worker completes a therapeutic intervention checklist for each family visit, the worker will have a total of 40 data collection sheets for the total intervention period for this one family alone. Given this large volume of data, it is likely that scoring will simply involve a count of the number of therapeutic interventions used. Summary data can show which intervention strategies the worker relied on the most. Because the dates of when data were recorded are on the data collection instrument, we could compare the worker's interventions that were used at the beginning, in the middle, and at end of treatment.

Other analyses are also possible if the data are grouped by client characteristics. For example: Do single-parent families receive more or less of a particular intervention, compared to two-parent families? Do families where children have behavior problems take more or less worker time? What is the pattern of time spent with families over the 10-week intervention period? Questions can also be asked in relation to any outcome data collected. Is the amount of time spent with a family related to success? What therapeutic interventions, if any, are associated with successful client outcomes? Once data are collected and entered into a computer database system, summaries and analyses are simple matters.

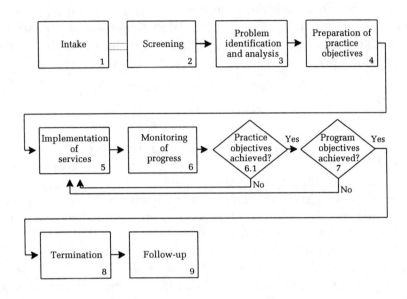

FIGURE 5.3   STAGES OF A PROGRAM THAT NEED TO BE
                                 CONSIDERED IN A PROCESS EVALUATION

STEP 5: DEVELOPING A FEEDBACK SYSTEM

Because a process evaluation focuses on the inner workings of a
social service program, the data collected should be shared with the
workers within the program. The data collected on worker activities
will not likely reveal any unknowns about how workers function on
a day-to-day basis. Rather, the data are more likely to confirm workers' and administrators' preformed hunches. Visually seeing data in
graphs and charts provides a forum for discussion and presents an
aggregate picture of the program's structure—which may or may not
be different from individual perspectives.

We have already discussed the utility of how process evaluations
can help supervisors and their supervisees in supervisory meetings.
Process data provide an opportunity to give feedback to individual
workers and can form the basis of useful discussions. Program-level
feedback can be provided to workers in program meetings. Ideally,
programs should set aside one-half day every one or two months for

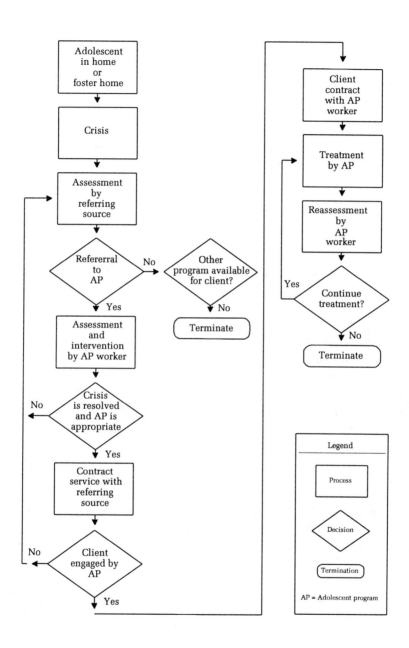

FIGURE 5.4   EXAMPLE OF A CLIENT PATH FLOW

program development. During the program development meetings, program administrators could present data summaries for relevant or pressing questions. In addition, these meetings can be used to problem-solve difficulties in creating an efficient monitoring system.

Figure 5.3 presents the general stages of client service delivery for a social service program. Figure 5.4 shows a detailed example of how clients can go through the same program. Both figures are useful guides when considering the components of a program that need to be addressed when doing a process evaluation—they both show the key events in the program's client service delivery approach.

STEP 6: DISSEMINATING AND COMMUNICATING RESULTS

Data collected through process evaluations can provide important clues as to what intervention(s) works with what particular client problem(s). These data are a first step to uncovering the mystery of the "black box" of intervention mentioned earlier in this chapter. The results of a process evaluation, therefore, should be made available to social service programs that offer similar services. By disseminating the results of a process evaluation in social work professional journals, at professional conferences, or through workshops, a social service program can take a leadership role in increasing our understanding of how to help specific groups of clients with specific problems.

SUMMARY

Process evaluations are aimed at improving services to clients. Data can be collected on many program dimensions in an effort to make informed decisions about a program's operations. Designing a process evaluation involves the participation of the program's administrators and workers. Program staff must decide what questions they want to ask, how data will be collected, who will be responsible for monitoring data collection activities, how the data will be analyzed, and how the results will be disseminated.

PART **II**

IMPLEMENTING EVALUATIONS

MEASURING PRACTICE AND PROGRAM OBJECTIVES

ACONCEPT SUCH AS DEPRESSION can be defined in words and, if the words are sufficiently well chosen, the reader will have a clear idea of what depression is. When we apply this definition to a particular client, however, words may be not enough to guide us. The client may seem depressed, according to the definition, but many questions may still remain. Is the client more or less depressed than the average person? If more depressed, how much more? Is the depression growing or declining? For how long has the client been depressed? Is the depression continuous or episodic? If episodic, what length of time usually elapses between depressive episodes? Is this length of time increasing or diminishing? How many episodes occur in a week? To what degree is the client depressed? Answers to questions such as these enable a social worker to obtain greater insight into the client's depression—an insight essential for planning and evaluating a treatment intervention.

WHY MEASUREMENT IS NECESSARY

An evaluation is an appraisal: an estimate of how effectively and efficiently practice objectives (and program objectives) are being met in a practitioner's individual practice (or in a human service program). In other words, an evaluation compares the change that has actually taken place against the predicted, desired change. Thus, an evaluation requires knowledge of both the initial condition and the present condition of the objective undergoing the proposed change. Therefore, it is necessary to have two measurements, one at the beginning of the change process and one at the end. In addition, it is always useful to take measurements of the objectives during the change process as well. Measurement, then, is not only necessary in the quality improvement process—it is the conceptual foundation, without which the evaluative structure cannot exist.

A definition, no matter how complete, is useful only if it means the same thing to different people. We could, for example, define a distance in terms of the number of days a person takes to walk it, or the number of strides needed to cross it, or the number of felled oak trees that would span it end to end. But since people, strides, and oak trees vary, none of these definitions is very exact. To be useful to a modern traveler, a distance must be given in miles or some other precisely defined unit.

Similarly, shared understanding and precision are very important in our profession. A social worker who is assessing a woman's level of functioning needs to know that the results of the assessment are not being affected by the worker's feelings toward the woman, the worker's knowledge of the woman's situation, or any other biasing factor; that any other worker who assessed the same woman under the same conditions would come up with the same result.

Further, we need to know that the results of the assessment will be understood by other professionals; that the results are rendered in words or symbols that are not open to misinterpretation. If the assessment is to provide the basis for decisions about the woman's future, via the treatment intervention chosen, objectivity and precision on our part are even more important.

OBJECTIVITY

Some social work practitioners believe that they are entirely objective; that they will not judge clients by skin color, ethnic origin, religious persuasion, sexual orientation, socioeconomic status, income level, marital status, education, age, gender, verbal skill, or personal attractiveness. They may believe they are not influenced by other people's opinions about a client—statements that the client has severe emotional problems or a borderline personality will be disregarded until objective data are gathered. No judgments will be made on the basis of the worker's personal likes and dislikes, and stereotyping will be avoided at all costs.

Social workers who sincerely believe that their judgment will never be influenced by any of the factors mentioned are deluding themselves. Everyone is prejudiced to some degree in some area or another; everyone has likes and dislikes, moral positions, and personal standards; everyone is capable of irrational feelings of aversion, sympathy, or outrage. Workers who deny this run the risk of showing bias without realizing it, and a worker's unconscious bias can have devastating effects on the life of a client.

A client may unwittingly fuel the bias by sensing what the social worker expects and by answering questions in a way that supports the worker's preconceptions. In extreme cases, clients can even become what they are expected to become, fulfilling the biased prophecy. The art of good judgment, then, lies in accepting the possibility of personal bias and trying to minimize its effects. What is needed is an unprejudiced method of assessment and an unbiased standard against which the client's knowledge, affects, or behaviors can be gauged. In other words, we require a measurement method from which an impartial measure can be derived.

PRECISION

The other ingredient of the quality improvement process is precision, whose opposite is vagueness. A vague statement is one that uses general or indefinite terms; in other words, it leaves so many details to be filled in that it means different things to different people. There are four sources of vagueness in our profession.

The first source of vagueness is terms such as *often, frequently, many, some, usually,* and *rarely,* which attempt to assign degrees to a client's affects or behaviors without specifying a precise unit of measurement. A statement such as "John misses many appointments with his worker" is fuzzy; it tells us only that John's reliability may leave much to be desired. The statement "John missed two out of 10 appointments with his worker" is far more precise and does not impute evil tendencies to John.

The second source of vagueness is statements that, although they are intended to say something about a particular client, might apply to anyone; for example, "John often feels insecure, having experienced some rejection by his peers." Who has not experienced peer rejection? Nevertheless, the statement will be interpreted as identifying a quality specific to John. Statements like this are as damaging to the client as they are meaningless.

A third source of vagueness is professional jargon, the meaning of which will rarely be clear to a client. Often professionals themselves do not agree on the meaning of such phrases as "expectations–role definition" or "reality pressures." In the worst case, they do not even know what they mean by their own jargon; they use it merely to sound impressive. Jargon is useful when it conveys precise statements to colleagues; when misused, it can confuse workers and alienate clients.

The last source of vagueness is tautology—a meaningless repetition disguised as a definition. For example: A delinquent is a person who engages in delinquent behaviors," "John is agoraphobic because he is afraid of open spaces," "Betty is ambivalent because she cannot make up her mind," "Marie hits her brother because she is aggressive," "John rocks back and forth because he is autistic." Obviously, tautological statements tell us nothing and are to be avoided.

In summary, we need to attain objectivity and precision and to avoid bias and vagueness. Both objectivity and precision are vital in the quality improvement process and are readily attainable through the measurement process.

THE MEASUREMENT PROCESS

The word *measurement* is often used in two different senses. In the first sense, a measurement is the result of a measuring process:

the number of times Bobby hits his brother in a day (a possible *frequency* practice objective); the length of time for which Jenny cries (a possible *duration* practice objective); the intensity of Ms. Smith's depression (a possible *magnitude* practice objective). In the second sense, measurement refers to the measuring process itself; that is, it encompasses the event or attribute being measured, the person who does the measuring, the method employed, the measuring instrument used, and often also the result. Measurement is the entire process of measuring something, excluding only the results. The results of any measurement process are called *data.* In other words, measurement is undertaken in order to obtain objective and precise data.

In any profession, from the social services to plumbing, an instrument is a tool designed to help the user perform a task. A tool need not be a physical object; it can just as easily be a perception, an idea, a new synthesis of known facts, or a new analysis of a known whole. In our profession, however, a tool used to obtain data—a measuring instrument—is a physical object. It is a piece of paper, or a form, on which the client's affects, perceptions, or behaviors can be recorded in various ways.

STANDARDIZED MEASURING INSTRUMENTS

A *standardized measuring instrument* is one that has been constructed by researchers to measure a particular knowledge level, affect, or behavior of clients (Jordan, Franklin, & Corcoran, 1997). It is a paper-and-pencil instrument and may take the form of a questionnaire, checklist, inventory, or rating scale. Two factors differentiate a standardized measuring instrument from any other: the effort made to attain uniformity in the measuring instrument's application, scoring, and interpretation; and the amount of work that has been devoted to ensuring that the instrument is valid and reliable.

Every measuring instrument, whether standardized or not, is designed to measure some specific quality; if it is valid, it will measure only that quality. The information sheet that usually accompanies a standardized measuring instrument will state the instrument's purpose: to measure anxiety about academic achievement, say, or to measure three aspects of assertiveness. In addition, the sheet will usually describe how the questions (items) on the instrument relate to that purpose and will say something about the clinical implications of the quality being measured.

The information sheet may also indicate what the instrument does not measure. A description of an instrument to measure aggression, for example, may specifically state that it does not measure hostility. This statement of purpose and the accompanying description improve chances that the instrument will be used as it was intended, to measure what it was designed to measure. In other words, it is more likely that the application of the instrument will be uniform.

The information sheet may also discuss the research studies done to ensure the instrument's validity, often including the instrument's ability to discriminate between clinical and nonclinical populations. It may mention other measuring instruments or criteria with which the instrument was compared, so that users will better understand what validity means in this particular instance. Information about reliability will usually be given via descriptions of the research studies undertaken to ensure reliability, and their results. Again, this information will help the worker who uses the instrument to know what kind of reliability can be expected.

Information will also be given about the characteristics of people on whom the instrument was tested. An instrument to measure loneliness, for example, may be accompanied by the information that it was tested on a sample of 399 undergraduate students (171 males, 228 females) from three large, urban-based university campuses. An instrument to measure self-esteem may have been tested on a sample of 240 eighth graders, 110 African Americans, and 130 Caucasians. In each case, scores will be given for the tested group and subgroups, so that the user can see what the norms are for people with particular demographic characteristics. A norm is an established score for a particular group against which the score of a client can be measured (Jordan, Franklin, & Corcoran, 1997).

Let us say, for example, that the average score of African-American eighth graders on the self-esteem measuring instrument was 40. In comparison, the average score for Caucasian eighth graders was 60. A practitioner who read this information on the sheet accompanying the instrument would know that an African-American client's score should be compared with the African-American average score of 40, and a Caucasian client's score should be compared with the

Caucasian average of 60. Without this information, the worker might think that an African-American client who scored 42 was suffering from low self-esteem—although, in such a case, 42 is really close to the average self-esteem score for African-American eighth graders.

The concept of norms has an important place in our profession, particularly in the administering of standardized measuring instruments. What is normal for an African-American child from a poor, urban neighborhood is not necessarily normal for a Caucasian child from a prosperous rural neighborhood; what is normal for one ethnic group may not be normal for another; what is normal for an adolescent female may not be normal for an adolescent male. It is very important that a client's score be compared with the average score of people with similar demographic characteristics. If this information is not available, as it sometimes is not, the social worker should bear in mind that an "unusual" score may not be at all unusual; it may be normal for the type of client being measured. Conversely, a normal-looking score may turn out to be unusual when the demographic characteristics of the client are taken into account.

The documentation sheet should also explain how to score the instrument and how to interpret the score. Scoring may be simple or relatively complex; it may involve summing specific items, reversing entered scores, or following a preset template. Often, it may also be accomplished on a computer. Some measuring instruments may yield one global score while others may provide several scores, each representing a dimension such as self-esteem or assertiveness.

Interpretation of the scores also varies depending on the instrument. When interpreting scores, it is particularly important to be aware that some scores represent the magnitude of problems, while others indicate the magnitude of positive attributes such as skills or knowledge. Depending on what is measured, increasing scores may indicate improvement or deterioration; the same is true for decreasing scores.

A standardized measuring instrument, then, should be accompanied by at least six kinds of information: (1) the purpose of the instrument, (2) a description of the instrument, (3) the instrument's validity, (4) the instrument's reliability, (5) norms, and (6) scoring and interpretation procedures. The amount and quality of information provided may be taken as an indicator of whether an instrument is standardized or not and, if it is, to what degree.

RATING SCALES

Rating scales use judgments by self or others to assign an individual (or program) a single score in relation to the program or practice objective being measured. What the various types of rating scales have in common is that they all rate clients on various traits or characteristics by locating them at some point on a continuum or in an ordered set of response categories, where numerical values are assigned to each category.

Rating scales may be completed by the person being evaluated (self-rating) or by some significant other, such as a parent, supervisor, spouse, or practitioner. Sometimes a client and a significant other are asked to complete the same rating scale in order to provide the worker with two different views. There are two types of rating scales that are useful for evaluative purposes: graphic rating scales and self-anchored rating scales.

GRAPHIC RATING SCALES

Graphic rating scales are structured with a practice or program objective described on a continuum from one extreme to the other, such as "low to high" or "most to least." The points of the continuum are ordered in equal intervals and are assigned numbers. Some points have descriptions to help people locate their positions.

Below is one such scale that asks children to rate their level of anxiety from "very anxious" to "very calm" (Kidder & Judd, 1986).

Check below how anxious you are.

```
100 ____    Very anxious
 90 ____
 80 ____
 70 ____
 60 ____
 50 ____    Neither anxious nor calm
 40 ____
 30 ____
 20 ____
 10 ____
  0 ____    Very calm
```

A second example of a graphic rating scale asks clients to rate their individual counseling sessions on a scale ranging from "not productive" to "very productive." The objective could be to increase a worker's understanding of how clients view his or her effectiveness.

> Please circle the number that comes closest to describing your feelings about the session you just completed.
>
> | 1 | 2 | 3 | 4 | 5 |
> |---|---|---|---|---|
>
> | Not productive | | Moderately productive | | Very productive |

The major advantage of graphic rating scales is that they are easy to use, though one must take care to develop appropriate descriptive statements. For example, end statements so extreme that it is unlikely anyone would choose them, such as "extremely hot" or "extremely cold," should not be used.

Note that the first graphic rating scale above provides data about a client, whereas the second scale provides data about a service.

SELF-ANCHORED RATING SCALES

Self-anchored rating scales are similar to graphic rating scales in that clients are asked to rate themselves on a continuum, usually a 7- or 9-point scale from low to high. They differ in that clients define the specific referents, or anchors, for three points on the continuum on a self-anchored scale. An anchor point is the point on a scale where a concrete descriptor is given to define the condition represented by that point. This type of scale is often used to measure such attributes as intensity of affect or pain. A self-anchored scale is an excellent source of data, because it is essentially developed by the person most familiar with the subtleties of the problem—the client.

A client who has difficulty being honest in group sessions, for example, could complete the following question (the three anchor points are put in by the client), which is intended to measure personal perceptions of his or her honesty. In the example below, the client writes in the three anchor points (i.e., can never be honest, can sometimes be honest, and can always be completely honest). A practice objective could be to increase his or her honesty within the group.

Indicate the extent to which you feel you can be honest in the group.

1	2	3	4	5	6	7	8	9

Can never be honest			Can sometimes be honest			Can always be completely honest		

Suppose that a client is feeling trapped in her marriage and in her role as a homemaker. She might develop a 9-point scale such as the one shown below, ranging from "I feel completely trapped," through "I feel I have some options," to "I do not feel trapped at all." If she is not able to analyze her feelings well enough to identify three distinct emotional levels between 5 and 9 or 1 and 5, she may prefer to use a 5-point scale instead. She should certainly be told that the intervals are equal; the distance between 8 and 9 is the same as the distance between 7 and 8, and so forth.

1	2	3	4	5	6	7	8	9

I Do not feel trapped at all			I Feel I have some options			I Feel completely trapped		

If the problem is not the extent to which the woman feels trapped but the intensity of the trapped feelings, she might consider what sort of emotions she experiences when she feels most and least trapped. If being most trapped involves desperate or suicidal feelings, these feelings will define the high end of the scale.

From this example, we can deduce the two major advantages of self-anchored scales. First, they are specific to the client in a way that a scale developed by someone else cannot be. They measure emotions known only to the client, and may therefore yield the most complete and accurate portrayal of the situation. Second, they can measure the intensity of an affect or attitude. Clients who suffer from feelings of anxiety or guilt or from physical ailments are often primarily concerned with intensity, and they may be more willing to fill out an instrument that reflects this concern.

There are also disadvantages to an instrument that is completed by the client. One major drawback is that clients may consciously or unconsciously distort their responses so as to appear more worthy or more deserving in the eyes of the worker. Analyzing an emotion thoroughly enough to rate it on a scale may result in changes to the emotion. This problem is known as "reactivity."

Self-anchored scales, then, are of particular value when the quality being measured is an emotion or thought pattern known only to the client, or when intensity is the primary concern. These scales can be used alone or in conjunction with other types of measuring instruments. They can also be used to supply data peripheral to the central problem: A client whose practice objective is weight loss, for example, might use a self-anchored scale to measure changes in self-esteem associated with the weight loss.

SUMMATED SCALES

Where rating scales obtain data from one question about the practice or program or objective, summated scales present multiple questions to which the client is asked to respond. Thus, summated scales combine responses to all of the questions on an instrument to form a single, overall score for the objective being measured. The responses are then totaled to obtain a composite score indicating the individual's position on the objective of interest.

Summated scales are used to assess individual or family problems, for needs assessment, and for other types of case- and program-level evaluation efforts. The scale poses a number of questions and asks clients to indicate the degree of their agreement or disagreement with each. Response categories may include such statements as "strongly agree," "agree," "disagree," and "strongly disagree."

FEATURES OF GOOD MEASURING INSTRUMENTS

As one might expect, some measuring instruments are better than others. There are five main features that distinguish a good instrument from a poor one: (1) validity, (2) reliability, (3) sensitivity, (4) nonreactivity, and (5) utility.

VALIDITY

A social worker who cannot find a measuring instrument to measure a particular practice or program objective—to decrease social isolation, for example—may be tempted to use an instrument that measures something closely related, say, loneliness. If instruments and concepts were really as interchangeable as that, we would never be quite sure what we are measuring. Note how the objective to "decrease social isolation" can be a practice objective as well as a program objective.

It is important to know that the instrument we choose will measure what we want it to measure and not anything else. An instrument that measures what it is supposed to measure, and measures only that, is called a valid instrument (Kyte & Bostwick, 1997).

If a number of questions on a measuring instrument are intended to measure the degree of loneliness, and if the instrument is valid, these questions should adequately reflect the true substance of loneliness. For instance, people who are lonely tend to feel that they have no one to turn to; they feel misunderstood and out of tune with the people around them; they feel withdrawn and are unhappy about being withdrawn; and they feel that their relationships are superficial. Each of these feelings, common to lonely people, contributes to the overall concept of loneliness.

If a measuring instrument is to truly measure loneliness, it must tap each one of these feelings, or at least an adequate sample of them. That is, it must reflect what loneliness really is and enable the clients to measure their feelings of loneliness against the entire spectrum of loneliness. A person who feels misunderstood, for example, is lonely; a person who feels misunderstood and also feels withdrawn is more lonely; a person who feels misunderstood and withdrawn and has no one to talk to is still lonelier. The measure is all a matter of degree.

Note that in order to construct an instrument to measure loneliness, we have to first operationalize the concept of loneliness, that is, to decide what specific feelings comprise that concept. An instrument purporting to measure loneliness will therefore be valid to the extent that its creators have identified all the requisite feelings and have included an adequate sample of them in the instrument. An instrument containing such an adequate sample is said to be content valid. Because it is almost impossible to identify all of the feelings that make up a complex concept like loneliness or depression, no instrument will be entirely content valid, only more or less so.

RELIABILITY

We have seen that, in testing for change, at least two and preferably more measurements are required. A social worker who uses the same measuring instrument more than once with the same client wants to assume that differences in the results (first measurement – second measurement = difference) are due to changes in the client. If this assumption is false—if the differences instead reflect, say, boredom with the questions—the instrument's results will give a false impression of the client's progress. It is therefore important that a measuring instrument gives the same result with the same unchanged client every time it is administered. An instrument that can do this is said to be reliable.

Of course, no client remains completely unchanged from one day to the next. The problem level may not have changed—the client may be just as depressed—but the client may be more tired or less anxious about taking the test, or more physically uncomfortable because the day is hotter. These random and irrelevant changes will probably affect a client's score to some degree, but if the instrument is reliable, this degree will not be large. In fact, an instrument is said to be reliable to the extent that results are not affected by random changes in the individual.

SENSITIVITY

Because changes in a client's problem level are often small, it is important that a measuring instrument be able to detect small changes. What is needed, in fact, is an instrument that is stable or reliable enough to ignore irrelevant changes and sensitive enough to detect small changes in the level of the real problem.

The key to achieving such subtlety of discrimination is to select an appropriate measurement method. Suppose, for example, that a practice objective is to reduce the number of nights on which a child wets his bed. The measure selected might be a count of the number of mornings on which the bed is dry. If the bed is wet every morning for a month despite the worker's intervention, we could assume that the intervention is ineffective.

But, if before the intervention started the child was wetting his bed five times a night and after intervention only once a night, the intervention has been successful in reducing the wetting episodes. This success was overlooked, however, because the measurement method selected was in this context insensitive. It measured whether the problem occurred, which it either does or does not; there are no degrees of change in between.

The same considerations apply when a problem is indicated by more than one behavior. A child may indicate problems with his or her teacher, for example, both by skipping the particular teacher's class and by being rude to the teacher when the child is in class. If the rudeness occurs more often than the skipping, it is sensible to count incidents of rudeness rather than of skipping, because the high-frequency behavior is more likely than the low-frequency behavior to reveal small changes in the child's attitude toward the teacher.

NONREACTIVITY

Sometimes the very act of measurement affects the behavior, affect, or knowledge-level objective that is being measured. Cigarette smokers who begin to count the number of cigarettes they smoke, for example, may smoke fewer cigarettes simply as a result of the counting, without any other intervention being involved. Staff being evaluated may change their routine because they know they are being evaluated. A child who knows that television watching is being monitored by a parent may watch television less to please or more to spite the parent, but in either case, the amount of television watching will have changed. It is therefore important that the measuring instrument chosen be nonreactive or not affect the behavior, affect, or knowledge objective being measured. A synonym for nonreactive is unobtrusive. Put another way, a worker's aim is to record a measurement as unobtrusively as possible.

UTILITY

Utility means usefulness. If a measuring instrument is to be useful, it also has to be practical in a particular situation with a particular client. The best way to demonstrate to the client such changes as improved posture or more frequent eye contact, for example, may be by making video recordings of successive interviews. If the client refuses to be videotaped, however, this particular measurement method cannot be used. It may be a perfectly valid and reliable measure, but it lacks utility.

To give another example, a practitioner may discover a perfect measuring instrument for measuring depression: It is valid, reliable, nonreactive, and sensitive to small changes, but it is also five pages long. In addition, it takes a long time to score and the numerical score, once obtained, is difficult to translate into a meaningful assessment of the client's depression. This instrument, though perfect in every other respect, is useless in practice because it takes too long to complete and too long to tabulate and interpret. Instruments that have utility are acceptable to the client; they are easy and quick to administer and score; and they give results that reveal the client's current state.

Naturally, an instrument that is short enough to have utility may be too short to be entirely valid. It may be impossible, for example, to sample loneliness adequately in a 10-item questionnaire. As is often the case, this is a matter for compromise: a situation in which the instrument developer's best judgment is the only real guide.

LOCATING STANDARDIZED MEASURING INSTRUMENTS

Once the need for measurement has been established, the next consideration is locating appropriate standardized measuring instruments from which to choose. The two general sources for locating such instruments are commercial or professional publishers and professional literature (Jordan, Franklin, & Corcoran, 1997).

PROFESSIONAL PUBLISHERS

Numerous commercial and professional publishing companies specialize in the production and sale of standardized measuring instruments for use in our profession. The cost of instruments purchased from a publisher varies considerably, depending on the instrument, the number of copies needed, and the publisher. The instruments generally are well developed and their psychometric properties are supported by the results of several research studies. Often they are accompanied by manuals that include the normative data for the instrument. As well, publishers are expected to comply with professional standards such as those established by the American Psychological Association and the National Association for Social Workers. These standards apply to claims made about the instrument's rationale, development, psychometric properties, administration, and interpretation of results.

Standards for the use of some instruments have been developed to protect the interests of clients. Consequently, purchasers of instruments may be required to have certain qualifications, such as possession of an advanced degree in a relevant field. A few publishers require membership in particular professional organizations. Most publishers will, however, accept an order from a social work student if it is cosigned by a qualified person, such as an instructor who will supervise the use of the instrument.

PROFESSIONAL JOURNALS AND BOOKS

Standardized measuring instruments are most commonly reproduced in professional journals; in fact, most commercially marketed instruments first appear in one of these publications. The instruments usually are supported by evidence of their validity and reliability, although they often require cross-validation and normative data from more representative samples and subsamples.

Locating instruments in journals or books is not easy. Of the two most common methods—computer searches of databanks and manual searches of the literature—the former is faster, unbelievably more thorough, and easier to use. Unfortunately, financial support for the development of comprehensive databanks has been limited and intermittent. Another disadvantage is that many articles on instruments are not referenced with the appropriate indicators for computer retrieval. These limitations are being overcome by the changing technology of computers and information retrieval systems. Several services now allow for a complex breakdown of measurement need; databanks that include references from over 1,300 journals, updated monthly, are now available from a division of Psychological Abstracts Information Services and Bibliographic Retrieval Services.

Nevertheless, most social workers will probably rely on manual searches of references such as *Psychological Abstracts*. Although the reference indices will be the same as those in the databanks accessible by computer, the literature search can be supplemented with appropriate seminal (original) reference volumes.

EVALUATING STANDARDIZED MEASURING INSTRUMENTS

A literature search should produce several instruments suitable for measuring a particular program or practice objective. The choice of one instrument over others depends on the strength of the quantitative data the instrument provides as well as its practicality in application. These two dimensions can be evaluated by asking a number of questions pertaining to the validity and reliability of the instrument, the population sample to be used, and the practicality of administering the instrument. The validity and reliability of both the instrument and the data collected by it are the most crucial concerns in evaluating any instrument. As these factors were discussed in detail above, the following discussion is confined to issues of sampling and practicality.

REPRESENTATIVENESS OF THE SAMPLE

One aspect of evaluating standardized instruments is the extent to which the data collected in setting the norms for the instrument represent the same types of individuals who are being measured. if the instrument being considered was formulated and tested on a sample drawn from a white Anglo-Saxon population, for example, it might give perfectly valid results when administered to white Anglo-Saxons, but not if it is administered to Native Americans, African Americans, or social minorities such as women. In general terms, the samples used in setting the norms for an instrument must reflect a population that is similar to those who will complete that instrument. Demographic characteristics such as age, gender, race, and socioeconomic status must also be considered.

Another consideration is the size of the sample: the larger the sample, the better. A further concern is when the data were collected from the sample. Data based on samples selected a long time ago may not be an adequate basis for accepting the instrument as psychometrically sound for contemporary use.

Practicality of Application

An instrument's practicality of application depends on its ease of implementation and ease of analysis of the data it generates. Practicality of application is the likelihood that the client will complete the instrument, for even the most valid and reliable instrument has no practical utility if it is left unanswered.

Likelihood of Completion

A longer instrument is usually more reliable than a shorter one, but it is also more time-consuming and so may not be completed by the client. This fact is especially important in case-level designs where multiple measures are needed.

The social acceptability of a measuring instrument turns on the client's, not the worker's, view of the appropriateness of the content. The content's perceived appropriateness as a measure of the practice or practice objective of interest—not what the instrument in fact measures but what it appears to measure—is referred to as *face validity*. In addition, an instrument that is offensive or insulting to clients will not be completed. Instruments should also be easy for clients to complete, with content and instructions that are neither above nor below their typical level of functioning, as well as questions that can be easily answered.

INTERPRETATION OF RESULTS

Interpretation is easiest when the instrument provides direct measurements, has utility, is nonreactive, is sensitive to small changes, and is easy to score.

Practice and program objectives that can be measured directly are often behavioral. Other objectives, such as self-esteem or depression, can be measured only indirectly, or through some behavior that is believed to be associated with the objective.

A measuring instrument is considered to have utility if the results provide some practical advantage or useful data. The significance of the results is obviously influenced by whether the instrument is reactive. The instrument has to be sensitive enough to pick up small changes in the practice or program objective being measured.

A final consideration is what is done with the instrument after it has been completed. It may seem self-evident that if an instrument is to provide meaningful data it must be possible to score it. The scoring procedures of many instruments, however, are too complicated and time-consuming to be practical in practice situations. Even though they are psychometrically sound, they should be eliminated in favor of others that can more easily be scored.

SUMMARY

This chapter discussed the concept of measurement: what measurement is, what a measuring instrument is, what will be measured, and by what method it will be measured. Rating scales, including graphic rating scales and self-anchored scales, were discussed along with summated scales. In addition, we considered the features required of a good measuring instrument.

C H A P T E R 7

UTILIZING CASE-LEVEL EVALUATIONS

THE PREVIOUS CHAPTER PRESENTED the measurement process: what and how program and client practice objectives (client target problems) can be measured, who should measure them, when and where they can be measured, and what measuring instruments can be used. This chapter discusses how the measurement process helps us to informally and formally evaluate our practice efforts with our clients—that is, at the case level.

INFORMAL, OR "SUBJECTIVE," CASE-LEVEL EVALUATIONS

An "objective" method of evaluation is one in which the evaluation is based on the analysis of systematically collected valid and reliable data, that is, on the collation and interpretation of data

173

generated by standardized measuring instruments. Correspondingly, "nonobjective" evaluations are derived from information developed from theories and descriptions considered relevant by the practitioner. Because nonobjective data collection is relatively less formal and rigorous than its objective data collection counterpart, it is also known as *informal evaluation*. Informal evaluation takes two forms: private case consultations and case conferences.

CASE CONSULTATIONS

Many professional social workers consult informally with others regarding their cases. These requests for advice are usually accompanied by a description of the client's circumstances, the interventions the worker has tried so far, and the present condition of the client as perceived by the practitioner. Sometimes these descriptions are written, but, more often than not, communication is verbal. In either case the consultation is informal because no authority structure mandates or controls it. And, it is "nonobjective" because the information exchanged is not derived from data obtained through standardized measurement.

The disadvantages of case consultations lie in their lack of objectivity and precision, or, in other words, in their "nonobjective" nature. Their main advantage is their efficiency, which is a function of their informal nature: Rapid exchange of ideas and information is facilitated by the absence of formal documentation and procedures.

CASE CONFERENCES

Case conferences tend to be more formal than private consultations in that the social worker and other professionals are usually required to attend, and minutes may be taken and disseminated to participants. Nevertheless, the presentation of the case tends to remain "nonobjective," a description reflecting the practitioner's point of view. Concurring and opposing viewpoints are generally couched in the same lack of precision. Although much information of value may be exchanged, it is not data derived from standardized measurements and, therefore, its reliability and validity are unknown.

The major advantage of a case conference is that all workers involved with a particular client can meet face to face, share their perceptions or concerns, and perhaps leave the conference feeling that they have been heard, something has been resolved, and future client problems can be addressed with the help of people who have already shown themselves to be caring and cooperative. As before, the disadvantages are lack of objectivity and lack of precision.

While private consultations and case conferences are a very important part of professional practice, these two informal evaluation methods should be used in conjunction with formal case-level evaluations.

FORMAL, OR "OBJECTIVE," CASE-LEVEL EVALUATIONS

Formal case-level evaluations—the main topic of this chapter—are used by social workers in many ways. Unlike case consultations and case conferences mentioned above, they are formal and "objective" methods of evaluation, based on the analysis of collected data usually generated by standardized measuring instruments. They are sometimes known as single-system designs, single-case designs, single-subject designs, ideographic designs, $N = 1$ designs, interrupted time-series designs, and subject-replication designs.

Whatever name is used, a formal case-level evaluation is a study of one entity—*a* single client, *a* single group, *a* single couple, *a* single family, *a* single organization, or *a* single community—involving repeated measurements over time in order to measure change. The results of a number of evaluations can be aggregated to assess the effectiveness of a program as a whole. Formal case-level evaluations, however, are, first and foremost, used to measure client practice objectives, hereafter called *client target problems.*

Formal case-level evaluations focus on practitioners' activities and their clients' target problem outcomes so that cause-effect relationships can be established in some cases. There are a large number of case-level evaluations, ranging from the qualitative to the quantitative and from the exploratory to the explanatory.

As we know, the term *qualitative* refers to a description in words, which is less precise than a quantitative description, or one given in numbers. An explanatory study is one in which we manipulate certain factors in order to gain a greater degree of control over the treatment process. A descriptive study involves less manipulation and hence less control, and an exploratory study involves no manipulation and virtually no control. The case consultations and case conferences mentioned earlier in this chapter fall into the qualitative, exploratory category. The following diagram represents the relationship among the three knowledge levels:

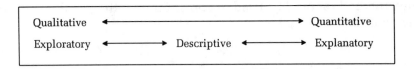

An evaluation continuum is only a continuum; that is, there is no point at which qualitative becomes quantitative or descriptive becomes explanatory. Various case-level evaluation designs are placed on the continuum according to the degree to which they manifest descriptive and manipulative qualities. These degrees merge and blend with one another. The following discussion on pages 176-207 has been taken and slightly modified from Williams, Tutty, and Grinnell (1995).

REQUIREMENTS OF FORMAL CASE-LEVEL EVALUATIONS

In order to carry out a single-case evaluation, the client's target problem must be identified, the desired target problem to be achieved must be decided upon, the intervention that is most likely to eliminate the client's target problem must be selected, the intervention must be implemented, and the client's progress must be continually monitored to see if the client's target problem has been resolved, or at least reduced. If practitioners are careful to organize, measure, and record what they do, single-case evaluations, will naturally take shape in the clients' files, and the results can be used to guide future interventive efforts.

Formal case-level evaluations are one of the most promising

evaluative tools available to line-level practitioners. A number of features are integral to these designs: (1) establishing baselines; (2) setting reliable, valid, and measurable target problems; (3) using repeated measurements of the practice target problems; (4) graphically displaying data; and (5) making comparisons across phases.

ESTABLISHING BASELINES

A baseline is essentially a measure of the client's problem before the worker provides a service. By establishing a baseline, we attempt to find out how long the problematic event lasts, how often it occurs and at what intensity, or whether it occurs at all in the client's normal life.

Suppose, for example, that a child throws temper tantrums. Before intervening, the worker will want to know how frequent and intense these tantrums are, when and where they occur, and for how long they last, in addition to trying to gain insight into the events that precipitate or alleviate them. An obvious way to gain such knowledge is to do nothing in the way of intervention while collecting the necessary data. The parents might be asked to keep a client log in which they record the day, date, and start and finish time of each episode together with the events that occurred immediately preceding, during, and after it.

Alternatively, a standardized measuring instrument might be used, over a period of time, to measure the magnitude of the target problem. In either case, at the end of the period, the practitioner will have baseline data on the tantrums as well as some data about possible precipitating events. These data provide a standard against which change can be measured, and provide some indication of the most effective interventive method to use.

SETTING RELIABLE, VALID, AND MEASURABLE TARGET PROBLEMS

One of the first tasks a worker does when initially seeing a client is to establish the purpose of why they are together. Why has the client approached the worker? Or, in many nonvoluntary situations, such as in probation and parole or child abuse situations, why has the worker approached the client? The two need to formulate target problems for their mutual working relationship. Client target problems are affects, knowledge levels, or behaviors that need to be changed.

Many times, clients do not have just one target problem, they have many. They sometimes have a number of interrelated target problems and, even if there is only one that is more important than the rest, they may not know what it is. Nevertheless, they may be quite clear about the desired outcome of their involvement with social work services. They may want to "fix" their lives so that, "Johnny listens when I ask him to do something," or "My partner pays more attention to me," or "I feel better about myself at work."

Unfortunately, many clients express their desired target problems in vague, ambiguous terms, possibly because they themselves do not know exactly what they want to change; they only know that something should be different. If a worker can establish (with the guidance of the client) what should be changed, why it should be changed, how it should be changed, and to what degree it should be changed, the solution to the target problem will not be far away.

Consider Heather, for example, who wants her partner, Ben, to pay more attention to her. Heather may mean sexual attention, in which case the couple's sexual relations may be the target problem. On the other hand, Heather may mean that she and Ben do not socialize enough with friends, or that Ben brings work home from the office too often, or that Ben has hobbies she does not share, or any of a host of things.

Establishing clearly what the desired change would look like is the first step in developing the target problem. Without this, the worker and client could wander around forever through the target problem maze, never knowing what, if anything, needs to be solved. Desired change cannot occur if no one knows what change is desired. It is, therefore, very important that the target problem to be solved be precisely stated as early as possible.

Continuing with the above example of Heather and Ben, and after a great deal of exploration, the worker agrees that Heather and Ben have many target problems to work on, such as improving their child discipline strategies, improving their budgeting skills, improving their communication skills, and many other issues that, when dealt with, can lead to a successful marriage. For now, however, they agree to work on one target problem of increasing the amount of time they spend together with friends. To do this, the worker, Heather, and Ben must conceptualize and operationalize the term "increasing the amount of time they spend together with friends." As we know, a variable is conceptualized by defining it in a way that is relevant to the situation and operationalized in such a way that it can be measured.

Heather may say that she wishes she and Ben could visit friends together more often. The target problem has now become a little more specific: It has narrowed from "increasing the amount of time they spend together with friends" to "Heather and Ben visiting friends more often.""Visiting friends more often with Ben," however, is still an ambiguous term. It may mean once a month or every night, and the achievement of the target problem's solution cannot be known until the meaning of "more often" has been clarified.

If Heather agrees that she would be happy to visit friends with Ben once a week, the ambiguous target problem may be restated as a specific, measurable target problem—"to visit friends with Ben once a week." The social worker may discover later that "friends" is also an ambiguous term. Heather may have meant "her friends," while Ben may have meant "his friends," and the social worker may have imagined that the "friends" were mutual.

The disagreement about who is to be regarded as a friend may not become evident until the worker has monitored their progress for a month or so and found that no improvement was occurring. In some cases, poor progress may be due to the selection of an inappropriate interventive strategy. In other cases, it may mean that the target problem itself is not as specific, complete, and clear as it should be. Before deciding that the interventive strategy needs to be changed, it is always necessary to clarify with the client exactly what it is that specifically needs to be achieved.

USING REPEATED MEASUREMENTS
OF THE PRACTICE TARGET PROBLEMS

Formal case-level evaluations rely on repeated valid and reliable measurements; change is perceived and measured by repeated administrations of the same measuring instrument under the same conditions. Repeated measurements document trends (if any), as well as how the target problem is changing over time.

GRAPHICALLY DISPLAYING DATA

As we know, the word *measurement* is the process of assigning a number to a variable. If the variable (target problem) being considered is depression as rated by the *GCS* (General Contentment Scale), and if Bob scores 72, then 72 is the number assigned to Bob's initial level of depression. The worker will try to reduce his initial score of 72 to at least 30—the minimum desired score. The worker can then select and implement an intervention and ask Bob to complete the *GCS* again, say once a week, until the score of 30 has been reached. Bob's depression levels can be plotted (over a 12-week period) on a graph, such as the one shown in Figure 7.1.

In the graph, Bob's depression level for each week is plotted on the y-axis, while time, in weeks, is plotted on the x-axis. There is a reason for this. Obviously, the social worker is hoping that the selected intervention will result in lowering Bob's level of depression, over time, as measured by the *GCS*. In other words, the worker is hypothesizing that: If Intervention *A* is implemented, Bob's depression will decrease. In evaluation terminology, the independent variable in this hypothesis is the intervention (*X*) and the dependent variable (*Y*) is Bob's depression level. The frequency of Bob's 10-minute crying spells per day, as recorded by Bob's wife, Maria, could also be graphed.

MAKING COMPARISONS ACROSS PHASES

A phase is any distinct part of the contact between a social worker and a client. The first few weeks of service, for example, may be spent collecting baseline data: This is one phase. Then an intervention (services) may be tried: This is the second phase. If the services do not seem to be effective, a different intervention may be tried: This is the third phase.

It is customary to use letters to designate the different phases. The letter *A* represents the baseline phase. Successive interventions are represented by successive letters: *B* for the first, *C* for the second, *D* for the third, and so on. A case-level evaluation design in which a baseline phase is followed by an interventive phase is therefore called an *AB* design. Similarly, an *ABC* design is one in which a baseline phase (*A*) is followed by two different interventive phases (*B* and *C*).

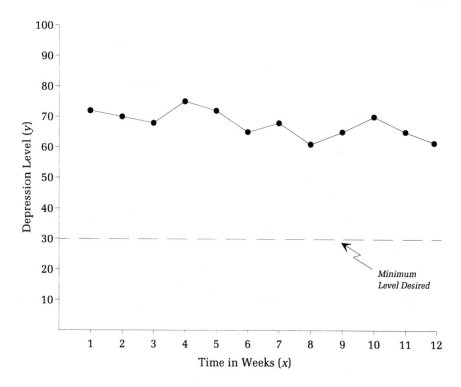

FIGURE 7.1   BOB'S DEPRESSION LEVEL OVER TIME

If an intervention is not really different but is merely a slight variation of one tried before, it is represented by the original letter plus a subscript. One way of improving knowledge in a certain area, for example, may be to set homework assignments. This may be the first intervention tried, or Phase *B*. If understanding does not improve to the desired degree, the number of homework assignments set may be increased.

This second intervention is merely an intensified version of the first and would be designated Phase B_2, with the first intervention now considered B_1. Phases are usually represented and labeled on a graph by dashed vertical lines (see Figures 7.4 and 7.5 for examples).

EXPLORATORY FORMAL CASE-LEVEL EVALUATIONS

As discussed, exploratory, descriptive, and explanatory research studies fall on a knowledge-level continuum. To review briefly, exploratory studies begin with little knowledge in the target problem area and produce only uncertain knowledge. Descriptive studies provide further descriptive facts, while explanatory studies attempt to explain the facts already gathered and produce the most certain level of knowledge.

Case evaluations are categorized as exploratory, descriptive, or explanatory, depending on the level of certainty they provide regarding the effectiveness of the intervention in resolving the client's target problem. Inevitably, the least complex designs, at the exploratory level, provide the least certainty about whether the intervention was effective in bringing about the desired change.

There are three kinds of exploratory formal case-level evaluation designs: (1) the *B* design, (2) the *BC* design, and (3) the *BCD* design.

THE B DESIGN

The first type of exploratory case-level evaluation design is the *B* design, which is the simplest of all case-level evaluation designs. The italicized letter *B* refers to the fact that an intervention of some kind has been introduced. Let us take a simple example of how a *B* design works.

A couple, David and Donna, have had a long history of interrupting one another while the other is talking. They have tried to stop the pattern of this destructive behavior, to no avail. They have finally decided to do something about this and have sought out the services of a social worker. After some exploration, it becomes apparent that the couple need to concentrate on their interruptive behaviors. In short, the worker wishes to reduce the frequency with which David and Donna interrupt each other while conversing. This could be observed and measured by having them talk to each other while in weekly, one-hour sessions.

The worker teaches basic communication skills (the intervention) to the couple and has them practice these skills during each weekly session while other marital relationship issues are being addressed. Each week during therapy, while the couple is engaged in conversation, the worker makes a record of how many times each partner interrupts the other. Thus, in this situation, the worker is trying to reduce the number of interruptions—the target problem. For now, suppose that the data for David and Donna over a 12-week period look like those displayed in Figure 7.2.

Figure 7.2 shows that the number of times interruptions occurred decreased gradually over the 12-week period until it reached zero in the twelfth week—that is, until the goal of therapy had been achieved. Even so, the worker could continue to record the level of the target problem for a longer period of time to ensure that success was being maintained.

In this case, the worker hypothesized that if the intervention—teaching communication skills—were implemented, then the number of times the couple interrupted each other while conversing during therapy sessions would be reduced. Figure 7.2 shows that the target problem was achieved for both partners, but it does not show that the worker's hypothesis was in fact correct. Perhaps teaching communication skills had nothing to do with reducing the couple's interruptions.

The interruptions may have been reduced because of something else the worker did (besides the communication skills training), or something the couple did, or something a friend did. There is even the possibility that their interruptions would have ceased if no one had done anything at all. Be that as it may, extraneous variables have not been controlled for. Thus, we cannot know how effective this particular intervention is in solving this particular target problem for this particular couple.

If we use the same interventive strategy with a second couple experiencing the same target problem and achieve the same results, it becomes *more likely* that the intervention produced the results. If the same results follow the same intervention with a third similar couple, it becomes *more likely* still. Thus, we can become more certain that an intervention causes a result the more times the intervention is successfully used with similar target problems.

If an intervention is used only once, however, as is the case with the exploratory B design, no evidence for causation can be inferred. All that can be gleaned from Figure 7.2 is that, for whatever reason, David's and Donna's target problem was reduced. Or,

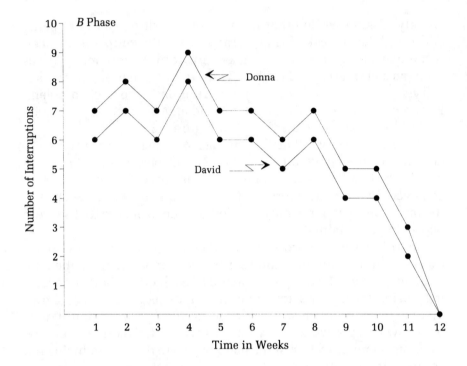

FIGURE 7.2   *B* DESIGN: FREQUENCY OF INTERRUPTIONS FOR A
COUPLE DURING ONE INTERVENTION,
INDICATING AN IMPROVEMENT

if a graph such as Figure 7.3 is obtained instead, this indicates that
the target problem has not been resolved, or has been only partly
resolved. If David and Donna continued to interrupt each other,
week after week, a graph like the one shown in Figure 7.3 would be
produced.

The data from graphs, such as the data presented in Figures 7.2
and 7.3, are extremely useful since a worker will be better able to
judge whether the intervention should be continued, modified, or
abandoned in favor of a different interventive strategy. In the simplest of terms, the *B* design only monitors the effectiveness of an
intervention over time and indicates when the desired level of the
target problem has been reached.

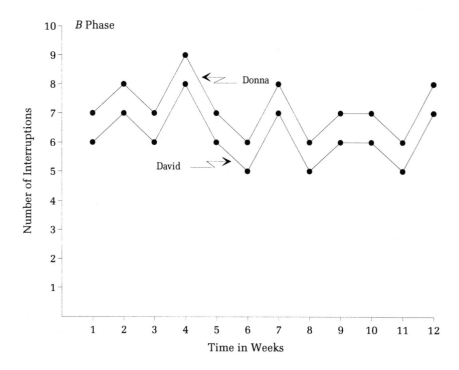

FIGURE 7.3   *B* DESIGN: FREQUENCY OF INTERRUPTIONS FOR A
COUPLE DURING ONE INTERVENTION, INDICATING
NO IMPROVEMENT

THE BC *AND* BCD *DESIGNS*

The second and third types of exploratory case-level evaluation
designs are the *BC* and *BCD* designs. As we know, in the *B* design
previously described, the italicized letter *B* represents a single
interventive strategy. Suppose now that a *B* intervention, such as
communication skills training, is implemented with David and
Donna, and a graph like the one shown in Figure 7.4 is obtained.
The left side of the graph shows that the target problem is not being
resolved with the implementation of the *B* intervention, and the
social worker may feel that it is time to change the intervention, so
a *C* intervention is tried starting the fifth week. Four weeks, for
example, may have been as long as the worker was prepared to wait
for the hoped-for change to occur as the result of the *B* intervention.

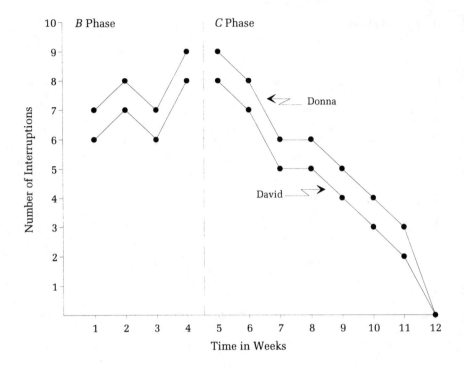

FIGURE 7.4   *BC* DESIGN: FREQUENCY OF INTERRUPTIONS FOR
                     A COUPLE AFTER TWO INTERVENTIONS,
                     INDICATING AN IMPROVEMENT WITH THE SECOND
                     INTERVENTION

As can be seen in Figure 7.4, the worker implemented a second
different intervention, *C*, starting the fifth week and measured the
target problem in the same way as before, by making weekly recordings of the number of times that each partner interrupts the other
during the course of therapy sessions. These measurements are
graphed as before, plotting the level of the client's target problem
along the *y*-axis and the time in weeks along the *x*-axis. The data
are shown in the *C* phase of Figure 7.4.

Figure 7.4 shows that no change occurred in the target problem
after Intervention *B* was implemented, but that the target problem
was resolved following the implementation of Intervention *C*. As
before, extraneous variables have not been considered, and Figure
7.4 does not show that Intervention *C* caused the target problem to

be resolved: It shows only that success occurred during Intervention *C* but not during Intervention *B*.

In order to demonstrate causation, the worker would have to obtain successful results with Intervention *C* on a number of occasions with different couples experiencing the exact same target problem. Similarly, the inherent uselessness of Intervention *B* could be shown only if it was implemented unsuccessfully with other couples—an unlikely event since the most hopeful intervention surely would be implemented first.

If Intervention *C* does not work either, the worker will have to try yet another intervention (Intervention *D*). Combined graphs may be produced, as in Figure 7.5, illustrating the results of the entire *BCD* case-level evaluation design.

Since the *BC* and *BCD* designs involve successive, different interventions, they are sometimes known as successive interventions designs. It is conceivable that an *E* intervention might be necessary, forming a *BCDE* design, and even an *F*, forming a *BCDEF* design. Multiple-treatment interference, discussed in Chapter 8, is a major threat to the external validity of successive intervention designs. Let us now turn our attention to descriptive case-level evaluations.

DESCRIPTIVE FORMAL CASE-LEVEL EVALUATIONS

One of the difficulties with the three exploratory case-level evaluations previously discussed (*B*, *BC*, and *BCD* designs) is that they provide no data about the level of the client's target problem *before* the intervention was introduced. Bob, for example, might show himself to be severely depressed, according to his initial score of 72 on the *GCS* (Figure 7.1). Perhaps the cause of his depression, however, is the recent death of his 20-year-old cat, Teddy, and the target problem will resolve itself naturally as he recovers from Teddy's loss.

Or perhaps, on the day that he approached the worker, he was more depressed than he usually is. Thus, it would have been useful if we had had an accurate measure of Bob's depression levels over time *before* he received social work services. Descriptive case-level evaluations provide such a procedure. We will briefly discuss two

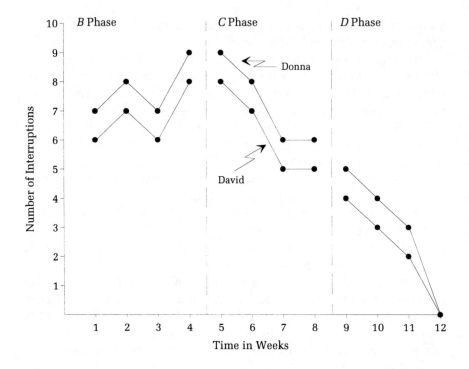

FIGURE 7.5   *BCD* DESIGN: FREQUENCY OF INTERRUPTIONS FOR
A COUPLE AFTER THREE INTERVENTIONS,
INDICATING THE BEST IMPROVEMENT WITH THE
THIRD INTERVENTION

types of descriptive case-level evaluation designs: (1) the *AB* design
and (2) the *ABC* design.

THE AB DESIGN

An *AB* design is useful when we can afford to monitor a client's
target problem for a short time *before* implementing an intervention. Suppose a social worker is seeing Juan, who experiences a
great deal of anxiety in social situations, for example. He is nervous
when he speaks to his teacher or boss or when he meets people for
the first time, and the prospect of speaking in public appalls him.
The worker could decide that progress for Juan's target problem

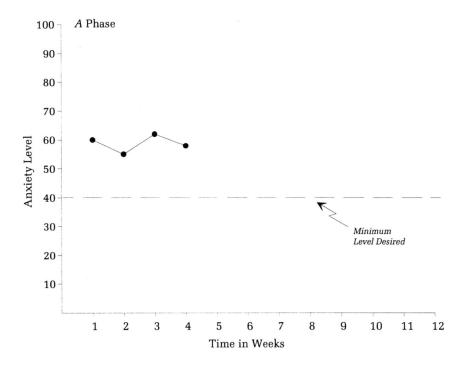

FIGURE 7.6   MAGNITUDE OF JUAN'S ANXIETY LEVEL BEFORE
AN INTERVENTION, INDICATING A STABLE
BASELINE

might be measured in two ways: first, Juan will complete the Interaction and Audience Anxiousness Scale (*IAAS*) that measures
social anxiety. For the first four weeks, the worker will not intervene at all. The purpose of the worker's contact, in these weeks,
will be merely to gather data on the initial level of Juan's anxiety—that is, to gather baseline data.

The period in which initial data are being gathered is known as
the *A* phase of the study. The italicized letter *A* symbolizes no
intervention—in the same way as the letters *B, C,* and *D* symbolize
the first, second, and third interventive strategies, respectively.
Suppose, now, that Juan scores 60 on the *IAAS* the first week he is
assessed, 55 the second week, 62 the third, and 58 on the fourth.
Juan's anxiety scores for this four-week period before an intervention was introduced can be graphed as shown in Figure 7.6.

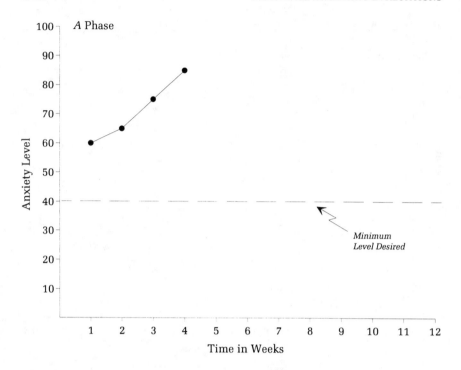

FIGURE 7.7   MAGNITUDE OF JUAN'S ANXIETY LEVEL BEFORE
                     AN INTERVENTION, INDICATING A
                     DETERIORATING BASELINE

Taken together, the four scores in Figure 7.6 show that Juan's anxiety level is reasonably stable at about an average of 59. Since it has remained relatively stable over a four-week period, the likelihood is that it will continue to remain at the same level if a social worker does not intervene: That is, Juan's target problem will not solve itself. The worker would be even more justified to intervene immediately if Juan achieved anxiety scores as illustrated in Figure 7.7. Here, Juan's anxiety level is getting worse.

Conversely, if he achieved the four scores shown in Figure 7.8, the worker might be reluctant to intervene, because Juan's anxiety level is decreasing anyway. If the worker did intervene, however, and his anxiety level continued to decrease, we would never know if the worker's intervention had a positive effect or if the same result would have been achieved without it.

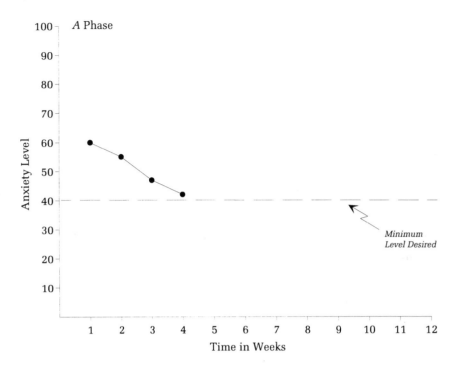

FIGURE 7.8   MAGNITUDE OF JUAN'S ANXIETY LEVEL BEFORE
AN INTERVENTION, INDICATING AN IMPROVING
BASELINE

The first four scores shown in Figure 7.9 vary to such an extent that it is not possible to tell how anxious Juan really is. Again, we would be reluctant to intervene because there would be no way of knowing whether Juan was making progress or not, and whether the intervention was helpful or not. In order to conduct an *AB* single-case research study—and in order to be helpful to a client—the level of the target problem must be stable (e.g., Figure 7.6), or getting worse (e.g., Figure 7.7) in the *A* phase.

Suppose that it has been established that Juan's target problem level is stable, as illustrated in Figure 7.6. A target problem may then be set: to reduce Juan's social anxiety level to 40. Forty has been selected because people who suffer from social anxiety at a clinically significant level tend to score *above* 40 on the *IAAS*, while people whose social anxiety is not clinically significant score

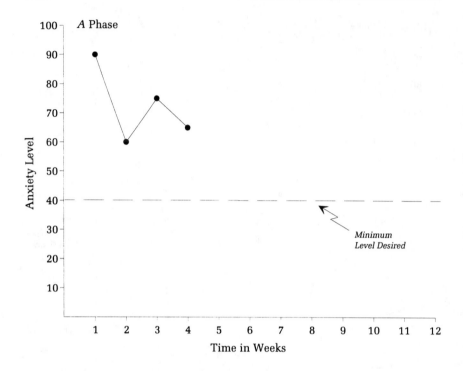

FIGURE 7.9 MAGNITUDE OF JUAN'S ANXIETY LEVEL BEFORE
AN INTERVENTION, INDICATING A FLUCTUATING
BASELINE

below 40. It will not really matter whether the target problem is
precisely met. If Juan becomes more confident in social situations,
feels more ready to meet people, and only reaches a score of 45,
this may be good enough to warrant termination of services.

Having produced a baseline graph and established a target
problem, the worker can now implement an intervention package
that could include such activities as role playing through anxiety-
producing situations and coping strategies. Whatever the intervention package, it is important that a record of its process is made so
that another worker will know, in the future, exactly what the
specific intervention was.

Once the baseline, or *A* phase, has been established, the *B*
phase will proceed as in the three exploratory *B* designs previously
discussed. Juan will complete the *IAAS* weekly, or every two

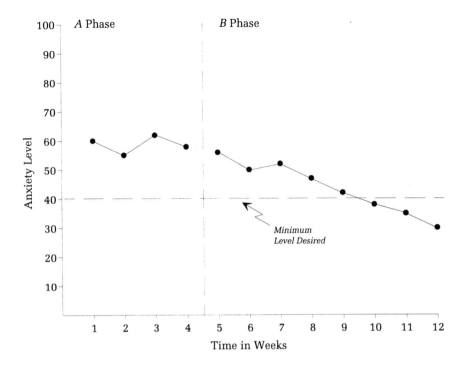

FIGURE 7.10   *AB* DESIGN: MAGNITUDE OF JUAN'S ANXIETY LEVEL BEFORE AND AFTER AN INTERVENTION, INDICATING AN IMPROVEMENT

weeks, or however often is appropriate, and the scores will be graphed. Figure 7.10 shows a relatively stable *A* phase over the first four weeks (from Figure 7.6), and a decreasing anxiety level over the next eight weeks, while the intervention is being implemented. The dashed vertical line on the graph indicates the time at which the intervention was begun.

The worker could continue to monitor the level of Juan's target problem after it has been achieved in order to ensure that progress is being maintained. We cannot adequately judge the usefulness of an intervention until it is known not only that it works, but that it continues to work when it is no longer the focus of our attention. It is, therefore, essential to make follow-up measurements whenever possible, perhaps a month, six months, and a year after the client's target problem appears to have been resolved. The actual

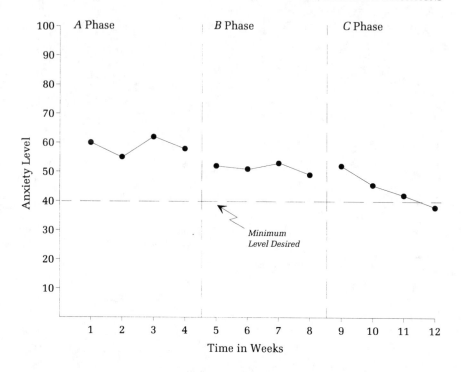

FIGURE 7.11   *ABC* DESIGN: MAGNITUDE OF JUAN'S ANXIETY
LEVEL BEFORE AND AFTER TWO
INTERVENTIONS, INDICATING AN IMPROVEMENT
WITH THE *C* INTERVENTION

number and frequency of follow-up measurements will depend on
the type of target problem and the client's situation.

THE ABC DESIGN

The second type of descriptive case-level evaluation design is
the *ABC* design. Figure 7.11 shows the same *A* phase as in Figure
7.10, but now the *B* phase indicates that Juan's target problem is
not being satisfactorily resolved. In this case, his worker will probably want to change the *B* intervention, initiating a *C* intervention.
Juan's target problem level will be continually measured over time
and may progress to the level set in the target problem. On the

other hand, if there is still no improvement, or an insufficient improvement, a *D* intervention may need to be implemented.

As with the exploratory *BC* and *BCD* designs presented earlier, descriptive *ABC* and *ABCD* case-level evaluation designs involve trying successive interventions until the target problem level is reached, or almost reached. Exploratory designs, however, only enable workers to compare the progress made in each new phase with progress in the previous phase or phases. Look at Phase *B* in Figure 7.11. Juan's *B*-phase scores are slightly lower than his *A*-phase scores. Some improvement has occurred, although a worker may not have been able to judge that from the *B*-phase if baseline scores were not established. When the results are not clear-cut, it is the *A* phase that enables us to see whether there has been a little progress from the initial target problem level, no progress at all, or perhaps even a regression.

When a new intervention is initiated in the *C* phase, the social worker is not really starting again from the beginning. The worker is starting from where the target problem level was at the end of the *B* phase. If the *C* intervention is successful in resolving the target problem, it is impossible to tell, without further studies, whether the *C* intervention would have worked alone or whether it was the combination of *B* and *C* that did the trick. If a *D* intervention is employed as well, the various effects of *B*, *C,* and *D* grow even more intertwined, so that we cannot know which intervention had what effect—even supposing that a given intervention had any effect whatsoever. We will now turn our attention to explanatory case-level evaluations.

EXPLANATORY FORMAL CASE-LEVEL EVALUATIONS

Explanatory case-level evaluations attempt to come to grips with the problem of cause and effect. If a worker wants to know whether a particular intervention is effective in a particular target problem area, the following question needs to be answered: Did intervention *X* cause result *Y*? At an explanatory level, the worker needs to be sure that nothing other than the intervention caused the result.

In order to conduct an internally valid study, three factors need to be taken into account. First, we must show that the independent variable occurred before the dependent variable. Second, the inevitable cohort of extraneous variables must be identified and dealt with. Third, a worker will need to consider other general factors that may pose a threat to internal validity. An improvement in a client's level of self-esteem, for example, may occur not only from the interventive efforts. The improvement may be due to changes in another aspect of the client's life, such as getting a new job, or an intervention by another practitioner such as being placed on medication. Alternatively, things may improve spontaneously.

Explanatory case-level evaluations attempt to control for such other occurrences by showing that there were two or more times in which improvement was noted in the client after a given intervention. If such is the case, then the likelihood of the improvement being related to other rival hypotheses is decreased. There are three types of explanatory case-level evaluation designs: (1) the *ABAB* design, (2) the *BAB* design, and (3) the *BCBC* design.

THE ABAB DESIGN

As the name might imply, an *ABAB* case-level evaluation design is simply two descriptive *AB* designs strung together. This design is most appropriate with interventions that produce temporary or easily removable effects, or when an intervention is withdrawn but measurements on the client's target problem continue to be made.

Referring back to Juan, whose target problem is social anxiety, Figure 7.10 illustrates a descriptive *AB* design as previously described. It shows a stable *A* or baseline phase, followed by a successful *B* phase, where his social anxiety level is gradually reduced to below 40 during the 10th week. It cannot be certain, however, that the intervention caused the reduction in anxiety until the same intervention has been tried again and has achieved the same result. The more times the same intervention is followed by the same result, the more certain it will become that the intervention caused the result.

Suppose, now, that Juan successfully reached his target problem score of 40 during the first *B* phase (6th week), as illustrated in Figure 7.12. After services are withdrawn, Juan then experiences

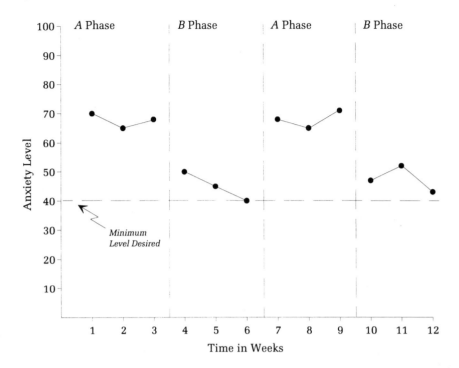

FIGURE 7.12   *ABAB* DESIGN: MAGNITUDE OF JUAN'S ANXIETY LEVEL BEFORE AND AFTER AN INTERVENTION, INDICATING HIGH DETERIORATION IN THE SECOND *A* PHASE

some social reversals as his anxiety mounts once more, as indicated in the second *A* Phase in Figure 7.12. The worker provides services for the second time and has Juan complete the same *IAAS* during the second *B* phase.

The worker goes through the same process as was done the first time, establishing a baseline score, or *A* phase, in the first few weeks before the introduction of an intervention. The same intervention is implemented, and measurements of Juan's progress are obtained through the *B* phase, producing almost the same result.

We can now be more certain that the intervention caused the result since the same intervention was followed by the same result on two separate occasions. In this example, Juan's social anxiety level returned to the original baseline level—the level established

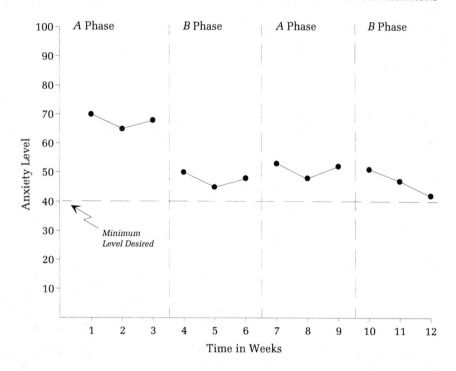

FIGURE 7.13   *ABAB* DESIGN: MAGNITUDE OF JUAN'S ANXIETY
                        LEVEL BEFORE AND AFTER AN INTERVENTION,
                        INDICATING LOW DETERIORATION IN THE
                        SECOND *A* PHASE

in the first *A* phase. From an evaluation perspective, this is an ideal
state of affairs, since the first *AB* study can now be duplicated
almost exactly. From a practice perspective, however, it is worri-
some, as we would like to think that a client will continue to benefit from an intervention after it has been withdrawn.

In fact, many clients do continue to benefit. Juan may have
learned and remembered techniques for reducing his anxiety, and
it would be unusual for his target problem to return to its exact
original level. Figure 7.13 illustrates a scenario in which Juan's
anxiety target problem did not return to its original level.

In a case such as that shown in Figure 7.13, it is still quite
possible to conduct an *ABAB* study. The baseline scores in the
second *A* phase are relatively stable, even though they show an

improvement over the first *A* phase; and the second *B* phase shows once again that the intervention has been followed by a reduction in Juan's social anxiety level.

Sometimes it is important to continue to measure the target problem even after it appears to have been resolved and the intervention has been withdrawn. Those workers who continue to measure a client's target problem, perhaps while working on a different issue, are essentially constructing another baseline. This can be used as an additional *A* phase if the client suffers a regression and needs the intervention to be repeated.

An *ABAB* design in which the target problem, once resolved, reverts to its original level, is known as a reversal design. Such a design may be implemented accidentally. We never intend that the client's target problem should reoccur. If an *ABAB* design is to be conducted purposefully, in order to attain more certainty about the effectiveness of an intervention, then another way to proceed is to use a multiple-baseline design.

MULTIPLE-BASELINE DESIGNS   In multiple-baseline designs, the *AB* phase is duplicated not with the same client and the same target problem but with two or more different clients (e.g., Figure 7.14), across two or more different settings (e.g., Figure 7.15), or across two or more different target problems (e.g., Figure 7.16).

Two or More Clients.   Suppose a worker has not just one client with a social anxiety target problem but two or more. The worker could establish a baseline with each client, implement an identical intervention with each one, and compare several *AB* designs with one another. If the *B* phases show similar results, the worker has grounds to speculate that the intervention caused the result.

As always, we must take care that the effect ascribed to the intervention did not result, instead, from extraneous variables. If the worker's socially anxious clients all happened to be residents of the same nursing home, for example, some event in the nursing home could have contributed to the reduction in their anxiety: perhaps a newly instituted communal activity. This possibility can be controlled for—that is, we can ensure that extraneous variables have not occurred—by introducing the same intervention with each client at different times. Figure 7.14 illustrates an example of a

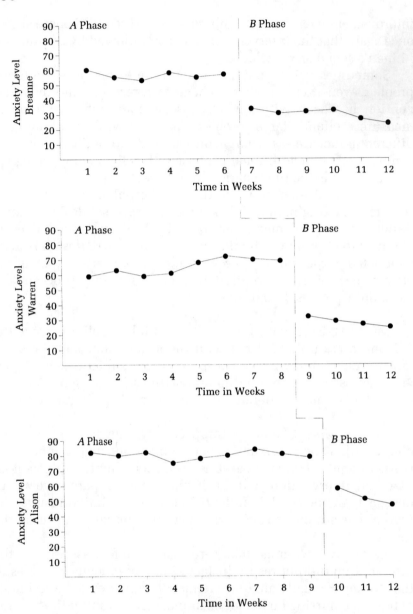

FIGURE 7.14   MULTIPLE-BASELINE DESIGN ACROSS
                        CLIENTS: MAGNITUDE OF ANXIETY LEVELS
                        FOR THREE CLIENTS, INDICATING AN
                        IMPROVEMENT

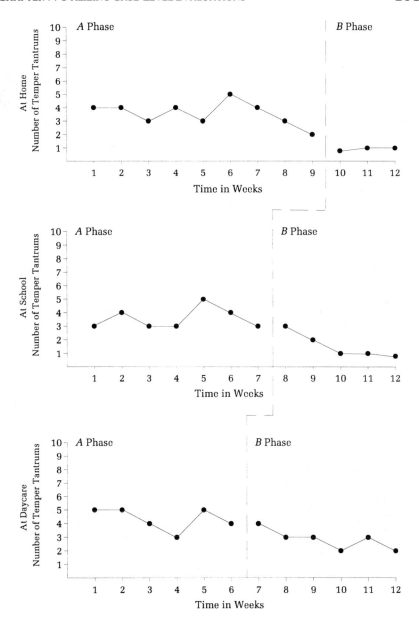

FIGURE 7.15 MULTIPLE-BASELINE DESIGN ACROSS SETTINGS: NUMBER OF TEMPER TANTRUMS FOR ONE CLIENT IN THREE SETTINGS, INDICATING AN IMPROVEMENT

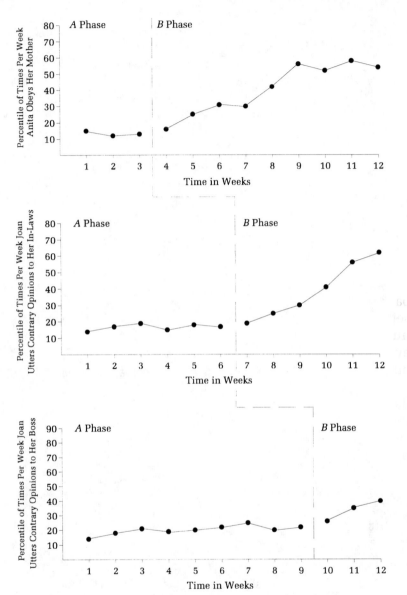

FIGURE 7.16   MULTIPLE-BASELINE DESIGN ACROSS
                       CLIENT TARGET PROBLEMS: MAGNITUDE OF
                       THREE CLIENT TARGET PROBLEM AREAS
                       FOR ONE CLIENT, INDICATING AN
                       IMPROVEMENT

multiple-baseline design across three clients who are being seen by a social worker for anxiety target problems.

Had an extraneous variable been responsible for the reduced anxiety demonstrated by Breanne, the other two clients, Warren and Alison, would also have demonstrated reduced anxiety, even though the worker was not intervening on their behalf. The fact that the baseline scores of the second two clients remained stable until the introduction of the intervention is a good indication that no extraneous variables were present, and that the intervention is a probable cause of the result.

While a multiple-baseline design requires more effort than a simple *AB* design, it is often clinically feasible. A multiple-baseline study across clients can sometimes be carried out by several workers at the same time.

Two or More Settings.   Another way to conduct a multiple-baseline evaluation is to use not separate clients, but two or more separate settings. Suppose that a target problem is to reduce the number of a child's temper tantrums. Three parallel case-level evaluations could be conducted: one at home, one at school, and one at the day-care center where the child goes after school. At home, a parent might count the number of temper tantrums per day, both before and during the intervention. A teacher might do the same thing at school, as would a staff member at the day-care center. Again, extraneous variables can be controlled for by beginning the *B* phase at different times, as illustrated in Figure 7.15.

Two or More Target Problems.   A third way to conduct a multiple-baseline evaluation is to use the same intervention to tackle different target problems. Suppose that Joan is having trouble with her daughter, Anita.

In addition, Joan is having trouble with her in-laws and with her boss at work. After exploration, a worker may believe that all these troubles stem from her lack of assertiveness. Thus, the intervention would be assertiveness training.

Progress with Anita might be measured by the number of times each day she is flagrantly disobedient. Progress can be measured with Joan's in-laws by the number of times she is able to utter a contrary opinion, and so on. Since the number of occasions on which Joan has an opportunity to be assertive will vary, these figures might best be expressed in percentiles. Figure 7.16 illustrates an example of a multiple-baseline design that was used to assess the effectiveness of Joan's assertiveness training in three target problem areas.

Whether it is a reversal design or a multiple-baseline design, an *ABAB* explanatory design involves establishing a baseline level for the client's target problem. This will not be possible if the need for intervention is acute, and sometimes the very thought of an *A*-type design will have to be abandoned. It is sometimes possible, however, to construct a retrospective baseline—that is, to determine with a reasonable degree of accuracy what the level of the target problem was *before* an intervention is implemented.

The best retrospective baselines are those that do not depend on the client's memory. If the target problem occurs rarely, memories may be accurate. Tai, a teenager, and his family may remember quite well how many times he ran away from home during the past month, for example. They may not remember nearly so well if the family members are asked how often he behaved defiantly. Depending on the target problem, it may be possible to construct a baseline from archival data—that is, from written records, such as school attendance sheets, probation orders, employment interview forms, and so forth.

Although establishing a baseline usually involves making at least three measurements before implementing an intervention, it is also acceptable to establish a baseline of zero, or no occurrences of a desired event. A target problem, for example, might focus upon the client's reluctance to enter a drug treatment program. The baseline measurement would then be that the client did not go (zero occurrences) and the desired change would be that the client did go (one occurrence). A social worker who has successfully used the same tactics to persuade a number of clients to enter a drug treatment program has conducted a multiple-baseline design across clients.

A usable baseline should show either that the client's target problem level is stable (e.g., Figure 7.6) or that it is growing worse (e.g., Figure 7.7). Sometimes an *A*-type design can be used even though the baseline indicates a slight improvement in the target problem (e.g., Figure 7.8). The justification must be that the intervention is expected to lead to an improvement that will exceed the anticipated improvement if the baseline trend continues.

Perhaps a child's temper tantrums are decreasing by one or two a week, for example, but the total number per week is still 18 to 20. If a worker thought the tantrums could be reduced to four or five a week, or they could be stopped altogether, the worker would be justified in implementing an intervention even though the client's target problem was improving slowly by itself.

In a similar way, a worker may be able to implement an *A*-type design if the client's baseline is unstable, provided that the intervention is expected to exceed the largest of the baseline fluctuations. Perhaps the child's temper tantrums are fluctuating between 12 and 20 per week in the baseline period and it is hoped to bring them down to less than 10 per week.

Nevertheless, there are some occasions when a baseline cannot be established or is not usable, such as when a client's behaviors involve self-injurious ones. Also, sometimes the establishment of a baseline is totally inappropriate.

THE BAB DESIGN

As the name suggests, a *BAB* design is an *ABAB* design without the first *A* phase. Many times a social worker may decide that immediate intervention is needed and that there is not time to collect baseline data. The client's progress can be monitored, as is done in a *B* design, and the intervention can be withdrawn later when the target problem appears to be resolved. Previous experience has indicated that sometimes even the best-resolved client target problems tend to reoccur, however, and the worker, therefore, continues to measure the target problem level, constructing an *A* phase almost incidentally. When the client's target problem does reoccur, the worker still has a good record of what happened to the target problem level after the intervention was withdrawn. Figure 7.17 illustrates an example of a *BAB* design.

Since there is no initial baseline data, we cannot know whether the resolution of the client's target problem on the first occasion had anything to do with the intervention. The target problem may have resolved itself, or some external event may have resolved it. Nor can we know the degree to which the target problem level changed during the intervention, since there was no baseline data with which to compare the final result. An indication of the

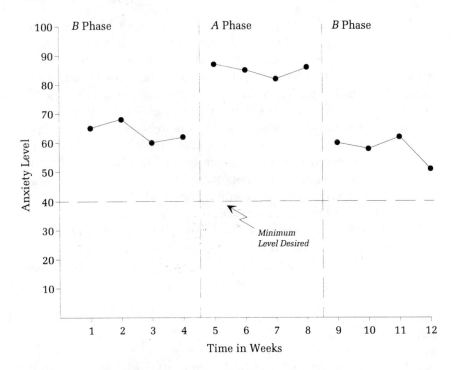

FIGURE 7.17   *BAB* DESIGN: MAGNITUDE OF JUAN'S ANXIETY
LEVEL DURING AND AFTER AN INTERVENTION IN
THE *A* PHASE

amount of change can be obtained by comparing the first and last
measurements in the *B* phase, but the first measurement may have
been an unreliable measure of the client's target problem level. The
client may have felt more or less anxious that day than usual; and
a baseline is necessary to compensate for such fluctuations.

Since the effectiveness of the intervention on the first occasion
is unknown, there can be no way of knowing whether the intervention was just as effective the second time it was implemented, or
less or more effective. All we know is that the target problem level
improved twice, following the same intervention; and this is probably enough to warrant using the intervention again with another
client.

THE BCBC DESIGN

In the same way that an *ABAB* design comprises two *AB* designs, a *BCBC* design is simply two *BC* designs strung together. In order to conduct a *BC* design, we can implement an intervention without collecting baseline data, and subsequently introduce a second intervention, both of which may be potentially useful. Although the social worker does not have baseline data, and thus has no record of how serious the target problem was initially, the worker is able to use this design to compare the efficacy of the two or more different interventions.

ADVANTAGES OF FORMAL CASE-LEVEL EVALUATIONS

Formal case-level evaluations provide the methods by which we can evaluate our success with individual clients. This approach has advantages for the worker, the client, and the social service program as: (1) the practitioner is responsible for data collection, (2) formal case-level evaluations are "theory free," (3) the focus is on the client, (4) clinical decisions are based on the data collected, (5) target problem analysis is facilitated, (6) the cost is small in time and disruptiveness, (7) the client's situation can be taken into account, and (8) data collected are useful for program-level evaluations.

THE PRACTITIONER IS RESPONSIBLE FOR DATA COLLECTION

Although data may be collected by the client or others in the client's environment, the practitioner has both control over and responsibility for the data. That is, the worker decides what data should be collected where, when, under what conditions, and by whom. Given this, it is possible to organize data collection so that if conformational data are needed (from, say, a teacher or relative), they can be obtained efficiently in time to assist decision making. In addition, workers are free to follow their own theoretical approaches to practice. The data collected will not determine the practice approach utilized but will be determined by it.

FORMAL CASE-LEVEL EVALUATIONS ARE "THEORY FREE"

Formal case-level evaluations have a second advantage. They do not limit a worker to any particular theoretical or practice approach. The worker can intervene in any way desired, as long as he or she knows exactly what was done, and in what sequence. In addition, the graphed results build up a repertoire of successful intervention strategies. If client records are adequate, a worker can look back at a specific target problem that the worker may have encountered a year ago. This process would help remind the worker about what worked and what did not, and how former clients progressed.

THE FOCUS IS ON THE CLIENT

All formal case-level evaluations are developed for or can be adapted to an individual case. Standardized measuring instruments can be chosen that are specific to the client's target problem or, if no instruments exist, the worker and client can develop them together. Self-anchored scales are a good example of this individualized approach to measurement.

Usually, clients are able to recognize that the interventions and measuring methods are specially tailored to them. Their belief that something relevant is being done will often increase their motivation, allowing them to participate more fully in solving their own target problems.

Formal case-level evaluations can also be adapted to the client. It may be necessary to intervene with a particular client at once, for example, without establishing a baseline. If the client can provide reliable data about the duration, frequency, or intensity of the target problem prior to the interview, for example, a retroactive baseline may be established on the strength of the client's recollection. The design is adaptable in a further sense: It may begin as *AB* (because a practitioner obviously hopes the first intervention will be effective), but if measurements indicate that it is not effective, it may become *ABC* or *ABCBC* or *ABCD*, depending on the professional's judgment and the client's response.

CLINICAL DECISIONS ARE BASED ON THE DATA COLLECTED

Formal case-level evaluations provide continuous data to social workers so that they can monitor clients' progress and alter their interventions if that progress is slower than expected. In addition, the collected data can be useful in making decisions to terminate or initiate different treatment interventions.

TARGET PROBLEM ANALYSIS IS FACILITATED

Formal case-level evaluations require that measurable target problems be set. Formulating a specific measurable target problem compels the worker to think the client's target problem through. What is it precisely about Gino's aggression that needs to be measured? Is Gino aggressive in the sense that he is hostile or in the sense that he is overassertive? It is obviously necessary to decide this, as interventions aimed at reducing hostility will differ from those intended to reduce overassertiveness. If Gino is hostile, is he hostile only to certain people in certain situations—for example, his mother or teacher—or is he generally hostile? Again, we need to know this in order to plan.

Once the target problem is defined, the worker will be able to devise an appropriate intervention. If a similar target problem has occurred with another client, the worker may well have formed a hypothesis about the most effective intervention. The intervention can be used again and its effectiveness measured; in other words, the hypothesis can be tested. Data serving to strengthen or weaken the hypothesis will enable the worker to reassess his or her own theoretical bases or practice approaches.

Case-level evaluations also require that a careful, visual record be kept of whatever change occurs in the client's target problem. When graphs are produced, everyone concerned can see what changes have really occurred and what changes they only think are occurring. Possibly, the study will not be very successful. There might be fluctuations in the baseline data, for example, that make it impossible to carry out an intended *AB* study. These very fluctuations, however, may throw light upon the target problem. A client named Darcy, for example, may discover that she is more depressed on days when she visits her sister in the nursing home. Her worker may then be able to trace Darcy's depression to an unadmitted fear of dependency and death.

As findings from single-case evaluation studies are duplicated, they offer increasing guidance as to what specific interventions work with what specific kinds of clients in what specific circumstances. They can also generate more precise hypotheses for testing in the increasingly complex group evaluation designs discussed in the following chapter.

THE COST IS SMALL IN TIME AND DISRUPTIVENESS

There is no doubt that making measurements takes more time than not making them. This time, however, must be compared to time that is inevitably wasted when the practitioner does not really know how the target problem is progressing, whether the intervention is working, and whether or not it is time to try something else. Nor should measurement be considered disruptive. A disruption is, by definition, something that disturbs the normal course of events; if measurement is a part of the normal course of events, it is not a disruption, but only a continuous record of progress made.

An important advantage of case-level evaluations is that they can be undertaken by line-level social workers seeing clients on a day-to-day basis. They are consistent with case needs in everyday practice situations, and they are neither expensive to implement nor time-consuming.

THE CLIENT'S SITUATION CAN BE TAKEN INTO ACCOUNT

One of the major advantages of formal case-level evaluations is that they are infinitely flexible and the client's unique situation can always be taken into account. For example, a rating scale that the practitioner knows will be completed by the client's mother can be designed to fit the mother's capabilities; instruments can be completed at home at times convenient for the client; and designs can always be adapted to fit the client's individual needs.

DATA COLLECTED ARE USEFUL
FOR PROGRAM-LEVEL EVALUATIONS

As we know, data collected on individual clients can be aggregated to provide program evaluation data. A charitable organization that funds a number of agencies, for example, might require member agencies to document a minimum level of objectively verified successful case outcomes in order to qualify for re-funding. The operative words here are *objectively verified.* Individual practitioners would have to provide evidence of successful case outcomes, complete with data clearly displayed on graphs. Formal case-level evaluations lend themselves to such documentation. An agency staffed with professional social workers who all use case-levels evaluations will have less difficulty in demonstrating success and obtaining funding than those agencies that do not use them.

Data collected on clients over time can also be useful in determining eligibility criteria for a social service program as a whole. It may have been found, for example, that clients who achieved a certain score on a particular standardized measuring instrument tended to do better in the program than clients who achieved a lower score. A minimum score might then be set as a criterion for admittance.

DISADVANTAGES OF FORMAL
CASE-LEVEL EVALUATIONS

There are advantages and disadvantages to most things in life, and case-level evaluations are no exception. Several of their disadvantages are: (1) the intervention may not work, (2) they have limited generalizability, (3) explanatory designs are difficult to implement, (4) there may be problems with operational definitions and measurement, and (5) they work best with specific client target problems.

THE INTERVENTION MAY NOT WORK

The first and most obvious limitation of a formal case-level evaluation is that it may not work. The client may have a target problem that cannot be changed in the 4-to-12-week period that is normal for an *AB* study. Or the selected intervention, and the next one, and the one after that may be unsuccessful in bringing about the desired change. Of course, an evaluation can continue for longer than twelve weeks—it can continue for as long as necessary—but often clients, and social workers too, tire of making measurements after the first three months, and the study will die a natural death if it is not brought to a planned conclusion.

THERE IS LIMITED GENERALIZABILITY

Second, simply because an intervention worked with one client does not necessarily mean that it will be as effective with a similar client. The issue of generalizability to other cases, or the external validity, is described in Chapter 8. Suffice it to say that in case-level evaluations we sacrifice concerns about generalizability and focus on how well an intervention works for one client system. Generalizability is essentially impossible to establish in case-level evaluations; we would have to be able to demonstrate that the clients to whom the intervention is given are representative of a larger group of clients to whom the intervention might be applied.

As will be discussed in the next chapter, when a study is conducted at the explanatory level with such controls as random sampling and random assignment to groups, the results of the study apply not just to the group being tested but to the entire population from which the sample was drawn. When a case-level evaluation is conducted with an individual client, the results apply only to that client. Thus, evaluations have limited generalizability from one client to the next or from one target problem to the next. This is a major drawback of formal case-level evaluations. Obviously, this is also true for informal case-level evaluations.

A number of similar results obtained in similar situations with similar clients make it more likely that the findings are generally applicable; but an individual worker may not have such comparative data available. Workers should therefore resist the temptation to assume that because an intervention worked once it must necessarily work again.

EXPLANATORY DESIGNS ARE DIFFICULT TO IMPLEMENT

Only in exceptional circumstances is it ethical to deliberately implement such explanatory designs as the *ABA* and *ABAB* designs, where a successful intervention is removed and the target problem allowed to return to the baseline level. Because of ethical difficulties, such designs usually come into being accidentally; consequently, rigor suffers. Very often, measurement of the target problem level does not continue between the first *B* phase and the second *A* phase, as a client who believes that a target problem has been solved will not continue to keep records between the apparent solution and the reappearance.

There is, therefore, a gap in the data, and it is not possible to say with certainty that the reappearance of the target problem had anything to do with the removal of the intervention. Perhaps the target problem would have reappeared even if the intervention had been continued. An accidental application of an *ABAB* design thus eliminates one argument for causality: that the target problem reappears when the intervention is removed.

Descriptive formal case-level evaluations are easier to implement than explanatory ones because they require only a baseline phase followed by as many intervention phases as are necessary to solve the client's target problem. They do not provide causal data, however, and practitioners who want to know whether a particular intervention solved a particular target problem cannot rely on these more practical designs.

THERE MAY BE PROBLEMS WITH
OPERATIONAL DEFINITIONS AND MEASUREMENT

Then, there may be target problems with operational definitions and with measurements. A mother who is asked to keep count of her daughter's temper tantrums may exaggerate in order to impress the worker with the severity of her daughter's target problem. Or she may forget to count and invent a figure in order to save herself embarrassment. Or she may merely be unsure of just what constitutes "a temper tantrum." Does shouted defiance count, or improper language, or a covert kick at the child's little brother, or must it be a prolonged assault on furniture or persons? However minutely we try to define these, there is often a period of confusion at the beginning of the study, when the hoped-for baseline data never actually seem to be collected.

The usual problems with measurement also apply. Measuring instruments may not be reliable or valid, measurements may not be taken regularly, or the act of measuring may influence the target problem being measured.

THEY WORK BEST WITH SPECIFIC CLIENT TARGET PROBLEMS

Finally, case-level evaluations work best for interventions that are specific to certain client target problems, rather than to general methods of problem solving. Thus, for example, teaching behavioral skills to become more assertive, or relaxation training to help overcome phobias, fits with case-level evaluations nicely, since the intervention can be easily withdrawn by not providing the intervention in a particular session. If a social worker is using generic counseling methods, though, these may not be as easily withdrawn without a concern for the client.

SUMMARY

Case-level evaluations are undertaken for the purpose of monitoring client progress up to, and sometimes beyond, the point of termination. Data gained in this way help to judge whether our intervention should be changed, modified, or terminated, and whether it is good enough to use with another client. A number of features are integral to these designs: (1) establishing baselines, (2) setting reliable, valid, and measurable target problems, (3) using repeated measurements of the target problems, (4) graphically displaying data, and (5) making comparisons across phases.

The following chapter expands upon this one by presenting how social work programs are evaluated through the use of program-level evaluation designs.

C H A P T E R **8**

UTILIZING PROGRAM-LEVEL EVALUATIONS

T HE LAST CHAPTER DISCUSSED simple approaches to case-level evaluations. This chapter is a logical extension of the previous one in that it presents various approaches to program-level evaluations that emphasize the use of groups of clients or cases instead of one client (e.g., one individual, one couple, one family, one group, one community, one organization). As the previous chapter pointed out, case-level evaluations are used mainly to evaluate practice objectives, whereas program-level evaluations are used mainly to evaluate program objectives.

The key difference between case-level and program-level evaluations is the kind of objectives they measure. It should be noted, however, that case-level designs described in the last chapter can also be used to evaluate program-level objectives.

THE EVALUATION CONTINUUM

When the focus and purpose of an evaluation have been determined, the program objectives have been formulated, and instruments have been selected to measure the objectives, it is time to select a program-level evaluation design. Essentially, a design is selected for the specific purpose of an evaluation, or the use to which the results will be put. If the purpose is to make decisions about continuing, abandoning, or replicating the program, the decision makers will need to be very confident about the validity and reliability of the evaluation, and a rigorous design may be required.

Like formal case-level designs, there are three levels of program-level evaluation designs: explanatory, descriptive, and exploratory. All three design levels can focus on the evaluation of a program's objectives to some degree; that is, they all can be used to generate useful data that can help human service programs deliver better services to the clients they serve.

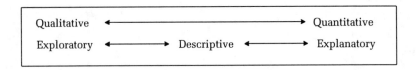

EXPLANATORY EVALUATION DESIGNS

Explanatory evaluation designs are sometimes called "ideal" evaluative experimental designs. They involve random assignment of clients (or case files) to groups. It is rarely possible to implement them in program settings, and less powerful designs, such as descriptive and exploratory designs that are usually less intrusive, will have to be chosen.

Explanatory program-level evaluation designs have the largest number of "design requirements." They are best used in confirmatory or causal evaluation studies where the program objective being evaluated is well developed, theories abound, and testable hypotheses can be formulated on the basis of previous work or existing theory. These designs usually seek to establish causal relationships between the program objectives and the activities the workers perform to achieve them (interventions).

DESCRIPTIVE EVALUATION DESIGNS

Descriptive program-level evaluation designs have the advantage of being practical when conditions prevent implementation of an explanatory evaluation design. They do not control as strictly for the effects of extraneous factors as explanatory designs and are thus less "rigorous." Nevertheless, they are very useful and practical in the evaluation of the human services.

EXPLORATORY EVALUATION DESIGNS

A third type of program-level evaluation design is the exploratory design. These designs only provide an estimate of the relationship between the program objectives and the workers' activities (interventions) with no defense at all against the effects of extraneous factors. Such a design, however, can be used for a preliminary "nonscientific" look at their relationship to see if it is worthwhile using more rigorous, and also more costly and time-consuming, designs.

Exploratory designs do not produce statistically definitive data or conclusive results; they are not intended to. Their purpose is to build a foundation of general ideas and tentative theories that can be explored later with more precise and hence more complex evaluation designs and their corresponding data-gathering techniques. As is stressed throughout this book, monitoring designs, a form of exploratory designs, are extremely useful in determining if interventive efforts are having an effect on a program's objectives.

CHOOSING AN EVALUATION DESIGN

The two most important considerations in choosing a program-level evaluation design are the purpose of the evaluative effort and how the data obtained will be used. In addition, ethical issues must be taken into account along with political, social, and practical considerations.

Before a discussion of using program-level evaluation designs can occur, it is necessary to distinguish what comprises an "ideal" evaluation (explanatory design), because any evaluation design finally selected should come as close to an "ideal" evaluation as possible—given the social, political, ethical, and practical constraints that surround any evaluative effort. In short, it is useful to understand what an "ideal" evaluation is, so comparisons can be made between the program-level evaluation design selected and the requirements of an "ideal" evaluation. Or, to put it another way, it is always helpful to know how far the evaluation design selected is from an "ideal" evaluation.

"IDEAL" PROGRAM-LEVEL EVALUATIONS

An "ideal" evaluation is one in which a study approaches certainty about the relationship between the workers' activities and the program objectives they are trying to achieve. The purpose of doing any "ideal" evaluation is to ascertain whether the conclusions derived from the findings that the workers' activities (their interventions or independent variables) are or are not the only cause of the change they are trying to achieve in the program objectives (dependent variables).

This concept is introduced with the word "ideal" in quotes because an "ideal" evaluation study is rarely achieved in the human services. On a general level, in order to achieve this high degree of certainty and to qualify as an "ideal" evaluation, a design must meet the following six conditions:

1. The time order of the intervention (independent variable) must be established.
2. The intervention must be manipulated.
3. The relationship between the intervention and program objective(s) must be established.
4. The design must control for rival hypotheses.
5. At least one control group should be used.
6. Random assignment procedures (and random sampling from

a population if possible) must be employed in choosing the sample for the study.

TIME ORDER OF THE INTERVENTION

In an "ideal" program-level evaluation, the independent variable must precede the dependent variable. Time order is crucial if the evaluation is to show that one variable causes another, because something that happens later cannot be the cause of something that occurred earlier. Thus X, the independent variable, or intervention, must occur before Y, the dependent variable, or degree of the achievement of the program objective.

Suppose we want to find out if a specific treatment intervention, Intervention X (independent variable), reduces our clients' depression levels (dependent variable) and formulate the following hypothesis:

Intervention X will cause a reduction in our clients' depression levels.

In this hypothesis, the independent variable is the intervention, and the program's objective, or the dependent variable, is the clients' depression levels. The intervention must come before a reduction in the clients' depression, because the hypothesis states that the intervention will cause a reduction of depression in our clients.

MANIPULATION OF THE INTERVENTION

Manipulation of the intervention, or independent variable, means that something must be done with the intervention to at least one group of clients in the evaluation study. In the general form of the hypothesis, if X occurs then Y will result, the intervention (X) must be manipulated in order to effect a variation in the program's objective (Y). There are essentially three ways in which human service interventions can be manipulated:

1. *X present versus X absent.* If the effectiveness of a specific treatment intervention is being evaluated, an experimental

group and a control group could be used. The experimental group would be given the intervention (presence of *X*) and the control group would not (absence of *X*).

2. *A small amount of X versus a larger amount of X.* If the effect of treatment time (independent variable) on client outcomes (dependent variable) is being evaluated, two experimental groups could be used, one of which would be treated for a shorter period of time (small amount of *X*) and the other being treated for a longer period of time (larger amount of *X*).

3. *X versus something else.* If the effectiveness of two different treatment interventions is being evaluated, Intervention X_1 could be used with Experimental Group 1 and Intervention X_2 with Experimental Group 2.

There are certain demographic characteristics, such as the gender or race of clients participating in evaluations, that obviously cannot be manipulated because they are fixed. They do not vary, so they are called constants, not variables. Other constants, such as socioeconomic status or IQ, may vary for clients over their life spans, but they are fixed quantities at the beginning of the study, probably will not change during the study, and are not subject to alteration by the evaluator.

Any variable that is subject to alteration by the evaluator (treatment time, for example) is an independent variable. At least one independent variable must be manipulated in an "ideal" evaluation.

Relationships between Interventions and Objectives

The relationship between the intervention and the attainment of the program's objective(s) must be established in order to infer a cause-effect relationship within a "true" evaluation. If the intervention is considered to be the cause in the change of the program objective, there must be some pattern in the relationship between them. An example is the hypothesis: "The more time clients spend in treatment (the intervention or the independent variable), the better the program objective will be (the dependent variable)."

CONTROL OF RIVAL HYPOTHESES

Rival, or alternative, hypotheses must be identified and eliminated in an "ideal" program-level evaluation. The logic of this requirement is extremely important, because this is what makes cause-effect statements possible in "ideal" evaluations.

The prime question to ask when trying to identify a rival hypothesis is, "What other independent variables might affect the dependent variable?" (What else might affect the client's outcome besides treatment time?) With the risk of sounding redundant, "What else besides X might affect Y?" Perhaps the client's motivation for treatment, in addition to the time spent in treatment, might affect the client's outcome. If so, motivation for treatment is another independent variable; it could be used to form the rival hypothesis, "The higher the client's motivation for treatment, the better his or her progress."

Perhaps the practitioner's attitude toward the client might have an effect on the client's outcome, or the client might win the state lottery and ascend abruptly from depression to ecstasy. These and other potential independent variables could be used to form rival hypotheses. They must all be considered and eliminated, before it can be said with reasonable certainty that a client's outcome resulted from the length of treatment time and not from any other independent variables contained within the rival hypotheses.

Control over rival hypotheses refers to efforts on the evaluator's part to identify and, if at all possible, to eliminate the independent variables in these hypotheses. Three of the ways most frequently used to deal with rival hypotheses are (1) to keep the variables in them constant, (2) to use correlated variation, or (3) to use analysis of covariance. This text will not discuss how to control for rival hypotheses, as this discussion can be found elsewhere.

USE OF A CONTROL GROUP

An "ideal" program-level evaluation should use at least one control group in addition to the experimental group. This is one of the principal differences between an "ideal" evaluation and formal case-level designs discussed in the previous chapter. Instead of controlling for rival hypotheses and achieving internal validity by comparing baseline and intervention phases as in case-level designs, program-level evaluation designs can accomplish the same purposes by comparing outcomes between two or more equivalent groups. The experimental group may receive an intervention that is withheld from the control group, or an equivalent group may receive a different intervention.

A social worker who initiates a treatment intervention is often interested in knowing what would have happened if the intervention had not been used or if some different intervention had been substituted. Would Ms. Gomez have recovered from alcoholism anyway—without the worker's efforts? Would she have recovered faster or more completely had family counseling (Intervention *A*) been used instead of a support group (Intervention *B*)?

The answer to these questions will never be known if only Ms. Gomez is studied, because there is only one of her and it is not possible, at the same time, to treat her, not treat her, and treat her in different ways. But if more than one group of alcoholics are studied, we have a better idea of the outcome of the treatment, because groups can be made equivalent in respect to important variables. Random assignment procedures (see next section) may be used to assure that the groups are not only equal but are representative of all others with similar problems of alcoholism.

In a typical program-level evaluation design with a control group, two equivalent groups, 1 and 2, can be formed, and both are administered the same pretest to ensure that they are the same in all important respects. Then an intervention is initiated with Group 1 but not with Group 2. The group treated, Group 1 or the experimental group, receives the independent variable (the intervention). The group not treated, Group 2 or the control group, does not receive it. At the conclusion of the treatment, both groups are given a posttest (the same measure as the pretest). Some kind of standardized measuring instrument can be used for the pretest and posttest.

Like formal case-level designs, program-level evaluation designs can also be written in symbols. With the notation scheme used later in this chapter, this design is written as follows:

> Experimental Group: R O_1 X O_2
> Control Group: R O_1 O_2

Where:

R = Random assignment to one of two groups

O_1 = First measurement of the program objective, the dependent variable

X = Intervention (program or activity), the independent variable

O_2 = Second measurement of the program objective, the dependent variable

The two Rs in this design indicate that the clients are to be randomly assigned to each group. The symbol X, which, as usual, stands for the interventive efforts, or the independent variable, indicates that an intervention, or service, is to be given to the experimental group after the pretest (O_1) and before the posttest (O_2). The absence of X in the control group indicates that the intervention is not to be given to the control group. Thus, one group receives the services (the experimental group) and the other group does not receive them (the control group).

Table 8.1 displays results from a program-level evaluation study of this type. If the experimental group is equivalent to the control group, the pretest results should be approximately the same for both groups. Within an acceptable margin of error, 24 can be considered approximately the same as 26. Since the control group has not been given any services, the posttest results for this group would not be expected to differ appreciably from the pretest results. In fact, the posttest score, 27, differs little from the pretest score, 26, for the control group.

Because the experimental and control groups are considered equivalent, any rival hypothesis that affected the experimental group would have affected the control group in the same way. No rival hypothesis affected the control group, as indicated by the fact that, without the intervention, the pretest and posttest scores did not differ. Therefore, it can be concluded that no rival hypothesis affected the experimental group, either, and the difference (–44)

TABLE 8.1   Clients' Outcomes
                       by Group

Group	Pretest	Posttest	Difference
Experimental	24	68	− 44
Control	26	27	− 1

between pretest and posttest scores for this group was probably due to the intervention and not to any other factor.

RANDOM ASSIGNMENT

Random assignment (and random sampling if possible) procedures are essential to assure that the results derived from a program-level evaluation study apply not only to the clients who actually took part in the program but to a much larger population. This makes it possible to generalize the findings to other program settings or other clients with similar characteristics, provided that the sample—those who are chosen to take part in a study—is representative of the population to whom the findings are to be generalized. A sample may also consist of cases or elements chosen from a set or population of objects or events, but most human service evaluations deal with people, individually or in groups.

Random sampling is the procedure used to select a sample from a population in such a way that the individuals (or objects or events) chosen accurately represent the population from which they were drawn. Once a sample has been randomly selected, the individuals in it are randomly assigned either to an experimental or to a control group in such a way that the groups are equivalent. This procedure is known as random assignment or randomization.

In random assignment, the word *equivalent* means equal in terms of variables that are important to the evaluation study, such as the clients' motivation for treatment or level of parenting skills.

If the effect of treatment time on clients' outcomes is being evaluated, for example, the evaluation design might use one experimental group that is treated for a comparatively longer time, a second experimental group that is treated for a shorter time, and a control group that is not treated at all. If we are concerned that the clients' motivation for treatment might also affect their outcomes, the clients can be assigned so that all the groups are equivalent (on the average) in terms of their motivation for treatment.

The process of random sampling from a population, followed by random assignment of the sample to groups, is illustrated in Figure 8.1. The design calls for a sample size of one-tenth of the population. From a population of 10,000, therefore, a random sampling procedure is used to select a sample of 1,000 individuals. Then random assignment procedures are used to place the sample of 1,000 into two equivalent groups of 500 individuals each. In theory, Group A will be equivalent to Group B, which will be equivalent to the random sample, which will be equivalent to the population in respect to all important variables studied.

MATCHED PAIRS

Another more deliberate method of assigning clients or other units to groups involves matching. The matched pairs method is suitable when the composition of each group consists of variables with a range of characteristics.

Sometimes trios and quartets can also be matched if more groups are required, but the matching process grows more complex and uncertain as the numbers in the matched set increase. It is usually not practical to match more than four clients. One of the disadvantages of matching is that some individuals cannot be matched and so cannot participate in the evaluation project. When available clients are few, this can be a serious drawback.

Suppose a new intervention program for depression is being evaluated, and it is important that the experimental and control groups have an equal number of more severely and less severely depressed clients. The clients chosen for the sample are matched in pairs according to level of depression; the two most severely depressed clients are matched, then the next two, and so on. One person in each pair of approximately equally depressed clients is then randomly assigned to the experimental group, and the other is placed in the control group.

An example of this procedure is as follows: A standardized

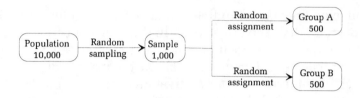

FIGURE 8.1   RANDOM SAMPLING AND
                      RANDOM ASSIGNMENT
                      PROCEDURES

measuring instrument that measures depression is administered to
a sample of ten clients. Their scores are then rank ordered, and one
of the clients with the two highest scores is selected to be assigned
either to the experimental group or the control group. It does not
make any difference which group the first client is randomly assigned to, as long as there is an equal chance that the client will go
to either the control group or the experimental group. In this example the first person is randomly chosen to go to the experimental
group, as illustrated below:

Rank Order of Depression Scores (in parentheses)

First Pair
    (69) Randomly assigned to the experimental group
    (68) Assigned to the control group
Second Pair
    (67) Assigned to the control group
    (66) Assigned to the experimental group
Third Pair
    (65) Assigned to the experimental group
    (64) Assigned to the control group
Fourth Pair
    (63) Assigned to the control group
    (62) Assigned to the experimental group
Fifth Pair
    (61) Assigned to the experimental group
    (60) Assigned to the control group

The client with the highest score (69) is randomly assigned to the experimental group, and this client's "match," with a score of 68, is assigned to the control group. This process is reversed with the next matched pair, where the first client is assigned to the control group and the match is assigned to the experimental group. If the assignment of clients according to scores is not reversed for every other pair, one group will be higher than the other on the variable being matched.

To illustrate this point, suppose the first person (highest score) in each match is always assigned to the experimental group. The experimental group's average score would be 65 (69 + 67 + 65 + 63 + 61 = 325/5 = 65), and the control group's average score would be 64 (68 + 66 + 64 + 62 + 60 = 320/5 = 64). If every other matched pair is reversed, however, as in the example, the average scores of the two groups are closer together—64.6 for the experimental group (69 + 66 + 65 + 62 + 61 = 323/5 = 64.6) and 64.4 for the control group (68 + 67 + 64 + 63 + 60 = 322/5 = 64.4). In short, 64.6 and 64.4 (difference of 0.2) are closer together than 65 and 64 (difference of 1).

INTERNAL AND EXTERNAL VALIDITY

In addition to the six characteristics of "ideal" program-level evaluation designs described above, an "ideal" evaluation study must also have both internal and external validity. Internal validity has to do with the provisions of the evaluation design for establishing that the introduction of the independent variable (such as a treatment intervention) alone can be identified as the cause of change in the dependent variable (such as the client's outcome). In contrast, external validity has to do with the extent to which the evaluation design allows for generalization of the findings of the study to other groups and other situations.

Both internal and external validity are achieved in a design by taking into account various threats that are inherent in the evaluation effort. A program-level evaluation design for a study with both types of validity will recognize and attempt to control for potential factors that could affect the study's outcome or findings.

Threats to Internal Validity

In an "ideal" program-level evaluation, the evaluator should be able to conclude from the findings that the intervention (independent variable) is or is not the only cause of change in the program's objective (dependent variable). If a study does not have internal validity, such a conclusion is not possible, and the study is not interpretable.

Internal validity is concerned with one of the requirements for an "ideal" evaluation—the control of rival hypotheses, or alternative explanations for what might bring about a change in the program's objective(s). The higher the internal validity of an evaluation study, the greater the extent to which rival hypotheses can be controlled; the lower the internal validity, the less they can be controlled. We must be prepared to rule out the effects of factors other than the intervention that could influence any changes in the program's objective(s).

History

History refers to any event that may affect the program's objective, and that could not be accounted for in the evaluation design. More specifically, it refers to events occurring between the first and second measurement of the program objective (the pretest and the posttest). If events occur that have the potential to alter the second measurement, there is no way of knowing how much (if any) of the observed change is a function of the intervention, and how much is attributable to these events.

Suppose, for example, that the effect of a certain educational program on racial tolerance is being evaluated. A pretest is given before the program is initiated, but before the posttest is administered, an outbreak of racial violence occurs in the community such as the one that happened in Los Angeles in 1992. This sequence of events may well counter the "true" effects of the educational program, so the posttest scores would indicate a lower level of racial tolerance than they would have otherwise. An earthquake, an election, an illness, or a marriage—any event, public or private— can be an example of this kind of history.

MATURATION

Maturation refers to changes, both mental and physical, that take place in clients who participate in an evaluation over the course of the project and which therefore can affect the outcome of the program's objective. Suppose a new interventive technique designed to improve behavior in adolescents who are physically challenged is being evaluated. Since adolescents tend to undergo rapid biological change, behavior changes noted in the experimental results may be due as much to their maturation as to the treatment intervention.

However, maturation refers not only to physical or mental growth. Over time, as clients grow older and (presumably) wiser, they also become more or less anxious, bored, happy, or rich, and more or less motivated to take part in an evaluation study. These variables and many more can affect the ways in which clients respond when the program objective is measured a second or third time.

TESTING

The pretests that are the starting point for some program-level evaluation designs are another potential threat to internal validity. One of the simplest descriptive evaluation designs involves three steps: measuring some program objective, such as learning behavior in school or attitudes toward work; initiating a program to change that variable; and then measuring the attainment of the objective again at the conclusion of the program. This simple design can be written in symbols as follows:

$$O_1 \quad X \quad O_2$$

Where:

O_1 = First measurement of the program objective, the dependent variable

X = Intervention, the independent variable (see Box 8.1)

O_2 = Second measurement of the program objective, the dependent variable

Testing can be a threat because taking the pretest can have an effect on posttest scores. Some clients might have a higher score on the posttest, for example, because they recall the questions (or items) on the pretest, or they might have a lower score because their experience with the pretest has made them anxious. In either case, the difference between pretest and posttest scores ($O_1 - O_2$ = difference, or effect of X) may not accurately reflect the effectiveness of the program.

In order to avoid the testing effect, an evaluation design could be used that does not require a pretest (to be discussed shortly). If a pretest must be used, the length of elapsed time between the pretest and the posttest should be considered. A pretest is far more likely to affect the posttest scores when the time between the two is short. The program objectives under study are another factor. The pretest is more likely to affect the posttest when the study is dealing with skill or knowledge levels—factual information that can be easily recalled and tested.

INSTRUMENTATION ERROR

The lack of validity or reliability in measuring instruments can invalidate the measurement of program objectives. Instrumentation error may be due to a mechanical device that malfunctions, a measuring instrument that has not been adequately standardized or pretested, or an observer whose observations are inconsistent throughout the course of the project. It may also occur if a measuring instrument that is perfectly reliable and valid in itself is not administered properly.

STATISTICAL REGRESSION

Statistical regression refers to the tendency of extremely low and extremely high scores to regress, or move toward the average score. Suppose Ray, a social work student, has to take a multiple-choice pretest exam in a research course about which he knows

---

BOX 8.1

TREATMENT: A VARIABLE OR A CONSTANT?

For instructional purposes, group designs are displayed using symbols where X is the independent variable (treatment) and O is the measure of the dependent variable. This presentation is accurate when studies are designed with two or more groups. When one-group designs are used, however, this interpretation does not hold. In one-group designs, the treatment, or program, cannot truly vary because all research participants have experienced the same event; that is, they all have experienced the program. Without a comparison or control group, treatment is considered a constant because it is a quality shared by all members in the research study. In short, *time* is the independent variable.

---

nothing at all. There are many questions, and each question has five possible answers. Since he has a 20 percent chance of guessing right on each question, he might expect to score 20 percent on the exam, just by guessing. If he is a bad guesser, he will score lower; if a good guesser, higher. The other members of his class, all of whom are just as confused as he is, take the same exam, and the score for the class averages out at 20 percent.

Suppose, now, that the research instructor separates the low scorers from the high scorers and tries to even out the academic level of the class by giving the low scorers special instruction. In order to see if this has been effective, the entire class then takes another multiple-choice exam.

According to the logic of statistical regression, both the low scorers and the high scorers would move toward the average score. Even without any special instruction and still in their state of ignorance, the low scorers would be expected to score higher than they did before; that is, by moving toward the average, their scores would increase. The high scorers would be expected to score lower than they did before.

It would be easy for the research instructor to assume that the low scores had increased because of the instruction and the high scores had decreased because of the lack of instruction. Not necessarily so, however; the instruction may have had nothing to do with it. It may all be due to statistical regression.

DIFFERENTIAL SELECTION

To some extent, the clients selected for a program-level evaluation study are different from one another to begin with. "Ideal" evaluations require random sampling and random assignment procedures to groups. This assures that the results of a study will be generalizable to a larger population (external validity). The threat to internal validity is failure to achieve or maintain equivalency among the groups, because clients assigned to them are not approximately equal.

This threat is present when the evaluator is working with preformed groups or groups that already exist, such as classes of students, self-help groups, or community groups. Formal case-level designs, especially, use such groups. When using case-level or program-level evaluation designs, the evaluator does not know whether the preformed groups used are representative of any larger population. Thus, it is not possible to generalize the evaluation's results beyond the clients (or objects or events) that were actually studied. In addition, it is very probable that different preformed groups will not be equivalent with respect to relevant variables, and these initial differences will invalidate posttest comparisons.

Accordingly, preformed groups should be avoided whenever possible. If it is not feasible to do this, rigorous pretesting must be done to determine in what ways the groups are (or are not) equivalent, and differences must be compensated for with the use of statistical methods.

MORTALITY

Mortality refers to the tendency of clients to drop out of a program-level evaluation study before it is completed. Their absence can have a significant effect on the study's findings.

The clients who drop out may be different from the other clients in some ways. For example, they may have been less motivated to begin with than those who stay in. If considerably more clients drop out of the experimental group than drop out of the control group (or vice versa), the evaluation project may end up with groups that are not as equivalent in variables such as motivation as the pretests indicated. Since dropouts often have such characteristics in common, it cannot be assumed that the attrition occurred in a random manner. An evaluation design that controls for mortality should be considered.

REACTIVE EFFECTS

Changes in the behaviors or feelings of clients may be caused by their reactions to the novelty of the situation or the knowledge that they are participating in an evaluation study of some kind. The evaluator may wrongly believe that such reactive effects are due to the intervention, the independent variable.

The classic example of reactive effects was found in a series of studies carried out at the Hawthorne plant of the Western Electric Company in Chicago many years ago. Researchers were investigating the relationship between working conditions and productivity. When they increased the level of lighting in one section of the plant, productivity increased; a further increase in the lighting was followed by an additional increase in productivity. When the lighting was then decreased, however, production levels did not fall accordingly but continued to rise. The conclusion was that the employees were increasing their productivity not because of the lighting level but because of the attention they were receiving as subjects in the study.

The term *Hawthorne effect* is still used to describe any situation in which the clients' behaviors are influenced not by the intervention but by the knowledge that they are taking part in a study of some kind. Another example of such a reactive effect is the placebo or sugar pill that produces beneficial results in patients because they believe it is medication.

Reactive effects can be controlled by ensuring that all clients in a program-level evaluation study, in both the experimental and control groups, appear to be treated equally. For example, if one group is to be shown an educational film, the other group should also be shown a film—some film carefully chosen to bear no relationship to the intervention being investigated. If the study involves a change in the clients' routine, this in itself may be enough to change behavior, and care must be taken to continue the study until novelty has ceased to be a factor.

INTERACTION EFFECTS

Interaction among the various threats to internal validity mentioned above can have an effect of its own. Any of the factors already described as threats may interact with one another, but the most common interactive effect involves differential selection and maturation.

Consider the example of an evaluator who is studying two groups of depressed clients. The intention was for these groups to be equivalent, in terms of both their motivation for treatment and their levels of depression. However, it turns out that Group A is more generally depressed than Group B. Whereas both groups may grow less motivated over time, it is likely that Group A, whose members were more depressed to begin with, will lose motivation more completely and more quickly than Group B. Inequivalent groups thus grow less equivalent over time as a result of the interaction between differential selection and maturation.

RELATIONS BETWEEN EXPERIMENTAL AND CONTROL GROUPS

The final group of threats to internal validity has to do with the effects of the use of experimental and control groups that receive different interventions. These effects include diffusion of services, compensation, rivalry, and demoralization.

Diffusion or imitation of services may occur when the experimental and control groups talk to each other about the evaluation's purpose. Suppose a study is designed that presents a new relaxation exercise to the experimental group and nothing at all to the control group. There is always the possibility that one of the clients in the experimental group will explain the exercise to a friend who happens to be in the control group. The friend explains it to another friend, and so on. This might be beneficial for the control group, but it invalidates the evaluation's findings.

Compensatory equalization of treatment occurs when an evaluator or staff member administering the service to the experimental group feels sorry for clients in the control group who are not receiving it and attempts to compensate them. For example, a worker might take a control group client aside and covertly demonstrate the relaxation exercise.

If an evaluation study has been ethically designed, there should be no need for guilt on the part of the practitioner because some clients are not being taught to relax. They can be taught to relax when the study is "officially" over. If the relaxation exercises are found to be helpful to those clients in the experimental group, there is no reason why the exercises cannot be given to the control group at a later date.

Compensatory rivalry is an effect that occurs when the control group becomes motivated to compete with the experimental group. For example, a control group in a program to encourage parental involvement in school activities might get wind that something is up and make a determined effort to participate also, on the basis that "anything they can do, we can do better." There is no direct communication between groups, as in the diffusion of treatment effect—only rumors and suggestions of rumors. However, rumors are often enough to threaten the internal validity of a study.

In direct contrast with compensatory rivalry, demoralization refers to feelings of deprivation among the control group that may cause them to give up and drop out of the evaluation project. In this case, this effect would be referred to as mortality. The clients in the control group may also act up or get angry.

Threats to External Validity

External validity is the degree to which the results of a program-level evaluation study are generalizable to a larger population or to settings outside the evaluative context, situation, or setting. If an evaluative design is to have external validity, it must provide for selection of a sample of clients for the study that is representative of the population from which it was drawn.

Generalizability is difficult to establish in case-level evaluations; we would have to be able to demonstrate that the clients on whom the intervention is to be tested are representative of a larger group of clients to whom the intervention might be applied. Program-level evaluation designs provide a much broader basis for generalization; if two or more groups are used, we must be able to demonstrate that groups formed for the evaluation project are not only representative of a larger population but are equivalent in all important variables. Moreover, it is necessary to establish that nothing happened during the course of the evaluation—except for the introduction of the intervention, the independent variable—to change either the representativeness of the sample or the equivalence of the groups.

PRETEST-TREATMENT INTERACTION

This threat is similar to the testing threat to internal validity. The nature of a pretest can alter the way clients respond to the experimental intervention, as well as to the posttest. Suppose, for example, that an educational program on racial tolerance is being evaluated. A pretest that measures level of tolerance could well alert the clients to the fact that they are going to be educated into loving all their neighbors. However, many people do not want to be "educated" into anything—they are satisfied with the way they feel and will resist the instruction. This will affect the level of racial tolerance registered on the posttest.

SELECTION-TREATMENT INTERACTION

Selection-treatment interaction commonly occurs when a program-level evaluation design cannot provide for random selection of clients from a population. Suppose we want to study the effectiveness of professional workers who work in family service agencies, for example. If our research proposal was turned down by 50 agencies before it was accepted by the 51st, it is very likely that the accepting program differs in certain important aspects from the other 50. It may accept the proposal because its workers are more highly motivated, more secure, more satisfied with their jobs, or more interested in the practical application of the study than the workers within the other 50 agencies.

As a result, we would be assessing the workers on the very

factors for which they were unwittingly (and by default) selected—motivation, job satisfaction, and so on. The evaluative study may be internally valid but, since it will not be possible to generalize the results to other family service agencies, it would have little external validity.

SPECIFICITY OF VARIABLES

The threat of specificity of variables has to do with the fact that an evaluation project conducted with a specific group of clients at a specific time and in a specific setting may not always be generalizable to other clients at a different time and in a different setting. For example, it has been demonstrated that an instrument developed to measure the IQ levels of upper-class, white, suburban children does not provide an equally accurate measure of IQ when it is applied to working-class children of racial minorities in the inner city.

REACTIVE EFFECTS

As with internal validity, reactive effects occur when the attitudes or behaviors of the clients who take part in a program-level evaluation are affected by their knowledge that they are taking part in an evaluation project. As in formal case-level evaluation designs, another threat to external validity is that clients are changed to some degree by the very act of taking a pretest. Thus, they are no longer exactly equivalent to the population from which they were randomly selected, and it may not be possible to generalize the results of the study to apply to that population. Because the pretest affects the clients who are being tested, the results may be valid only for those who were pretested.

MULTIPLE-TREATMENT INTERFERENCE

If a client is given two or more treatments in succession, the results of the first treatment may affect the results of the second treatment. A client attending treatment sessions, for example, may not seem to benefit from one therapeutic technique, so another is tried. In fact, however, the client may have benefited from the first technique, but the benefit does not become apparent until the second technique has been tried. As a result, the effects of both techniques become commingled, or the results may be erroneously ascribed to the second technique alone.

Because of this threat, experimental treatment interventions should be given separately if possible. If the design does not allow this, sufficient time should be allowed to elapse between treatments to minimize the possibility of multiple-treatment interference.

RESEARCHER BIAS

People who do evaluations, like people in general, tend to see what they want to see or expect to see. Unconsciously and without any thought of deceit, they can manipulate a program-level evaluation study so that the actual results agree with the anticipated results. A practitioner may favor an intervention so strongly that the evaluation design is structured to support it, or the results are interpreted favorably.

If the evaluator knows which individuals are in the experimental group and which are in the control group, this knowledge alone might affect the study's results. Students an instructor believes to be bright, for example, often are given higher grades than their performance warrants, while students believed to be dull are given lower grades. The way to control for such bias is to perform a double-blind experiment in which neither the evaluation clients nor the evaluator knows who is in the experimental or control group or who is receiving a specific treatment intervention.

PROGRAM-LEVEL EVALUATION DESIGNS

Examples of simple evaluation designs were introduced in the previous chapter with case-level designs, because they represent a class of designs that is comparatively consistent and uncomplicated. Many of these designs have the same purpose: to evaluate the effects of interventions on clients. Many have the same independent variable—the intervention—and the same dependent variable—the attainment of the practice objective. The study is done at the individual level—a single person, a single couple, a single group, a single family, a single community or a single organization.

Understanding formal case-level designs, therefore, lays a good foundation for understanding more complex program-level evaluation designs that use groups of clients rather than single clients. But only some of the program-level evaluation designs discussed in this chapter are complex; a design that is unnecessarily complex costs more, takes more time, and probably will not serve its purpose nearly as well as a simpler one.

In choosing an evaluation design, therefore, the principle of parsimony must be applied: As in formal case-level designs discussed in the previous chapter, the simplest and most economical route in order to gather the necessary data is the best choice. The order for the lists of group evaluation designs in Table 8.2 goes from simplest to most complex, and the descriptions of the designs in this and the following sections follow the same order.

A simple notation is used to write these designs in symbol form. Only three basic symbols are used:

X = Intervention, the independent variable
O = Measurement of the program objective, the dependent variable
R = Random selection from a population or random assignment to a group

EXPLORATORY EVALUATION DESIGNS

At the lowest level of the continuum of knowledge that can be derived from program-level evaluation studies are the exploratory studies. An exploratory study explores a program's objective about which little is already known, in order to uncover generalizations and develop hypotheses that can be investigated and tested later with more precise and hence more complex designs and data-gathering techniques.

TABLE 8.2　　KNOWLEDGE LEVELS AND CORRESPONDING
　　　　　　　　　RESEARCH DESIGNS

Knowledge Levels	Research Designs
1. EXPLORATORY	a: One-group posttest only
	b: Multigroup posttest only
	c: Longitudinal case study
	d: Longitudinal survey
2. DESCRIPTIVE	a: Randomized one-group posttest only
	b: Randomized cross-sectional and longitudinal survey
	c: One-group pretest-posttest
	d: Comparison group posttest only
	e: Comparison group pretest-posttest
	f: Interrupted time series
3. EXPLANATORY	a: Classical experimental
	b: Solomon four-group
	c: Randomized posttest-only control group

The examples of exploratory designs given in this section do not use pretests; they measure the program objective only after the introduction of the intervention, or the independent variable.

ONE-GROUP POSTTEST-ONLY DESIGN

The one-group posttest-only evaluation design (Design 1a) is sometimes called the one-shot case study or cross-sectional case study design. It is the simplest of all the program-level evaluation designs

Suppose in a particular community—Rome, Wisconsin—there are numerous parents who are physically abusive toward their children. The city decides to hire a school social worker, Antonia, to implement a program that is supposed to reduce the number of parents who physically abuse their children. She conceptualizes a 12-week child abuse prevention program (the intervention) and offers it to parents who have children in her school who wish to participate on a voluntary basis. A simple evaluation study is then conducted to answer the question, "Did the parents who completed the program stop physically abusing their children?" The answer to this question will determine the success of the intervention.

There are many different ways in which this program can be evaluated. For now, and to make matters as simple as possible, we are going to evaluate it by simply counting how many parents stopped physically abusing their children after they attended the program.

At the simplest level, the program could be evaluated with a one-group posttest-only design. The basic elements of this design can be written as follows:

$$X \quad O_1$$

Where:

X = Independent variable (child abuse prevention program, the intervention) (see Box 8.1)

O_1 = First and only measurement of the dependent variable (number of parents who stopped physically abusing their children, the program's outcome, or program objective)

All that this design provides is a single measure (O_1) of what happens when one group of people is subjected to one treatment or experience (X). The program's participants were not randomly selected from any particular population, and, thus, the results of the findings cannot be generalized to any other group or population.

It is safe to assume that all the members within the program had physically abused their children before they enrolled, since people who do not have this problem would not enroll in such a program. But, even if the value of O_1 indicates that some of the parents did stop being violent with their children after the program, it cannot be determined whether they quit because of the intervention (the program) or because of some other rival hypothesis.

Perhaps a law was passed that made it mandatory for the police to arrest anyone who behaves violently toward his or her child, or perhaps the local television station started to report such incidents on the nightly news, complete with pictures of the abusive parent. These other extraneous variables may have been more important in persuading the parents to cease their abusive behavior toward their children than their voluntary participation in the program. In sum, this design does not control for many of the threats to either internal or external validity. In terms of internal validity, the threats that are applicable and that are not controlled for in this design are history, maturation, differential selection, and mortality.

CROSS-SECTIONAL SURVEY DESIGN

Let us take another example of a one-group posttest-only design that *does not* have an independent or dependent variable. In survey research, this kind of a group research design is called a cross-sectional survey design. As presented in Chapter 2, it is used often in needs assessment studies.

In doing a cross-sectional survey, we survey *only once* a cross-section of some particular population. In addition to Antonia's child abuse prevention program geared for abusive parents, she may also want to start another program geared for all the children in the school (whether they come from abusive families or not)—a child abuse educational program taught to children in the school.

Before Antonia starts the program geared for the children, however, she wants to know what parents think about the idea. She may send out questionnaires to all the parents or she may decide to personally telephone every second parent, or every fifth or tenth, depending on how much time and money she has. The results of her survey constitute a single measurement, or observation, of the parents' opinions of her second proposed program (the one for the children) and may be written as:

$$\boxed{O_1}$$

The symbol O_1 represents the entire cross-sectional survey design since such a design involves making only a single observation, or measurement, at one time period. Note that there is no X, as there is really no independent variable. Antonia only wants to ascertain the parents' attitudes toward her proposed program—nothing more, nothing less.

MULTIGROUP POSTTEST-ONLY DESIGN

The multigroup posttest-only design (Design 1b) is an elaboration of the one-group posttest-only design (Design 1a) in which more than one group is used. To check a bit further into the effectiveness of Antonia's program for parents who have been physically abusive toward their children, for example, she might decide to locate several more groups of parents who had completed her program and see how many of them had stopped abusing their children—and so on, with any number of groups. This design can be written in symbols as follows:

> Experimental Group 1: X O_1
> Experimental Group 2: X O_1
> Experimental Group 3: X O_1
> Experimental Group 4: X O_1

Where:

X = Independent variable (child abuse prevention program, the intervention) (see Box 8.1)

O_1 = First and only measurement of the dependent variable (number of parents who stopped physically abusing their children, the program's outcome, or program objective)

With the multigroup design it cannot be assumed that all four Xs (the independent variables) are equivalent because the four programs might not be exactly the same; one group might have had a different facilitator, the program might have been presented differently, or the material could have varied in important respects.

In addition, nothing is known about whether any of the research participants would have stopped being violent anyway, even without the program. It certainly cannot be assumed that any of the groups were representative of the larger population from which they were drawn. The following discussion on pages 244-247 has been taken and slightly modified from Williams, Tutty, and Grinnell (1995).

LONGITUDINAL CASE STUDY DESIGN

The longitudinal case study design (Design 1c) is exactly like the one-group posttest-only design (Design 1a), except that it provides for more measurements of the dependent variable (Os). This design can be written in symbols as follows:

$$X \quad O_1 \quad O_2 \quad O_3 \ldots$$

Where:

X = Independent variable (child abuse prevention program, the intervention) (see Box 8.1)

O_1 = First measurement of the dependent variable (number of parents who stopped physically abusing their children, the program's outcome, or program objective)

O_2 = Second measurement of the dependent variable (number of parents who stopped physically abusing their children, the program's outcome, or program objective)

O_3 = Third measurement of the dependent variable (number of parents who stopped physically abusing their children, the program's outcome, or program objective)

Suppose that, in our example, Antonia is interested in the long-term effects of the child abuse prevention program. Perhaps the program was effective in helping some people to stop physically abusing their children, but will they continue to refrain from abusing their children? One way to find out is to measure the number of parents who physically abuse their children at intervals—say at the end of the program, the first three months after the program, then the next three months after that, and every three months for the next two years.

Design 1c can be used to monitor the effectiveness of treatment interventions over time and can be applied not just to groups but also to single client systems. However, all of the same threats to the internal and external validity that were described in relation to the previous two exploratory designs also apply to this design.

LONGITUDINAL SURVEY DESIGN

Unlike cross-sectional surveys, where the variable of interest (usually the dependent variable) is measured only once, longitudinal surveys (Design 1d) provide data at various points so that changes can be monitored over time. Longitudinal survey designs can be written as:

$$O_1 \quad O_2 \quad O_3$$

Where:

O_1 = First measurement of some variable
O_2 = Second measurement of some variable
O_3 = Third measurement of some variable

Longitudinal survey designs usually have no independent and dependent variables and can broken down into three types: (1) trend studies, (2) cohort studies, and (3) panel studies.

TREND STUDIES   A trend study is used to find out how a population, or sample, changes over time. Antonia, the school social worker mentioned previously, may want to know if parents of young children enroled in her school are becoming more receptive to the idea of the school teaching their children child abuse prevention education in the second grade. She may survey all the parents of Grade 2 children this year, all the parents of the new complement of Grade 2 children next year, and so on until she thinks she has sufficient data.

Each year the parents surveyed will be different, but they will all be parents of Grade 2 children. In this way, Antonia will be able to determine whether parents are becoming more receptive to the idea of introducing child abuse prevention material to their children as early as Grade 2. In other words, she will be able to measure any attitudinal trend that is, or is not, occurring. The research design can still be written:

$$O_1 \quad O_2 \quad O_3$$

Where:

O_1 = First measurement of some variable for a sample
O_2 = Second measurement of some variable for a different sample
O_3 = Third measurement of some variable for yet another different sample

COHORT STUDIES   Cohort studies are used over time to follow a group of people who have shared a similar experience—for example, AIDS survivors, sexual abuse survivors, or parents of grade-school children. Perhaps Antonia is interested in knowing whether parents' attitudes toward the school offering abuse prevention education to second-grade students change as their children grow older. She may survey a sample of the Grade 2 parents who attend a Parent Night this year, and survey a different sample of parents who attend a similar meeting from the same parents next year, when their children are in Grade 3.

The following year, when the children are in Grade 4, she will take another, different sample of those parents who attend Parent Night. Although different parents are being surveyed every year, they all belong to the same population of parents whose children are progressing through the grades together. The selection of the samples was not random, though, because parents who take the time to attend Parent Night may be different from those who stay at home. The research design may be written:

$$O_1 \quad O_2 \quad O_3$$

Where:

O_1 = First measurement of some variable for a sample drawn from some population

O_2 = Second measurement of some variable for a different sample drawn from the same population one year later

O_3 = Third measurement of some variable for a still different sample, drawn from the same population after two years

PANEL STUDIES   In a panel study, the *same individuals* are followed over a period of time. Antonia might select one particular sample of parents, for example, and measure their attitudes toward child abuse prevention education in successive years. Again, the design can be written:

$$O_1 \quad O_2 \quad O_3$$

Where:

O_1 = First measurement of some variable for a sample of individuals

O_2 = Second measurement of some variable for the same sample of individuals one year later

O_3 = Third measurement of some variable for the same sample of individuals after two years

A trend study is interested in broad trends over time, whereas a cohort study provides data about people who have shared similar experiences. In neither case do we know anything about *individual* contributions to the changes that are being measured. A panel study provides data that we can use to look at change over time as experienced by particular individuals.

DESCRIPTIVE EVALUATION DESIGNS

At the midpoint of the knowledge continuum are descriptive evaluation designs, which have some but not all of the requirements of an "ideal" evaluation. They usually require specification of the time order of variables, manipulation of the intervention (independent variable), and establishment of the relationship between the intervention and the attainment of the program objectives (dependent variables). They may also control for rival hypotheses and use a second group as a comparison (not a control). The requirement that these designs lack most frequently is random selection of clients from a population and random assignment to groups.

Human service evaluators often are not in a position to assign clients randomly to either an experimental or a comparison or control group. Sometimes the groups to be studied are already in existence; sometimes ethical issues are involved. For example, it would not be ethical to assign clients who need immediate help to two random groups, only one of which is to receive the intervention. Since a lack of random assignment will affect the internal and external validities of the evaluative effort, a descriptive evaluation design must try to compensate for this. The six examples of descriptive evaluation designs presented in this section do this in various ways.

Randomized One-Group Posttest-Only Design

The distinguishing feature of the randomized one-group posttest-only design (Design 2a) is that members of the group are randomly selected for it. Otherwise, this design is identical to the exploratory one-group posttest-only design (Design 1a). The randomized one-group posttest-only design is written as follows:

$$R \quad X \quad O_1$$

Where:

R = Random selection from a population
X = Independent variable (see Box 8.1)
O_1 = First and only measurement of the dependent variable

In the example of the child abuse prevention program, the difference in this design is that the group does not accidentally assemble itself by including anyone who happened to be interested in volunteering for the program. Instead, group members are randomly selected from a population, say, of all the 400 parents who were reported to child welfare authorities for having physically abused a child and who wish to receive voluntary treatment in Rome, Wisconsin, in 1998. These 400 parents comprise the population of all the physically abusive parents who wish to receive treatment in Rome, Wisconsin.

The sampling frame of 400 people is used to select a simple random sample of 40 physically abusive parents who voluntarily wish to receive treatment. The program (X) is administered to these 40 people, and the number of parents who stopped being abusive toward their children after the program is determined (O_1). The design can be written as:

$$R \quad X \quad O_1$$

Where:

R = Random selection of 40 people from the population of physically abusive parents who voluntarily wish to receive treatment in Rome, Wisconsin
X = Child abuse prevention program (see Box 8.1)
O_1 = Number of parents in the program who stopped being physically abusive to their children

Say that the program fails to have the desired effect, and 39 of the 40 people continue to physically harm their children after participating in the program. Because the program was ineffective for the sample and the sample was randomly selected, it can be concluded that it would be ineffective for the physically abusive parent population of Rome, Wisconsin—the other 360 who did not go through the program. In other words, because a representative random sample was selected, it is possible to generalize the program's results to the population from which the sample was drawn.

Since no change in the dependent variable occurred, it is not sensible to consider the control of rival hypotheses. Antonia need not wonder what might have caused the change—X, her program, or an alternative explanation. If her program had been successful, however, it would not be possible to ascribe her success solely to the program.

RANDOMIZED CROSS-SECTIONAL AND LONGITUDINAL SURVEY DESIGN

As discussed earlier, a cross-sectional survey obtains data only once from a sample of a particular population. If the sample is a random sample—that is, if it represents the population from which it was drawn—then the data obtained from the sample can be generalized to the entire population. A cross-sectional survey design using a random sample can be written:

$$R \quad O_1$$

Where:

R = Random sample drawn from a population
O_1 = First and only measurement of the dependent variable (see Box 8.1)

Explanatory surveys look for associations between variables. Often, the suspected reason for the relationship is that one variable caused the other. In Antonia's case, she has two studies going on: the child abuse prevention program for parents who have physically abused their children, and her survey of parental attitudes toward the school that is teaching second-grade children child abuse prevention strategies. The success of the child abuse prevention program (her program) may have caused parents to adopt more positive attitudes toward the school in teaching their children child abuse prevention (her survey). In this situation, the two variables, the program and survey, become commingled.

Demonstrating causality is a frustrating business at best because it is so difficult to show that nothing apart from the independent variable could have caused the observed change in the dependent variable. Even supposing that this problem is solved, it is impossible to demonstrate causality unless data are obtained from random samples and are generalizable to entire populations.

ONE-GROUP PRETEST-POSTTEST DESIGN

The one-group pretest-posttest design (Design 2c) is also referred to as a before-after design because it includes a pretest of the dependent variable, which can be used as a basis of comparison with the posttest results. It is written as:

$$O_1 \quad X \quad O_2$$

Where:

O_1 = First measurement of the dependent variable
X = Independent variable, the intervention (see Box 8.1)
O_2 = Second measurement of the dependent variable

The one-group pretest-posttest design, in which a pretest precedes the introduction of the independent variable and a posttest follows it, can be used to determine precisely how the independent variable affects a particular group. The design is used often in social work decision making—far too often, in fact, because it does not control for many rival hypotheses. The difference between O_1 and O_2, on which these decisions are based, therefore, could be due to many other factors rather than the independent variable.

Let us take another indicator of how Antonia's child abuse

prevention program could be evaluated. Besides counting the number of parents who stopped physically abusing their children as the only indicator of the program's success, she could have a second outcome indicator, such as reducing the parents' risk for abusive and neglecting parenting behaviors. This dependent variable could be easily measured by an instrument that measures their attitudes of physical punishment of children.

Let us say that Antonia had the parents complete the instrument *before* the child abuse prevention program (O_1) and *after* it (O_2). In this example, history would be a rival hypothesis or threat to internal validity because all kinds of things could have happened between O_1 and O_2 to affect the participants' behaviors and feelings—such as the television station deciding to publicize the names of parents who are abusive to their children. Testing also could be a problem. Just the experience of taking the pretest could motivate some participants to stop being abusive toward their children. Maturation—in this example, the children becoming more mature with age so that they became less difficult to discipline—would be a further threat.

This design controls for the threat of differential selection, since the participants are the same for both pretest and posttest. Second, mortality would not affect the outcome, because it is the differential drop-out between groups that causes this threat and, in this example, there is only one group.

COMPARISON GROUP POSTTEST-ONLY DESIGN

The comparison group posttest-only design (Design 2d) improves on the exploratory one-group and multigroup posttest-only designs by introducing a comparison group that does not receive the independent variable, but is subject to the same posttest as those who do (the experimental group).

A group used for purposes of comparison is usually referred to as a comparison group in an exploratory or descriptive design and as a control group in an explanatory design. While a control group is always randomly assigned, a comparison group is not. The basic elements of the comparison group posttest-only design are as follows:

> Experimental Group: X O_1
> Comparison Group: O_1

Where:

X = Independent variable, the intervention
O_1 = First and only measurement of the dependent variable

In Antonia's child abuse prevention program, if the January, April, and August sections are scheduled but the August sessions are canceled for some reason, those who would have been participants in that section could be used as a comparison group. If the values of O_1 on the measuring instrument were similar for the experimental and comparison groups, it could be concluded that the program was of little use, since those who had experienced it (those receiving X) were not much better or worse off than those who had not.

A problem with drawing this conclusion, however, is that there is no evidence that the groups were equivalent to begin with. Selection, mortality, and the interaction of selection and other threats to internal validity are, thus, the major difficulties with this design. The comparison group does, however, control for such threats as history, testing, instrumentation, and statistical regression.

COMPARISON GROUP PRETEST-POSTTEST DESIGN

The comparison group pretest-posttest design (Design 2e) elaborates on the one-group pretest-posttest design (Design 2c) by adding a comparison group. This second group receives both the pretest (O_1) and the posttest (O_2) at the same time as the experimental group, but it does not receive the independent variable. This design is written as follows:

Experimental Group: O_1 X O_2
Comparison Group: O_1 O_2

Where:

O_1 = First measurement of the dependent variable, the parents' scores on the measuring instrument
X = Independent variable, the intervention
O_2 = Second measurement of the dependent variable, the parents' scores on the measuring instrument

The experimental and comparison groups formed under this design will probably not be equivalent, because members are not randomly assigned to them. The pretest scores, however, will indicate the extent of their differences. If the differences are not statistically significant, but are still large enough to affect the posttest, the statistical technique of analysis of covariance can be used to compensate for this. As long as the groups are equivalent at pretest, then, this design controls for nearly all of the threats to internal validity. But, because random selection and assignment were not used, the external validity threats remain.

INTERRUPTED TIME-SERIES DESIGN

In the interrupted time-series design (Design 2f), a series of pretests and posttests are conducted on a group of research participants over time, both before and after the independent variable is introduced. The basic elements of this design are illustrated as follows:

$$O_1 \quad O_2 \quad O_3 \quad X \quad O_4 \quad O_5 \quad O_6$$

Where:

Os = Measurements of the dependent variable
X = Independent variable (see Box 8.1)
This design takes care of the major weakness in the descriptive

one-group pretest-posttest design (Design 2c), which does not control for rival hypotheses. Suppose, for example, that a new policy is to be introduced into a program whereby all promotions and raises are to be tied to the number of educational credits acquired by social workers. Since there is a strong feeling among some workers that years of experience should count for more than educational credits, the administrator of the program decides to examine the effect of the new policy on morale.

Because program morale is affected by many things and varies normally from month to month, it is necessary to ensure that these normal fluctuations are not confused with the results of the new policy. Therefore, a baseline is first established for morale by conducting a number of pretests over, say, a six-month period before the policy is introduced. Then, a similar number of posttests is conducted over the six months following the introduction of the policy. This design would be written as follows:

$$O_1 \quad O_2 \quad O_3 \quad O_4 \quad O_5 \quad O_6 \quad X \quad O_7 \quad O_8 \quad O_9 \quad O_{10} \quad O_{11} \quad O_{12}$$

The same type of time-series design can be used to evaluate the result of a treatment intervention with a client or client system, as in case-level designs described in the previous chapter. Again, without randomization, threats to external validity still could affect the results, but most of the threats to internal validity are addressed.

EXPLANATORY EVALUATION DESIGNS

Explanatory program-level evaluation designs approach an "ideal" evaluation most closely. They are at the highest level on the knowledge continuum, have the most rigid requirements, and are most able to produce results that can be generalized to other clients and situations. Explanatory designs, therefore, are most able to provide valid and reliable evaluation results that can add to our theoretical knowledge base.

The purpose of most explanatory designs is to establish a causal connection between the intervention (the independent variable) and the program objectives (the dependent variable). The attainment of the objectives could always result from chance rather than from the influence of the intervention, but there are statistical techniques for calculating the probability that this will occur.

CLASSICAL EXPERIMENTAL DESIGN

The classical experimental design (Design 3a), or classical evaluation design, is the basis for all explanatory designs. It involves an experimental group and a control group, both created by random sampling and random assignment methods. Both groups take a pretest (O_1) at the same time, after which the intervention (X) is given only to the experimental group, and then both groups take the posttest (O_2). This design is written as follows:

Experimental Group: R O_1 X O_2
Control Group: R O_1 O_2

Where:

R = Random selection from a population and random assignment to group
O_1 = First measurement of the dependent variable
X = Independent variable, the intervention
O_2 = Second measurement of the dependent variable

Because the experimental and control groups have been randomly assigned, they are equivalent with respect to all important variables. This group equivalence in the design helps control for rival hypotheses, because both groups would be affected by them in the same way.

SOLOMON FOUR-GROUP DESIGN

The Solomon four-group research design (Design 3b) involves four rather than two randomly assigned groups as in Design 3a. There are two experimental groups and two control groups, but the pretest is taken by only one of each of these groups. Experimental Group 1 takes a pretest, receives the independent variable, and then takes a posttest. Experimental Group 2 also receives the independent variable but takes only the posttest. The same is true for the two control groups; Control Group 1 takes both the pretest and posttest, and Control Group 2 takes only the posttest. This design is written in symbols as follows:

Experimental Group 1:	R	O_1	X	O_2
Control Group 1:	R	O_1		O_2
Experimental Group 2:	R		X	O_2
Control Group 2:	R			O_2

Where:

R = Random assignment to group
O_1 = First measurement of the dependent variable
X = Independent variable, the intervention
O_2 = Second measurement of the dependent variable

The advantage of the Solomon four-group research design is that it allows for the control of testing effects, since one of the experimental groups and one of the control groups do not take the pretest. All of the threats to internal validity are addressed when this design is used. It has the disadvantage that twice as many study participants are required, and it is considerably more work to implement than the classical experimental design.

RANDOMIZED POSTTEST-ONLY CONTROL GROUP DESIGN

The randomized posttest-only control group research design (Design 3c) is identical to the descriptive comparison group posttest-only design (Design 2d), except that the research participants are randomly assigned to two groups. This design, therefore, has a control group rather than a comparison group.

The randomized posttest-only control group research design usually involves only two groups, one experimental and one control. There are no pretests. The experimental group receives the independent variable and takes the posttest; the control group only takes the posttest. This design can be written as follows:

> Experimental Group: R X O_1
> Control Group: R O_1

Where:

R = Random selection from a population and random assignment to group

X = Independent variable, the intervention

O_1 = First and only measurement of the dependent variable

Suppose we want to test the effects of two different treatment interventions, X_1 and X_2. In this case, Design 3c could be elaborated upon to form three randomly assigned groups, two experimental groups (one for each intervention) and one control group. This design would be written as follows:

> Experimental Group 1: R X_1 O_1
> Experimental Group 2: R X_2 O_1
> Control Group: R O_1

Where:

R = Random selection from a population and random assignment to group

X_1 = Different independent variable than X_2

X_2 = Different independent variable than X_1

O_1 = First and only measurement of the dependent variable

In addition to measuring change in a group or groups, a pretest also helps to ensure equivalence between the control and experimental groups. As you know, this design does not have a pretest. The groups have been randomly assigned, however, as indicated by R, and this, in itself, is theoretically enough to ensure equivalence without the need for a confirmatory pretest. This design is useful in situations where it is not possible to conduct a pretest or where a pretest would be expected to strongly influence the results of the posttest due to the effects of testing. This design also controls for many of the threats to internal validity.

SUMMARY

Program-level evaluation designs are conducted with groups of cases rather than on a case-by-case basis. They cover the entire range of evaluation concerns and provide designs that can be used to gain knowledge on the exploratory, descriptive, and explanatory levels. The chapter presented the threats to internal and external validity and demonstrated how these threats can affect various evaluation designs.

The last chapter described how formal case-level evaluations can be used to enhance quality improvement at the line level; that is, it presented various evaluative designs that can be used to evaluate (or monitor) clients' practice objectives. This chapter presented various designs that can be used to evaluate program objectives. Thus, the two chapters complement one another as they both describe how evaluations can be used in the quality improvement process at the case level (practice objectives) and at the program level (program objectives). All of the evaluative designs presented in the last chapter and this one can be used to enhance the delivery of human services.

Most of the designs described in these two chapters can be used in the project and monitoring approaches to quality improvement (see Chapter 3), depending on when the evaluation takes place. Designs that reflect the project approach usually take place after a program is completed, whereas designs that reflect the monitoring approach usually take place while the program is underway.

CHAPTER 9

FROM DATA TO INFORMATION

ASOCIAL SERVICE AGENCY is a complex organization that usually contains numerous interlinking programs. The programs themselves can also be complex. A treatment program housed within an agency, for example, may have set procedures for client intake, assessment, intervention, termination, and follow-up. Other types of programs within the same agency may offer other sets of activities, each of which will also be undertaken according to set procedures. An educational program, for example, may operate a library, as well as organize workshops, seminars, and presentations for lay persons and professionals. A program for adolescents with developmental disabilities may operate a number of residential programs that may include a vocational component.

The procedures just listed above all have to do with client-related activities, but there are also procedures for staff-related activities, volunteer-related activities, community-related activities, and fund-raising activities, to list only a few. For example, procedures describe how staff are selected and trained; how volunteers are recruited, selected, trained, supervised, and acknowledged; and which fund-raising activities are undertaken using which methods.

Monitoring involves yet another set of procedures. These define what data are collected when, where, in what manner, and by whom; who will collate, analyze and interpret them; and how, and in what form, the results will be disseminated. Essentially, the procedures serve to operationalize two important features of any monitoring system: (1) the system should recognize that different data needs exist at different organizational levels, and (2) the system should be capable of delivering needed information to all levels within the organization in a timely manner and in a format useable at that level.

Specifically, the monitoring system should be designed in a way that data collected at any stage are demonstrably relevant to decisions to be made. Data collected by front-line workers, for example, should bear upon, in the first instance, decisions they are required to make. In other words, the data collected by workers must guide clinical decision making. At the same time, these data must be capable of being aggregated in a manner that is relevant to the program's administrators. Information at this level is used to guide planning as well as to meet external reporting requirements.

The important point here is that data are not collected indiscriminately in the hope that they will somehow be useful. Data collection procedures must reflect a careful analysis of information needs at all levels within the program and agency and should provide for the collection of needed data in the least disruptive and most economical and efficient manner.

STAFF ROLES IN DEVELOPING A MONITORING CAPACITY

Establishing and maintaining a monitoring system requires the cooperation of all program staff, from line-level workers through senior administrators. Inevitably, much of the burden of data collection falls on the line-level workers. Involving them in the planning and design of the monitoring system helps to ensure that information needs at the direct service level will be met and that data can be collected without undue disruption to service provision. Moreover, the involvement of line-level workers helps to secure their cooperation and commitment to the monitoring process.

Administrators must contribute by committing the necessary resources for the implementation of a monitoring system, in addition to providing worker training and support. The design and implementation of the monitoring system costs money; computer hardware and software must be purchased and consultation fees will be incurred. It will also cost money to train professional workers and support staff as well; this is a vital component on which administrators should resist the temptation to skimp. Training is particularly necessary if the new system introduces computerization.

As will be discussed in the next chapter, it is very important that monitoring be carried out within an organizational culture that acknowledges that all human service programs fall short of perfection. The purpose of monitoring is not to assign blame; it is to provide better services, by identifying strengths and limitations, so that the former can be reinforced and the latter corrected. The monitoring approach to quality improvement allows shortcomings to be identified not only by supervisors or administrators, but by the line-level workers themselves, allowing them to become more accountable for their own practice effectiveness. Among other benefits, this approach empowers staff members who have been disempowered by traditional evaluation approaches.

ESTABLISHING AN ORGANIZATIONAL PLAN FOR DATA COLLECTION

Any data collection plan must take into account at least three sets of needs:

- First, data collection must meet case-level decision-making needs, serving decisions to be made immediately as well as those made throughout the client's progress within the program. Certain data, for example, are required at client intake in order to decide whether to accept the referral. Once accepted, the client may go through a formal assessment procedure, at which point further data will likely be collected.

- Second, the system must be designed to accommodate the program-level decision-making responsibilities of the administrators. This often entails the aggregation of case-level data, permitting the development of reports for internal and external use.
- Third, technical requirements of the system must also be considered. The system requires certain types of information as well as specific formats.

The data collection system adopted must represent a balance between these three sets of needs, satisfying each to the extent possible. It is likely, however, that no one set of needs can be completely met. To come up with a data collection plan that is feasible, acceptable, and effective requires careful planning as well as negotiation and compromise. Early involvement in the planning of the system by front-line workers, administrators, as well as those designing the system helps to ensure that everyone's needs are met.

CASE-LEVEL DATA COLLECTION

Perhaps the best way to decide what data are needed at the case level is to follow a client through the program by way of a client case-flow analysis. Figure 9.1 (and Figure 5.4) presents an example, a case-flow chart illustrating the sequence of events in a child protection program.

The beginning of the process is the referral. Suspected abuse may be reported by a variety of sources, including teachers, neighbors, and health care workers. All referrals are immediately directed to the Screening Unit. Because every allegation of child abuse must be looked into, at this point the two most relevant pieces of data are the age and place of residence of the alleged victim. Within a short period, a screening worker normally contacts the referring source as well as the family to verify the complaint and to obtain further details. Based on this information, the worker decides whether a full investigation is warranted. If so, an investigating worker will likely interview the alleged victim and will probably also interview relevant others.

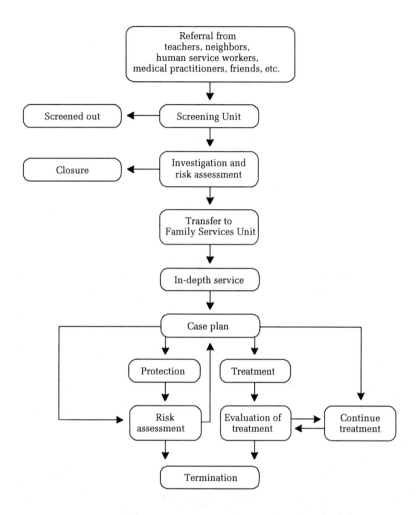

FIGURE 9.1   FLOW CHART FOR A CHILD PROTECTION
                     PROGRAM

As with every activity, each interview has a specific purpose.
The purpose of interviewing the alleged victim is fourfold:

- to verify that the alleged abuse has in fact occurred
- to ensure the immediate safety of the child
- to determine whether treatment is needed, and if so, what
  treatment would be best

- to inform the child and others connected to the case about what will happen next

The investigating worker will conduct this interview on the basis of data collected by the screening worker and will need data in the following general areas:

- the specific circumstances of the alleged abuse
- the specific circumstances in which it was disclosed
- data about the child
- data about the family

The screening form thus must be designed to incorporate these different data needs.

From a case-level perspective, then, the data collected at screening serves two broad purposes: (1) to ensure that the alleged victim is a child resident within the program's catchment area, and (2) to fulfill the investigating worker's data needs. Since a monitoring system is intended to provide needed and timely data to staff members, and since front-line workers themselves know best what data they need to help them in their decision-making efforts, front-line workers must be involved in designing forms.

When the investigation is complete, the data are used to assess the degree of continuing risk to the child. On this basis, the worker determines whether further services are required. Continuing cases are transferred from the Screening Unit to the Family Services Unit, where a worker is assigned to the family to coordinate protection and treatment functions. The Family Services Unit worker then conducts a full assessment based on the data provided by the investigating worker in the Screening Unit, as well as any additional data collected. The purpose of assessment is to develop an in-depth understanding of the situation and of child and family needs so that an appropriate intervention plan can be established. In other words, data collected during assessment are used in making decisions about the client's case plan.

As Figure 9.1 indicates, the case plan formulated may have both a protection component and a treatment component. Practice objectives are then established in relation to these components, and data collected during service provision are used to assess the degree to which interventions are achieving practice objectives. Case-level data also are collected for subsequent aggregation and used in a program evaluation(s). In addition, data collection is conducted with an eye to guiding the termination decision.

Termination criteria for protection and treatment can easily differ. Protection workers are likely to focus on the continuing safety of the child, whereas treatment workers may focus on family functioning. The family may therefore still be undergoing treatment when protection services have been discontinued. Ultimately, when the decision to terminate all services is made, the case can be closed.

Data collection is not a matter of randomly assembling whatever data come to hand. The data collected in each program phase must be fully and firmly linked to the objectives of the particular phase, the decisions to be made during the phase, and the informational needs of subsequent phases. Insufficient data lead to poor decision making; overly profuse and irrelevant data result in confusion and unnecessary costs.

To ensure that there is adequate congruence between the data collected and the decisions to be made, a data collection analysis can be undertaken. This analysis lists, in chronological order:

- the decisions to be made
- the data needed to make each decision
- the actual data collected

If there is a discrepancy between what is needed and what is being collected, data collection protocols need to be revised.

PROGRAM-LEVEL DATA COLLECTION

Data collection at any program stage must be designed to fulfill the informational needs of both line-level workers and administrators alike.

It is often useful to identify the main data collection events for each program. Typically, programs collect data at intake, at every contact with a client, as well as at termination. Other data collection events may be planned, depending on circumstances and worker's needs. A plan identifying the key data collection events for a family service agency, for example, across five of its programs, is presented

Forms	Information	Education	Parent Support	Counseling	Mediation
Registration	X	X	X	X	X
Assessment				X	X
Contact notes			X	X	X
Termination			X	X	X
Outcome: Self-report		X	X	X	X
Outcome: Measures				X	X
Satisfaction	X	X	X	X	X

FIGURE 9.2   EXAMPLE OF A DATA COLLECTION PLAN

in Figure 9.2. Each cell marked with an "X" in the grid represents a major data collection event for which a corresponding data collection instrument or form can be designed. In the case of the counseling program, for example, the major data collection events are intake, client contacts, termination, and client satisfaction survey. Data can then be collected, for each of these events, using specifically designed forms.

To illustrate this point, consider the counseling program operated by the agency. The service is funded by the Department of Social Services (DSS) to provide counseling services to DSS clients with psychosocial problems who need more help than the brief, instrumentally oriented counseling that can be provided by the DSS. Figure 9.3 shows part of an intake form that new clients might complete in the center's office while they are waiting for a first interview.

The intake form is usually the first document in the client's file. Of course, different programs need different or additional data. A job-training program, for example, will likely ask about jobs previously held, previous income, reason for present unemployment, and participation in other job-training programs.

An individual intake form provides beginning data for a case record, but it is not very useful for program evaluation purposes unless the data are aggregated with other intake forms. Figure 9.4 provides four simple tabular reports on the counseling service com-

Name: _____

Current Address: _____

_____

_____ Zip Code: _____

Home Telephone Number: _____

- TYPES OF SERVICE SOUGHT (circle one number below):
  1. Individual counseling
  2. Couple counseling
  3. Family counseling
  9. Other (please specify _____)

- SEX (circle one number below):
  1. Male
  2. Female

- BIRTH DATE _____

- REFERRAL SOURCE (circle one number below):
  1. Self
  2. Friends, family
  3. Physician
  4. Clergy
  5. Department of Social Services
  6. Other agency
  9. Other (please specify _____)

- REASONS FOR SEEKING SERVICES (circle one number below):
  1. Marital problems
  2. Family problems
  3. Problems at school
  4. Problems at work
  5. Parent-child problems
  6. Health problems
  7. Substance abuse
  8. Personal adjustment problems
  9. Other (please specify _____)

FIGURE 9.3   EXAMPLE OF A CLIENT INTAKE FORM

piled by aggregating the data from 200 individual client intake forms for the month of October 1997.

Figure 9.4 shows at a glance that 200 new clients were accepted into the program during the month of October, 63 percent of whom were referred by DSS. The program is thus able to document the degree to which it is achieving one of its maintenance objectives: providing services to clients referred by DSS. Equally important, if referrals from DSS begin to decline as the months go by, the program staff will be able to spot this trend immediately and take steps to better meet its mandate, or perhaps to negotiate an adjustment of this mandate if new circumstances have arisen. The general point of importance is that monitoring provides ongoing feedback that helps to ensure continuing achievement of a program's mandate—to see clients referred by DSS.

Contrast this with the situation of a program that undertakes biannual, project-type evaluations. By the time data indicating a problem with DSS referrals are analyzed and reported, the problem will have had a long time to get firmly established and is likely to be a very serious one. In all likelihood, the program's reputation among the DSS workers will have suffered. DSS may even have concluded that because this program is not providing adequate service, alternative services should be contracted.

The screening report also provides other useful data. Tables reporting the frequency distribution of the sex and age of new clients provide the data required to ensure that the program is attracting the type of clients for whom it was established. Assume that another one of the program's maintenance objectives is to attract 100 adolescents and young adults during October 1997. Figure 9.4 indicates that 54 percent of new clients are 29 years of age or under. This kind of data indicates that the program is on the right track.

If, on the other hand, the program's thrust were to provide services to a large number of senior citizens, data revealing that only 5 percent of new clients are 60 years of age or over would be cause for concern (Figure 9.4). A program is unlikely to undertake extensive changes on the basis of data for one month, but if several consecutive monthly reports indicate that older people constitute only a small percentage of new clients, staff may well conclude that a problem exists and needs to be addressed.

The course of service provision can be followed by completing, after each session, a client contact form such as the one illustrated

Sex of Client		
Sex	*Number*	*Percent*
Male	90	45
Female	110	55
Totals.........	200	100

Age of Clients		
Age Ranges	*Number*	*Percent*
10–19	30	15
20–29	78	39
30–39	42	21
40–49	28	14
50–59	12	6
60 +	10	5
Totals.........	200	100

Referral Sources of Clients		
Sources	*Number*	*Percent*
Self	8	4
Friends, family	12	6
Physicians	8	4
Clergy	10	5
DSS	126	63
Other agencies	28	14
Other	8	4
Totals.........	200	100

Reasons Clients Requesting Services		
Presenting Problems	*Number*	*Percent*
Marital problems	18	9
Family problems	40	20
Problems at school	28	14
Problems at work	12	6
Parent-child problems	30	15
Health problems	20	10
Substance abuse	22	11
Personal adjustment	20	10
Other	10	5
Totals.........	200	100

FIGURE 9.4   EXCERPTS FROM A MONTHLY INTAKE FORM FOR OCTOBER 1997 (FROM FIGURE 9.3)

in Figure 9.5. The client identification number (e.g., 144277) allows the data from this form to be related to data from the intake form and other contact forms prepared for this client. These data may subsequently be used to track the services provided and monitor the effects of the intervention(s).

Some of the most important data on this form concern outcomes. For one program, the program objective is to "increase client's functioning level." First, the client's score (recorded as "6" in Figure 9.5) represents the worker's current rating of the client's overall level of functioning. The scale has a range from 1 to 9, with higher numbers representing higher levels of functioning. Three points on the scale have been defined:

1. = totally dependent
2.
3.
4.
5. = minimally autonomous functioning
6.
7.
8.
9. = autonomous functioning

Clients may be considered for discharge at level 5, but will ideally attain level 7, 8, or 9 before service is terminated.

Scores from up to three additional standardized measuring instruments can also be recorded on this contact form. In Figure 9.5, the current week's score on a measuring instrument that measures self-esteem, 39, is recorded for one of the practice objectives that is considered to be directly related to this client's overall functioning. These data can be used to follow changes in practice objectives during the course of the intervention and, as well, can be aggregated into monthly summaries and other reports (as shown at the bottom of Figure 9.7).

When the case is closed, a termination form is completed. On this form, information regarding the nature of termination, as well as the final level of program and practice objectives, can be recorded. Moreover, the need for any follow-up can also be noted. An example of a termination form is provided in Table 9.6. Information from client terminations can also be aggregated and summarized.

Client's Name: *Jane Harrison*   Date (M-D-Y) **09 29 97**

Client Identification Number   **144277**

Program Objective: *Increase Client's Functioning Level*   **6**

Practice Objectives:

Objective	Score	Measuring Instrument
1. *Self-Esteem*	**39**	*Index of Self-Esteem*
2. _____	__	_____
3. _____	__	_____
4. _____	__	_____

Disposition (check one only):
✓ Continuing service
  Referred (if so, where? _____)
  Closed (if so, when? _____)

FIGURE 9.5   EXCERPTS FROM A CLIENT CONTACT FORM

Figure 9.7 provides excerpts from a summary report of cases closed in the counseling unit in the month of October 1997. These data are the result of aggregating data from clients' intake and termination forms. Aggregating data in this manner provides information that is very useful in understanding program functioning. We can readily see, for example, that over a third of the clients who terminated (36 percent) did so unilaterally.

Depending on program norms and expectations, and past experience, this information may be considered problematic. If the data are further analyzed to learn more about the termination process, program staff can determine whether unilateral termination is characteristic of any particular client group, such as males, older clients, or clients with a specific practice objectives. Such data are invaluable in diagnosing the problem and deciding on program adjustments and modifications. Data from subsequent reports will then shed light on the success of the measures adopted.

Client's Name: _____   Date (M-D-Y)   ___ ___ ___

Client Identification Number   _____

- CLOSURE DECISION WAS:
    1. Mutual
    2. Client's
    3. Worker's
    9. Other (specify _____)

- REASON FOR CLOSURE:
    1. Service no longer needed
    2. Further service declined
    3. Client stopped coming
    4. Client moved
    5. Referred elsewhere
    9. Other (specify _____)

- PROGRAM OBJECTIVE: (_____): _____

- PRACTICE OBJECTIVES:

Objective	Score	Measuring Instrument
1. _____	_____	_____
2. _____	_____	_____
3. _____	_____	_____
4. _____	_____	_____

- IS FOLLOW-UP REQUIRED?
    1. Yes (if so, how_____)
    2. No (if so, why not_____)

FIGURE 9.6   EXAMPLE OF A CLIENT TERMINATION FORM

Cases Terminated

Method of Termination	Number	Percent
Mutual consent	25	50
Client's decision	18	36
Worker's decision	7	14
Totals.......	50	100

Clients' Functional Levels (Program Objective)

Functioning Level	Beginning		Termination	
	Number	Percent	Number	Percent
1. Totally dependent	0	0	0	0
2.	1	2	1	2
3.	2	4	0	0
4.	20	40	10	20
5. Satisfactory	18	36	7	14
6.	6	12	20	40
7.	3	6	8	16
8.	0	0	3	6
9. Totally independent	0	0	1	2
Totals..........	50	100	50	100
Averages		4.7		5.7

Average of Clients' Practice Objectives

Practice Objectives	Beginning	End	n
Self-esteem	61	42	12
Peer relations	57	37	4
Depression	42	27	4
Marital satisfaction	51	48	6
Clinical stress	47	41	9
Alcohol involvement	40	31	4
Partner abuse	52	42	1
Sexual satisfaction	66	60	5
Anxiety	52	41	5
Total..........			50

Note: All practice objectives are measured with Hudson's Scales as reported in Nurius and Hudson, 1993. High scores = higher levels of problem.

FIGURE 9.7   EXCERPTS FROM A MONTHLY SUMMARY FORM OF CLOSED CASES FOR OCTOBER 1997

The summary report also provides data about program outcomes. Examining the data on client functioning levels at intake tells staff whether they are successfully targeting the clientele whom the program is intended to serve. In addition, functioning levels at termination provide a profile of how well client problems had been resolved by the time of termination. As can be seen in Figure 9.7, the average functioning level of the 50 clients who terminated in October 1997 went up by one full point, from 4.7 to 5.7.

As the data show, 36 percent of the clientele leave the program at or above the minimally autonomous functioning level of 5. However, only 24 percent of clientele attain the most desirable levels of 7, 8, or 9 at discharge. Contextual data, such as the practice objectives established and previous results, would be required to fully interpret these data. Nevertheless, it would not be unreasonable to conclude that, although the service is achieving acceptable results, there is room for further improvement.

Data pertaining to specific client practice objectives also provide useful information. Comparing the average practice objective score at the beginning with the average score at termination for a group of clients provides information about net change achieved with respect to each practice objective.

Of course, these data in themselves do not tell the whole story. They are indicators, and very useful indicators, but their full interpretation requires careful attention to contextual variables and issues. For instance, it is possible that the relatively modest results achieved with clients experiencing marital and family problems is attributable to factors other than the way in which the program is designed and delivered. It may be that two of the more experienced workers have been on leave for the past several months. Perhaps one of these positions was covered by temporarily reassigning a less-experienced worker, while the other one was left vacant. Thus, during the preceding several months, fewer marital counseling and family therapy hours have been delivered, by less experienced staff: This could obviously have affected client outcomes. In general, interpreting the information obtained through monitoring always requires consideration of contextual variables and cannot be done purely on the basis of quantitative results.

It should be pointed out that the practice objectives listed in Figure 9.7 may also serve as program objectives if the client was being seen only to work on one of those specific issues. If a client wanted help with depression, for example, then the program objective could be "to reduce depression to a score of 30 or less."

Staff members at the agency depicted in the illustrations above have also determined that they would like to obtain feedback from program participants regarding various aspects of their satisfaction. Consequently, a satisfaction survey was developed, which clients are asked to complete at the time of service closure. Excerpts from this instrument are provided in Figure 9.8.

Again, such data are most useful when aggregated across clients. An excerpt from such analysis is provided in Figure 9.9. As may be seen, a large majority of clients consider the services helpful, the staff members supportive, and think themselves better off as a result of services. As well, two thirds would recommend the services to others and about 68 percent indicate a high or very high level of overall satisfaction with the agency.

Staff members may react to summaries such as the one shown in Figures 9.7 and 9.9 in a number of ways. They may resent the fact that their work is being scrutinized, particularly if the monthly summary has been newly instituted. Where the results suggest that there is room for improvement (which is usually the case), they may be uncertain of their own competence and, perhaps, somewhat afraid of management's reaction. Alternatively, or perhaps in addition, they may be alerted to the fact that they need to modify their approaches to improve results.

Which one of these feelings predominates depends to some extent on the way the monitoring system was introduced to the practitioners. Workers who were consulted about the system's development, informed about its advantages, and involved in its design and implementation are more likely to regard the monthly summaries as useful feedback. Staff who were neither consulted nor involved are likely to regard it with apprehension and resentment.

Equally important in shaping attitudes to monitoring is how the agency's administration uses, or abuses, the data generated. If the data are used in a judgmental, critical manner, staff are likely to remain skeptical and defensive about the monitoring process. Where the data are regarded as useful feedback and are used in a genuine, cooperative effort to upgrade and further develop services, workers will likely welcome such reports as tools that can help them—and the agency—improve.

Please provide us with feedback on our services by completing the following five questions. Please answer each question by placing a number (1 through 4) on the right side of it that best represents your response:

    1. Strongly Disagree
    2. Disagree
    3. Agree
    4. Strongly Agree

1. The services I received were helpful.   _____

2. Staff members were supportive.   _____

3. I am better off as a result of your services.   _____

4. I would recommend your services to others.   _____

5. My satisfaction with your program is good.   _____

Further comments or suggestions:

FIGURE 9.8   EXAMPLE OF A CLIENT SATISFACTION SURVEY

These considerations suggest that administrators should view monitoring information as a means of assisting them in identifying areas for improvement and in identifying factors in problems and difficulties. Obviously, this approach is far more likely to evoke a positive response than one in which data are used to reveal worker inadequacies. An administrator's responsibilities do not, however, end here. To foster a truly positive environment for monitoring,

The services I received were helpful.

	Number	Percent
Strongly Disagree	22	11
Disagree	36	18
Agree	94	47
Strongly Agree	48	24
Totals......	200	100

Staff members were supportive.

	Number	Percent
Strongly Disagree	18	9
Disagree	38	19
Agree	88	44
Strongly Agree	56	28
Totals......	200	100

I am better off as a result of your services.

	Number	Percent
Strongly Disagree	30	15
Disagree	46	23
Agree	98	49
Strongly Agree	26	13
Totals......	200	100

I would recommend your services to others.

	Number	Percent
Strongly Disagree	40	20
Disagree	30	15
Agree	74	37
Strongly Agree	56	28
Totals......	200	100

My satisfaction with your program is good.

	Number	Percent
Strongly Disagree	24	12
Disagree	40	20
Agree	90	45
Strongly Agree	46	23
Totals......	200	100

FIGURE 9.9   RESULTS FROM A CLIENT SATISFACTION SURVEY
FOR OCTOBER 1997 (FROM FIGURE 9.8)

administrators should not only be concerned with pinpointing potential trouble spots, but should also be committed to supporting workers' efforts to improve program effectiveness.

DATA MANAGEMENT

Effective monitoring systems are powered by information gleaned from data. As programs become more complex, and as monitoring becomes an increasingly important function, organizations require increasingly sophisticated data management capabilities. Data management includes collection and recording; aggregation, integration and analysis; and reporting. These functions may be carried out manually, through the use of computers, or through a combination of manual and computer-based methods.

MANUAL DATA MANAGEMENT

Not long ago, most data management functions were undertaken manually. Data collection forms were designed, completed in longhand or by typewriter, and filed, usually in case files. The need to produce specific data—for example looking at the referral sources of all new cases in the last six months—usually entailed a manual search of all new case files, as well as manual aggregation and analysis of the data. While such a system could unearth the required data, the process was cumbersome and labor-intensive.

As organizations found that they were called upon to generate certain types of information on a regular basis, they developed methods for manually copying specific data (e.g., referral sources, age and sex of client, presenting problem) from client records onto composite forms or spreadsheets. In this way, manually searching files for the required data could be avoided. However, the composite forms or spreadsheets were still analyzed manually. While an improvement, such a system was limited not only because manual analysis was time consuming but also because it could provide only the data that had been identified for aggregation. A need for data other than that which had been presented still entailed a manual search of all relevant files.

Obviously, manual methods are labor-intensive and potentially disruptive to normal day-to-day operations. They are also limited in their flexibility and in their capacity to quickly deliver needed data. It is not surprising that, with the ready availability of powerful desktop computers, social service organizations have increasingly turned to computer-based data management systems.

COMPUTER-ASSISTED DATA MANAGEMENT

Computers can be used in both case- and program-level monitoring. Because they increase the capacity for data management and make the process more efficient, their use in recent years has become widespread.

Strictly speaking, few social service organizations rely entirely on computers for data management. Usually, their data management systems are a combination of manual and computer-based methods. Manual functions, however, are decreasing and, correspondingly, computer-based functions are increasing. The trend is clear: Computers are becoming increasingly important in evaluation. Typically, data are collected manually through the completion of standardized forms and standardized measuring instruments. At this point, the data are entered into the computer, which maintains and manages the data and carries out the required aggregation and analysis.

Most obviously, the computer can assist with the aggregation and analysis of case-level monitoring data. Figure 9.7 illustrated this process, using the example of a family service agency where workers routinely use standardized measuring instruments to track changes in clients' practice objectives. As may be seen, the computer has selected all clients who had practice objectives related to self-esteem and whose cases were closed in October 1997 and has calculated the average initial and final self-esteem scores for those clients. There were twelve clients in the group, and the average score for the group dropped from 61 at the beginning of service to 42 at termination, a considerable decline in problems with self-esteem. In this instance, the data management capabilities of the computer readily allowed a one-group pretest-posttest evaluation design to be carried out.

Further analyses can be conducted on these results to determine if the decline is statistically significant. A variety of computer programs can rapidly carry out such analyses. This represents a major advantage over manual data analyses, as most statistical computations tend to be complex, cumbersome, and time-consuming. With today's statistical software packages, the required computations can be easily and accurately accomplished and, indeed, more sophisticated procedures, prohibitively time-consuming when done by hand, also become possible.

There is a potential danger in the ready availability of such analytical power; people who have little knowledge or understanding of statistics can easily carry out inappropriate procedures that may serve to mislead rather than inform. Nevertheless, when used knowledgeably, such statistical power makes more incisive analyses possible.

Another group of software programs, known as *relational databases,* are also increasingly used in data management. As the name suggests, these programs enable the linking of disparate data in a way that makes it possible to look at and understand data in different ways. Through linking the information contained on contact forms with information on intake and termination forms, for example, it may be possible to analyze the relationship between initial presenting problems, the course of service provision, and outcomes. A virtually unlimited flexibility in analyzing data is provided by such programs, making them an ideal tool for responding to specific questions as they arise.

REPORTING

Regular reports provide continuous feedback, which is the essence of monitoring. Essentially, reports provide the same data, updated for new cases, on a regular basis. Examples of such reports were provided in Figures 9.7 and 9.9.

As with other data management, computers are particularly useful in generating such reports. Software packages used to conduct statistical analyses or to maintain relational data bases usually have provisions for repeating the same reports, using different data sets. Basically, once a data analysis is specified, it can be run over and over again using updated data. Moreover, formats for reports, whether tables, graphs, or charts, as well as headings and labels, can also be specified in advance. Using computers, there is little limit to the number of reports that can be generated, making it possible to provide timely information, tailored to the needs of staff members at all organizational levels. This, in turn, makes possible an on-going, organization-wide quality improvement process.

A LOOK TO THE FUTURE

It is probably safe to predict that over the next few years computers will play an increasingly important role in data management. With the ready availability of more powerful computer hardware (and software programs), it is likely that most organizations will attempt to automate many of their data management processes.

One prominent area for automation is in the data entry process. Laptop computers make direct data entry possible and feasible. Workers and clients will increasingly use electronic versions of forms, instruments, and questionnaires, entering data directly into laptop computers. These data will then be electronically transferred into the organization's data management system, eliminating the need for completing paper copies and manually entering data into the system. This development will not only make data management more accurate and efficient but will also make possible the creation of larger, more powerful systems.

Such developments are probably inevitable. Though potentially Orwellian, large comprehensive data management systems can also support quality improvement efforts. Ultimately, the technology represented by computerization is, in itself, neither good nor bad. Like most systems, it can be used well but it can also be misused. Clearly, social workers will need to keep a close eye on such developments and strive to ensure that they are congruent with the highest professional values and ethics.

SUMMARY

The development of a monitoring capacity in an existing social service program requires the full cooperation of both line-level workers and its administrators. Front-line workers have an important role to play in the design and development of the system. Administrators must be prepared to provide training, support, and resources in addition to demonstrating that the monitoring system is intended to improve the program, not to assign blame.

At the case level, data can be useful in making a variety of decisions. Whenever possible, these data should also be collected in a manner that allows aggregation for the purposes of a program evaluation(s). Staff agreement on the measurement instruments to be used for specific problem types will facilitate the aggregation process. Staff must decide, at both the case and program levels, what data are needed, when they will be collected, in what format, and by whom. The development of appropriate forms will guide data collection and ensure that the data are recorded in a consistent, standard format.

Both computerized and manual data management techniques will probably be used, although computers are increasingly becoming the method of choice. Computers can be used at the case level for administering measuring instruments, scoring, and graphing results; and at the program level for comprehensive data management, including aggregation and analysis.

CHAPTER 10

DECISION MAKING WITH OBJECTIVE AND SUBJECTIVE DATA

IDEALLY, ALL PROFESSIONAL DECISIONS should be arrived at via a rational process based on the collection, synthesis, and analysis of relevant, objective, and subjective data. Objective data are obtained by an explicit measurement process that, when carefully followed, reduces bias and increases the data's objectivity. Subjective data, on the other hand, are obtained from impressions and judgments which, by their very nature, incorporate the values, preferences, and experiences of the individuals who make them.

It is our position that objective data, when combined with subjective data, offer the best basis for decision making. The best practice- and program-relevant decisions are made when we understand the advantages and limitations of both objective and subjective data and are able to combine the two as appropriate to the circumstances.

OBJECTIVE DATA

The main advantage of using objective data when making decisions is in the data's precision and objectivity. At the program level, for example, an agency may receive funding to provide an employment skills training program for minority groups. If appropriate data are kept, it is easy to ascertain to what degree the eligibility requirement is being met, and it may be possible to state, for example, that 85 percent of service recipients are in fact from minority groups. Without objective data, the subjective impressions of community members, staff members, funders, and program participants would be the sources of the data. Individuals may use descriptors such as "most," "many," or "a large number" to describe the proportion of minority people served by the employment skills training program. Obviously, such subjective judgments are far less precise than objective data, and they are, also, subject to biases.

Objective data, however, are not without their own limitations. Among these are:

1. Some variables are difficult to measure objectively.
2. Data may be uncertain or ambiguous, allowing conflicting interpretations.
3. Objective data may not take all pertinent contextual factors into account.

Although considerable progress has been made in recent years in the development of standardized measuring instruments, not all variables of conceivable interest to social workers are convenient and feasible to measure. Thus, objective data may not be available to guide certain practice and program decisions. In the same vein, even if a variable can be measured, data collection plans may not call for its measurement—or, the measurement may have been omitted for any of a variety of reasons that arise in day-to-day professional activity. Consequently, objective data are not always available to guide practice and program decision making.

Where objective data are available, their meaning and implications may not always be clear. At the case level, a series of standardized measures intended to assess a 10-year-old's self-esteem may yield no discernable pattern. It would thus be difficult, on the basis of such objective data alone, to make decisions about further interventions and services. At the program level, objective data may indicate that, over a three-month period, people participating in a weight-loss program lose an average of five pounds a person. Although the results seem favorable, the average weight loss is not very great, making it unclear whether the program should be continued as is, or whether modifications should be considered.

Finally, objective data seldom provide contextual information—although the context relating to them is important in their interpretation. In the example of the weight-loss program, the average five-pound loss would probably be considered inadequate if the clientele were known to be a group of people who, for medical reasons, needed to lose an average of sixty pounds each. On the other hand, if the clientele were known to be a group of skiers preparing for the ski season, the program could be considered quite successful.

SUBJECTIVE DATA

Although it might seem desirable to base all decisions on logically analyzed objective data, such information on all factors affecting a given practice or program decision is seldom available. Consequently, objective data are often supplemented by more subjective types of data, such as the workers' impressions, judgments, experiences, and intuition.

As human beings, we assimilate subjective data continuously as we move through our daily life; competent social work professionals do the same, noting the client's stance, gait, gestures, voice, eye movements, and set of mouth, for example. At the program level, an administrator may have a sense of awareness of staff morale, history and stage of development of the organization, external expectations, and the ability of the organization to absorb change. Seldom are any of these subjective data actually measured, but all of them are assimilated. Some subjective data are consciously noted; some filter through subconsciously and emerge later as an impression, opinion, or intuition. Clearly, such subjective data may considerably influence case and program decision making.

At the case level, for example, perceptions, judgments, and intuition—often called clinical impressions—may become factors in decision making. A worker may conclude, based on body language, eye contact, and voice, that a client's self-esteem is improving. Further case-level decisions may then be based on these subjective impressions. At the program level, objective data may suggest the need to modify the program, in the face of inadequate results. The administrator, however, may put off making any modifications, on the basis of a subjective judgment that, because several other program changes had recently been implemented, the team's ability to absorb any more changes is limited.

To the extent that subjective data are accurate, such a decision is entirely appropriate. The main limitation of subjective data, however, is that impressions and intuition often spring to the mind preformed, and the process by which they were formed cannot be objectively examined. By their nature, subjective data are susceptible to distortion through the personal experience, bias, and preferences of the individual. These may work deceptively, leaving the worker unaware that the subjective data upon which they are relying actually distort the picture.

In reality, case- and program-level decision making uses a blend of objective and subjective data. Together, the two forms of data have the potential to provide the most complete information upon which to base decisions. Ultimately, the practitioner will have to use judgment in reconciling all relevant sources of data in order to arrive at an understanding of the situation. In building an accurate picture, it is important not only to consider all sources of data but also to be aware of the strengths and limitations of each of these sources. Quality case and program decisions are usually the result of explicitly sifting through the various sources of data and choosing those sources in which it is reasonable to have the most confidence under the circumstances.

Having considered decision making in general, we now turn to an examination of the process at the case and program levels, specifically.

CASE-LEVEL DECISION MAKING

If high-quality case level decisions are to be reached, the social worker should know what types of decisions are best supported by objective data and what types will likely require the use of subjective data.

A helping relationship with a client is a process that passes through a number of stages and follows logically one from the other. There are essentially four stages: (1) the engagement and problem-definition phase, (2) the practice objective–setting phase, (3) the intervention phase, (4) the termination and follow-up phase. In practice, these phases are not likely to follow a clear sequence. Engagement, for example, occurs most prominently at the beginning of the professional relationship, but it continues in some form throughout the entire helping process. Problem definition is logically the first consideration after engagement, but if it becomes evident during intervention that the client's problem is not clearly understood, the problem-definition and objective-setting phases will have to be readdressed. Nevertheless, discernible phases do exist. The following describes how case-level decisions can be made in each phase.

THE ENGAGEMENT AND PROBLEM-DEFINITION PHASE

Suppose a married couple, Mr. and Ms. Wright, come to a family service agency to work on their marriage problems and have been assigned to a worker named Maria. From Ms. Wright's initial statement, the problem is that her partner does not pay enough attention to her. In Maria's judgment, Ms. Wright's perception is a symptom of yet another problem that has not been defined. The client's perception, however, is a good starting point, and Maria attempts to objectify Ms. Wright's statement. In what ways, precisely, does her partner not pay enough attention to her? Ms. Wright obligingly provides data: Her partner has not gone anywhere with her for the past three months, but he regularly spends three nights a week playing basketball, two nights with friends, and one night at his mother's.

Mr. Wright, protestingly brought into the session, declares that he spends most nights at home and the real problem is that his partner constantly argues. Further inquiry leads Maria to believe that Mr. Wright spends more nights away from home than he reports but fewer than his partner says; Ms. Wright, feeling herself ignored, most likely is argumentative; and the underlying problems are actually poor communication and unrealistic expectations on the part of both. A host of other problems surfaced subtly during the interview and cannot be addressed until the communications problem is solved; communication, therefore, should be the initial target of the intervention—the first practice objective.

A second practice objective could be to reduce the Wrights' unrealistic expectations of each other. Let us consider that the Wrights have these two practice objectives that are specifically geared toward the program objective, "to increase their marital satisfaction." Maria believes that the attainment of the two practice objectives will increase the Wrights' marital satisfaction—the main purpose for which they are seeking services. Remember, the Wrights want a happier marriage (that is why they sought out services); they did not seek out help with their dysfunctional communication patterns and unrealistic expectations of one another. Thus, to increase their marital satisfaction becomes the program objective, and communications and expectations become the two practice objectives.

So far, Maria's conclusions have been based on her own impressions of the conflicting data presented by the Wrights. Unless the problem is straightforward and concrete, the engagement and problem definition phase often depends more on the worker's subjective judgment, experience, and intuition than it does on objective data. Even when standardized measuring instruments are used to help clients identify and prioritize their problems, the choice of the problem to be first addressed will largely be guided by the worker's subjective intuition and judgment. Once intuition has indicated what the problem might be, however, the magnitude of the problem can often be measured with more objectivity through the use of standardized measuring instruments.

In the Wrights' case, Maria has tentatively decided to formulate a practice objective of increasing the Wrights' communication skills. In order to confirm that communication skills are problematic, she asks Mr. and Ms. Wright to independently complete a 25-item standardized measuring instrument designed to measure marital communications skills. The instrument contains such items as, "How often do you and your spouse talk over pleasant things that happen during the day?" with possible responses of "very frequently," "frequently," "occasionally," "seldom," and "never." This instrument has a range of 0 to 100, with higher scores showing better communication skills. It has a clinical cutting score of 60, indicating effective communications above that level, and it has been tested on people of the same socioeconomic group as the Wrights and may be assumed to yield valid and reliable data.

The introduction of the measuring instrument at this stage serves two basic purposes. First, the scores will show whether communication is indeed a problem, and to what degree it is a problem for each partner. Second, the scores will provide a baseline measurement that can be used as the first point on a graph in whatever case-level design Maria selects (see Chapter 7).

THE PRACTICE OBJECTIVE–SETTING PHASE

In the Wrights' case, the program objective is to increase their marital satisfaction. Thus, a related practice objective (one of many possible) is to increase the couple's communication skills to a minimum score of 60, the clinical cutting score on the standardized measuring instrument. The practice objective–setting phase in this example thus relies heavily on objective data: It is framed in terms of a change from very ineffective communication (score of 0) to very effective communication (score of 100).

The same process applies in cases where the standardized measuring instrument selected is less formal and precise. Maria, for example, may ask each partner to complete a self-anchored rating scale indicating his and her level of satisfaction with the degree of communication achieved. The scoring range on this instrument could be from 1–6, with higher scores indicating greater levels of satisfaction and lower scores indicating lesser levels of satisfaction. If Mr. Wright begins by rating his satisfaction level at 3 and Ms. Wright indicates hers at 2, the practice objective chosen may be to achieve a minimum rating of 4 for each partner. Here again, practice objective–setting is based on objective data collected at the beginning of Maria's intervention.

THE INTERVENTION PHASE

The selection of the intervention strategy itself will be based on objective and subjective data only to a limited degree. Perhaps Maria has seen previous clients with similar practice objectives and also has objective evidence, via the professional literature, that a specific treatment intervention is appropriate to use in this specific situation. But even though the intervention is chosen on the basis of data accumulated from previous research studies and past experience, each intervention is tailored to meet the needs of the particular client system, and decisions about strategy, timing, and its implementation are largely based on subjective data—the worker's experience, clinical judgment, and intuition.

Although objective data may play only one part in the selection of an intervention strategy, once the strategy is selected, its success is best measured on the basis of consistently collected objective data. Ideally, objective data are collected using a number of different standardized measures. In the Wrights' case, for example, the scores from repeated administrations of the standardized instrument that measures the degree of communication will comprise one set of objective data for one particular practice objective.

Frequency counts of specifically selected behaviors may comprise another set: for example, a count of the number of conversations daily lasting at least five minutes, or the number of "I" statements made daily by each partner. The self-anchored rating scale, described in the previous section, could be a third source of data. These sets of data together provide considerable information about whether, and to what degree, progress is being made.

Maria is also likely to come to a more global opinion about how the couple is doing in regard to their communication patterns. This opinion will be based on a variety of observations and impressions formed as she works with the couple. The process by which such an opinion is formed is intuitive and, depending on the worker's skill, experiences, and the circumstances, may be quite accurate. The method by which it is arrived at, however, is idiosyncratic and is, therefore, of unknown validity and reliability. For this reason, relying on clinical impressions exclusively is inadvisable.

On the other hand, as we saw in Chapter 6, objective measures may have their own problems of validity and reliability. The best course is a middle one: Determination of a client's progress should be based on a combination of objective data *and* subjective data. Where objective and subjective data point in the same direction, Maria can proceed with considerable confidence that she has a clear and accurate picture of her client's progress. Where objective and

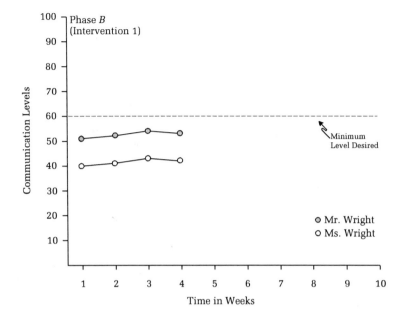

FIGURE 10.1   *B* DESIGN: THE WRIGHTS' COMMUNICATION
LEVELS OVER TIME, INDICATING NO CHANGE

subjective data diverge, Maria should first attempt to determine the reasons for the difference and ensure that she has a good understanding of her client's problems and needs.

When Maria is satisfied that she has an accurate grasp of her client system's progress, she is ready to proceed to decisions about the most appropriate treatment intervention to use. These decisions are guided by changes in the practice objective. Three patterns of change are possible: (1) deterioration, or no change; (2) insufficient, or slow change; and (3) satisfactory change.

DETERIORATION, OR NO CHANGE

Suppose that Ms. Wright scored a 40 on the first administration of the standardized measuring instrument that measures the degree, or level, of communication patterns, scores a 41 on the second, a 43 on the third, and a 42 on the fourth (see Figure 10.1). In addition,

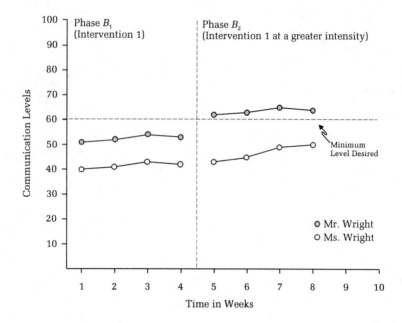

FIGURE 10.2 $B_1 B_2$ CHANGING INTENSITY DESIGN: THE
WRIGHTS' COMMUNICATION LEVELS OVER
TIME, INDICATING INSUFFICIENT CHANGE AT
B_1 FOLLOWED BY A MORE INTENSIVE B_2

Mr. Wright scores 50, 51, 53, and 52 respectively. How would Maria
analyze and interpret such data?

First, Maria will want to consider what the other available
sources of data indicate. Let us assume that, on the self-anchored
communication satisfaction scale, Ms. Wright still rates her satisfaction at 2 and that, during the sessions, she avoids eye contact with
Mr. Wright and tries to monopolize the worker's attention with
references to "he" and "him." In this situation, the data all seem to
point to the same conclusion: There has been virtually no change or
progress. Under such circumstances, it is reasonable to place considerable reliance on the data contained in Figure 10.1

As Figure 10.1 also indicates, the slope of the line connecting the
measurement points is virtually flat—that is, it is stable, indicating
neither improvement nor deterioration. Moreover, the level of the
problem is well below the desired minimum score of 60. Such data

would normally lead Maria to conclude that a change in the intervention is warranted—resulting in *BC* design.

Here qualitative considerations may also enter the case-level decision-making process. Maria, for example, may be aware of disruptions in the lives of Mr. and Ms. Wright. Perhaps Mr. Wright received a lay-off notice during the second week of the intervention. Maria may now need to consider whether the effects of the intervention might not have been counteracted by these adverse circumstances. Ultimately, she will need to decide whether to continue the intervention in the hope that, once the couple has dealt with the shock of the impending lay-off, the intervention will begin to have the desired effect.

It is also possible that the intervention is known to have a delayed impact. This characteristic could have been determined from the professional literature or from Maria's previous experience with using the intervention. Under such circumstances it may, again, be reasonable to maintain the intervention for some time longer and see whether movement toward the practice objective begins.

How long it is sensible to continue an intervention in the absence of documented progress is a matter best left to Maria's and the couple's judgment. As long as there is reason to believe that an intervention may yet have the desired impacts, it is justified to pursue that intervention. If there is no evidence of change for the better, however, the intervention will need to be changed. Note that data will provide objective evidence supporting the need for a change in the intervention, but they will not indicate what future intervention strategies might be used instead. Formulation of a new intervention strategy will again call upon Maria's and her clients' judgment.

INSUFFICIENT, OR SLOW CHANGE

Insufficient or slow change is a familiar scenario in the social services. A gradual but definite improvement in the communication scores may be noted, indicating that Mr. and Ms. Wright are slowly learning to communicate. Their relationship continues to deteriorate, however, because their communication scores are still below 60—the minimum level of good communication; progress needs to be more rapid if the marriage is to be saved.

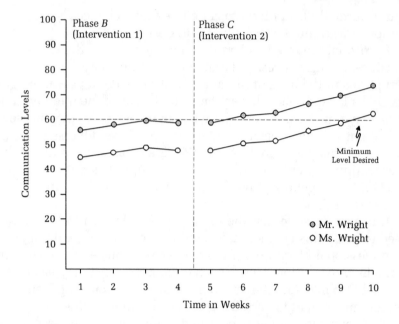

FIGURE 10.3   *BC* DESIGN: THE WRIGHTS'
COMMUNICATION LEVELS OVER TIME,
INDICATING INSUFFICIENT CHANGE AT THE *B*
INTERVENTION FOLLOWEDBY A *C*
INTERVENTION

In general, many clients improve only slowly, or improve in
spurts with regressions in between. The data will reflect what is
occurring—what the problem level is, and at what rate and in what
direction it is changing. No data, however, can tell a worker whether
the measured rate of change is acceptable in the particular client's
circumstances. This is an area in which subjective clinical judgment
again comes into play.

The worker may decide that the rate of change is insufficient, but
just marginally so; that is, the intervention is successful on the whole
and ought to be continued, but at a greater frequency or intensity.
Perhaps the number of treatment sessions can be increased, or more
time can be scheduled for each session, or more intensive work can
be planned. In other words, a *B* design will now become a B_1B_2
design (as illustrated in Figure 10.2) or, if baseline data have been

collected, an *AB* design will become an AB_1B_2 design. If, on the other hand, the worker thinks that intensifying the intervention is unlikely to yield significantly improved results, a different intervention entirely may be adopted. In this case, the *B* design will become a *BC* design (illustrated in Figure 10.3), or the *AB* design will become an *ABC* design.

Sometimes improvement occurs at an acceptable rate for a period and then the client reaches a plateau, below the desired minimal level; no further change seems to be occurring. The data will show the initial improvement and the plateau (see Figure 10.4), but they will not show whether the plateau is temporary, akin to a resting period, or whether the level already achieved is as far as the improvement will go. Again, this is a matter for clinical judgment. The worker and client system may decide to continue with the intervention for a time to see if improvement begins again. The exact length of time during which perseverance is justified is a judgment call. If the client system remains stuck at the level reached beyond that time, the worker and client system will have to decide whether to apply the intervention more intensively, try a new intervention, or be content with what has been achieved.

SATISFACTORY CHANGE

Frequently objective data will show an improvement. At times the improvement will be steady and sustained, and at other times an overall trend of improvement will be punctuated with periods of plateau or even regression. This latter scenario is illustrated in Figure 10.5. Essentially, continuation of the treatment intervention is justified by continuing client progress, although Maria may wish at times to make minor modifications in the intervention.

It is important to keep in mind that not all case-level designs permit the worker to conclude that the intervention has caused the change for the better (see Chapter 7). In the case of many designs that are likely to be used in the monitoring of human service interventions, it is possible to conclude only that the client's practice objective has changed for the better. This is the situation in the *B* design shown in Figure 10.4 where Mr. Wright has obtained communication scores over 60 but Ms. Wright has yet to reach the minimum acceptable level of 60. From a service perspective, however, evidence that

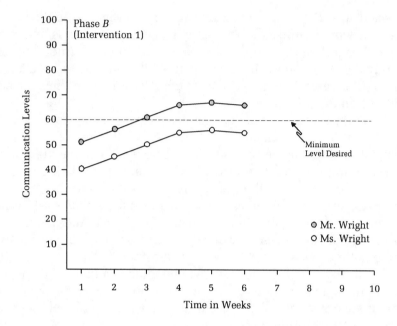

FIGURE 10.4   *B* DESIGN: THE WRIGHTS'
                       COMMUNICATION LEVELS OVER TIME,
                       INDICATING AN INITIAL IMPROVEMENT
                       LEVELING OFF TO A PLATEAU

Mr. and Ms. Wright are improving is sufficient justification for continuing the intervention; it is not necessary to prove that the intervention is causing the change.

When the data show that a client has reached the program or practice objective, the worker will, if possible, initiate a maintenance phase, perhaps gradually reducing the frequency of contact with a view to service termination, but also trying to ensure that the gains achieved are not lost. If other practice objectives need to be resolved, the maintenance phase for one objective may coincide with the baseline or interventive phase for another. It is quite possible to engage in a number of case-level designs at the same time with the same client; because client practice objectives are usually interrelated, data obtained in one area will often be relevant to another.

The maintenance phase is important, ensuring that the practice objective really has been satisfactorily resolved. Assume that data

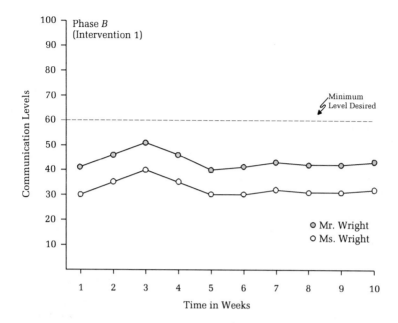

FIGURE 10.5   *B* DESIGN: THE WRIGHTS'S
COMMUNICATION LEVELS OVER TIME,
INDICATING SOME IMPROVEMENT WITH
PERIODS OF PLATEAUS AND REGRESSIONS

show a steady improvement, culminating at a point above the target range (as in Figure 10.3). One measurement below the minimum desired level means only that the practice objective was not at a clinically significant level when that measurement was made. Subsequent measurements may show that a significant problem still exists. A number of measurements are required before Maria can be confident that the practice objective has stabilized at the desired level. Similarly, where the trend to improvement included plateaus and regressions, measurements must continue beyond the achievement of the practice objective to ensure that the objective has indeed stabilized in the desired level and direction.

THE TERMINATION AND FOLLOW-UP PHASE

Once it is decided that the program objective (not the practice objective) has been accomplished, the next step is termination and follow-up. The termination decision is straightforward in theory: When the data show that the program objective has been achieved, via the attainment of practice objectives, and the objective level is stable, services can be terminated. In reality, however, other factors need to be taken into account, such as the number and type of support systems available in the client's social environment and the nature and magnitude of possible stressor events in the client's life. We must carefully weigh all these factors, including information yielded by objective and subjective data, in making a decision to end services.

Ideally, the follow-up phase will be a routine part of the program's operations. Many social work programs, however, do not engage in any kind of follow-up activities, and others conduct follow-ups in a sporadic or informal way. If the program does conduct routine follow-up, decisions will already have been made concerning how often and in what manner the client should be contacted after the termination of services. If no standardized follow-up procedures are in place, we will have to decide whether follow-up is necessary and, if so, what form it should take.

Data can help decide whether a follow-up is necessary. If data reveal that a client has not reached a program objective, or has reached it only marginally, a follow-up is essential. If data show a pattern of improvement followed by regression, a follow-up is also indicated, to ensure that regression will not occur again.

The follow-up procedures that measure program objectives may be conducted in a number of ways. Frequently used approaches include contacting former clients by letter or telephone at increasingly longer intervals after the cessation of services. A less frequently used approach is to continue to measure the program objectives that were taken during the intervention period. As services to the Wrights are terminated, Maria could arrange to have them each complete, at monthly intervals, the Marital Satisfaction Scale (the measure of the program objective). Maria could mail the scale to the Wrights, who, because they have already completed it during the course of the intervention, should have no problem doing so during follow-up.

The inclusion of a stamped, self-addressed envelope can further encourage them to complete this task. In this manner, Maria can determine objectively whether marital satisfaction gains made during treatment are maintained over time.

At a minimum, collecting program-level data (not case-level data) during follow-up results in a *BF* design, as illustrated in Figures 10.6 and 10.7. If an initial baseline phase had been utilized, the result would be an *ABF* design. Where follow-up data indicate that client gains are being maintained, a situation illustrated in Figure 10.6, termination procedures can be completed. Where follow-up data reveal a deterioration after termination, as illustrated in Figure 10.7, Maria is at least in a position to know that her clients are not doing well. Under such circumstances, complete termination is not warranted. Instead, Maria should consider whether to resume active intervention, provide additional support in the clients' social environment, or offer some other service. The follow-up data will not help Maria to decide what she should do next, but they will alert her to the need to do something.

It should be noted that Figures 10.6 and 10.7 provide data for marital satisfaction scores (the lower the score the better the marital satisfaction) and do not represent the couple's communication scores as in Figures 10.1–10.5 (the higher the score the better the communication). This is because follow-up data are concerned with program objectives (in this case, marital satisfaction), not practice objectives (in this case, communication and expectations of one another).

PROGRAM-LEVEL DECISION MAKING

The primary purpose of the monitoring approach at the program level is to obtain feedback on the program in an ongoing manner so that the services provided can be continually developed and improved.

In the first instance, the program may be assessed with regard to the achievement of process objectives. Process objectives are analogous to facilitative practice objectives; their achievement makes it more likely that program objectives will also be achieved. In a sense, they speak to the effectiveness and efficiency of the service operation. Process objectives, for example, might address the type of

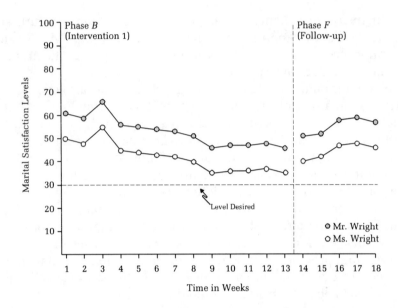

FIGURE 10.6   *BF* DESIGN: THE WRIGHTS' MARITAL
                        SATISFACTION LEVELS DURING TREATMENT
                        (*B*) AND AFTER TERMINATION (*F*),
                        INDICATING MAINTAINED IMPROVEMENT
                        AFTER TERMINATION

clientele to be served, indicating that a minimum of 75 percent should come from minority backgrounds. Or, these objectives could speak to the length of waiting lists, specifying that no one should have to wait longer than two weeks prior to the commencement of services. Other process objectives could deal with the number of continuing education hours provided to staff members, premature termination of cases, service hours provided, and similar other matters.

The actual program objectives may be assessed in various ways. Success rates may vary with problem type. A particular social service program, for example, may achieve good success with children who have family-related problems but less success with children whose problems are primarily drug-related. Or perhaps desirable results are achieved with one type of client but not another: A drug rehabilitation program may be more successful with adults than it is with adolescents. Or, again, a particular program within an agency

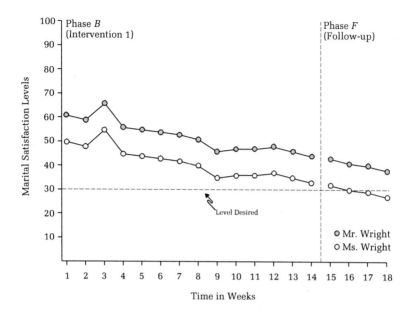

FIGURE 10.7   *BF* DESIGN: THE WRIGHTS' MARITAL
SATISFACTION LEVELS DURING
TREATMENT (*B*) AND AFTER TERMINATION
(*F*), INDICATING A DETERIORATION AFTER
TERMINATION

may achieve its program objectives better than another program within the same agency. A child welfare agency, for example, may successfully operate an adolescent treatment foster-care program but have less success with its adolescent group-care program. If several residential programs are operated, one may achieve its program objectives to a higher degree than another.

Finally, the agency must be considered as a whole. How successful is it when all of its programs are assessed together? What might be done on a general organizational level to improve the agency's effectiveness and efficiency?

A picture of results can be readily achieved through the collection and analysis of objective and subjective data. The kinds of data collected and analyses performed will depend on the program being considered. This section begins with a few words about process evaluation and then deals in detail with outcome evaluation.

PROCESS

Usually, data can be readily gathered on matters of interest in a process evaluation. Collecting data, for example, on the demographic characteristics of clients, the length of time spent on waiting lists, the types of services provided, and the total number of hours of each is a relatively straightforward matter. In the monitoring approach, these and similar data are collected continuously and analyzed on a regular basis. Reports available to staff members make clear to what degree process objectives are being met. Process objectives usually pertain to good and desirable practices that are thought to lead to desired results. A more in-depth discussion of process evaluations is found in Chapter 5.

OUTCOME

Outcomes can be classified into three nonmutually exclusive areas: (1) problems and cases, (2) program, and (3) agency.

PROBLEMS AND CASES

Many human service agencies offer services to people with a variety of needs: pregnant teens, disabled seniors, preadolescents with self-esteem problems, couples seeking help with their marriages, and people who are trying to stop smoking. The agency will be interested in knowing, and is usually required by funders to document, to what degree its programs are helping people with particular types of social problems.

The results achieved by any one client, satisfactory or not, do not say much about the general effectiveness of the program as a whole. Program effectiveness is determined only by examining data from groups of clients, often using simple aggregation methods that are described shortly.

Assume, for example, that during a six-month period of a smoking cessation program, the program served 80 clients, 40 male and 40 female. Using the case-level monitoring techniques previously described, data will be available showing the number of cigarettes

TABLE 10.1   AVERAGE
NUMBER OF CIGARETTES SMOKED AT
THE BEGINNING AND END OF THE
SMOKING CESSATION PROGRAM
($N = 80$)

Beginning	–	After	=	Difference
34		11		23

smoked by each client at the beginning and at the end of the intervention. Aggregating the individual client results indicates that the average number of cigarettes smoked daily at the beginning of the intervention was 34, and the average number smoked at the end of the program was 11. Thus, the clients smoked, on the average, 23 fewer cigarettes after they completed the stop-smoking program. These aggregated data, after analysis, provide a method of assessing the outcome of the program. The aggregated data and the results of the analysis for all 80 clients are presented in Table 10.1.

The analysis presented in Table 10.1 is a simple one—the calculation of the difference between beginning and ending average number of cigarettes smoked. The analysis could be extended to determine whether this difference might have come about by chance alone. This is what is meant by the term "statistical significance." Detailed treatment of statistical procedures is beyond the scope of this text but is readily available in any introductory statistics book (e.g., Weinbach & Grinnell, 1998)

To return to our example, the decline in smoking can be documented as a net change of 23 cigarettes, on the average, per client. Although the data available in this situation permit documentation of the program's objective, or outcome, it is not possible to attribute this change to the intervention. The particular evaluation design used was the descriptive one-group pretest-posttest design, and, as we saw in Chapter 8, such descriptive designs do not support inferences about causality. Nevertheless, this type of design enables staff members to document the overall results of their services.

Further analyses of these data may provide additional and more specific information. Suppose, for example, that program staff had the impression that they were achieving better results with female

TABLE 10.2   AVERAGE NUMBER OF
CIGARETTES SMOKED AT THE BEGINNING AND END
OF THE SMOKING CESSATION PROGRAM BY SEX
$(N = 80)$

Sex	Beginning	–	After	=	Difference	n
Males	34		18		16	40
Females	34		4		30	40
Totals	34		11		23	80

smokers than with male smokers. Examining the results of males and females as separate groups would permit a comparison of the average number of cigarettes each group smoked at the end of the program. The data for this analysis are presented in Table 10.2. Note that the average number of cigarettes smoked at the beginning of the program was exactly the same for the males and females, 34. Thus, it could be concluded that there were no meaningful differences between the males and females in reference to the average number of cigarettes they smoked at the start of the intervention.

As Table 10.2 shows, at the end of the program males smoked an average of 18 cigarettes daily and females an average of 4 cigarettes. On the average, then, females smoked 14 fewer cigarettes per day than did males. Essentially, this analysis confirms workers' suspicion that they were obtaining better results with female smokers than with male smokers.

The information obtained via the simple analysis presented above provides documentation of outcomes, a vitally important element in this age of accountability and increased competition for available funding. There is, however, a further advantage to compiling and analyzing evaluation data. By conducting regular analyses, social work administrators and workers can obtain important feedback about program strengths and weaknesses. These data can be used to further develop services. The data discussed above, for example, may cause the services to be modified in ways that would improve effectiveness with male clients while maintaining effectiveness with female clients. This would not only improve services to the male client group but would also boost overall program outcomes.

PROGRAM

As we know from Chapter 1, a program is a distinct unit, large or small, that operates within an organization. An agency, for example, may comprise a number of treatment programs, or a child welfare agency may operate a treatment foster-care program and a residential child abuse treatment program as part of its operations. The residential program itself may comprise a number of separate homes for children of different ages or different problem types.

These programs should be evaluated if the agency as a whole is to demonstrate accountability and provide the best possible service to its clientele. A thorough evaluation will include attention to needs, process, and outcomes as well as efficiency. Since the greatest interest is often in outcome, however, this section focuses on outcome evaluation (Chapter 4), where the question is, "To what degree has a program succeeded in reaching its program objectives?"

If this question is to be answered satisfactorily, of course, the program's objectives must be defined in a way that allows them to be measured (Chapter 3). Let us assume that one of the objectives of the residential child abuse treatment program is to enable its residents to return to their homes. The degree of achievement of this program objective can be determined through a simple count: What percentage of the residents returned home within the last year?

If the agency includes several programs of the same type, in different locations, lessons learned from one can be applied to another. In addition, similar programs will likely have the same program objectives and the same ways of measuring them, so that results can be aggregated to provide a measure of effectiveness for the entire agency. If the programs are dissimilar—for example, a treatment foster-care program and a victim-assistance program—aggregation will not be possible, but separate assessment of program outcomes will nevertheless contribute to the evaluation of the agency as a whole.

AGENCY

Outcome evaluation, whether in respect to an agency, a program, or a case, always focuses on the achievement of objectives. How well has the agency fulfilled its mandate? To what degree has it succeeded in meeting its goal, as revealed by the measurement of its program objectives? Again, success in goal achievement cannot be determined unless the agency's programs have well-defined, measurable program objectives that reflect the agency's mandate.

As seen in Chapter 3, agencies operate on the basis of mission statements, which often consist of vaguely phrased, expansive statements of intent. The mission of a sexual abuse treatment agency, for example, may be to ameliorate the pain caused by sexually abusive situations and to prevent sexual abuse in the future. Although there is no doubt that this is a laudable mission, the concepts of pain amelioration and abuse prevention cannot be measured until they have been more precisely defined.

This agency's mandate may be to serve persons who have been sexually abused and their families living within a certain geographical area. If the agency has an overall goal, "to reduce the trauma resulting from sexual abuse in the community," for example, the mandate is reflected and measurement is implied in the word "reduced." The concept of trauma still needs to be operationalized, but this can be accomplished through the specific, individual practice objectives of the clients whose trauma is to be reduced: The primary trauma for a male survivor may be fear that he is homosexual, whereas the trauma for a nonoffending mother may be guilt that she failed to protect her child.

If logical links are established between the agency's goal, the goals of the programs within the agency, and the individual practice objectives of clients served by the program, it will be possible to use the results of one to evaluate the other. Practice objective achievement at the case level will contribute to the success of the program, which will in turn contribute to the achievement of the agency's overall goal.

USING OUTCOME MONITORING DATA
IN PROGRAM-LEVEL DECISION MAKING

Just as a program outcome for any client may be acceptable, mixed, or inadequate, program-level evaluation results can also be acceptable, mixed, or inadequate, reflecting the degree to which its program objectives have been achieved.

ACCEPTABLE RESULTS

Before a result can be declared "acceptable," it is necessary to define clearly what counts as an acceptable result for a specific program objective. Let us return to the example of the residential program, where one of the program's objectives included enabling residents to return home: If 90 percent of residents succeed in making this move within six months of entry into the program, has the program's objective been achieved to an acceptable degree? What if 80 percent of residents return home within six months and a further 10 percent return home within a year? Or suppose that 100 percent return home within six months but half of the adolescents are eventually readmitted to the program?

Evidently, an acceptable result is largely a matter of definition. The program administrators and funders must decide what degree of objective achievement can reasonably be expected given the nature of the problems, the resources available, and the results of similar programs. Are the results for the smoking cessation program, for example, shown in Tables 10.1 and 10.2, indicative of success? If the program comprises a number of subprograms, the same considerations apply with regard to each.

Defining criteria for success should be done in advance of obtaining results, to avoid politicizing the results and to make it possible to set relevant program objectives.

Once the standards for an acceptable level of achievement have been set, evaluation becomes a matter of comparing actual outcomes against these standards. Where standards are met, program personnel can, with some degree of confidence, continue to employ existing procedures and practices. If a monitoring approach to evaluation is used and outcomes are analyzed on a regular basis, workers will be able to see not only whether program objectives are being achieved to an acceptable degree, but also whether the level of achievement is rising or falling. Any persistent trend toward improvement or decline is worth investigating so that more effective interventions and processes can be reinforced and potential problems can be detected and resolved.

MIXED RESULTS

Occasionally, the results of an outcome evaluation will show that the program is achieving its objectives only partially. A program may be successful in helping one group of clients, for example, but less successful with another. This was the situation in the smoking cessation program presented above: Female clients were being helped considerably, but male clients were obtaining much less impressive results (Table 10.2). Similarly, an evaluation may reveal seasonal variations in outcomes: At certain times of the year a program may achieve its program objectives to an acceptable degree, but not at other times. Clients in farming communities, for instance, may be able to participate in the program in the winter more easily than during the growing season, when they are busy with the tasks of farming. This factor alone may result in reduced achievement at both the case and program levels. It is also possible that one program within an agency is achieving its objectives to a greater degree than another similar program.

In such situations, staff members will undoubtedly wish to adjust practices and procedures so that the underperforming components can be upgraded. In making any adjustments, however, care must be taken not to jeopardize those parts of the operation that are obtaining good outcomes. In the case of the smoking cessation program, for example, the workers may be tempted to tailor several sessions more to the needs of male clients. Although this may indeed improve the program's performance with male clients, the improvement may come at the expense of effectiveness with females.

A preferable strategy might be to form separate groups for males and females during some parts of the program, leaving the program unchanged for female clients but developing new sessions for male clients to better meet their needs. Of course, it is impossible to predict in advance whether changes will yield the desired results, but ongoing monitoring will provide feedback about their efficacy.

INADEQUATE RESULTS

One of the strengths of a program-level monitoring system is that it takes into account the entire program process, from intake to follow-up. A low level of program objective achievement is not necessarily attributable to the interventions utilized by the workers with their clients. It is possible that the problem lies in inappropriate eligibility criteria, unsatisfactory assessment techniques, inadequate staff training, or a host of other factors, including unforeseen systematic barriers to clients' involvement in the program.

If an outcome evaluation shows that results are unsatisfactory, further program development is called for. To diagnose the problem or problems, the program administrator and workers will want to examine data concerning all the stages that lead up to intervention as well as the intervention process itself. Once they have ideas about the reasons for suboptimal performance, they are in a position to begin instituting changes to procedures and practices—and monitoring the results of those changes.

SUMMARY

One of the most important reasons for monitoring is to obtain timely data on which further decisions about intervention plans or program development can be based. At the case level, the worker will continually monitor changes in the client problem; at the program level, data relating to needs, processes, and outcomes can help staff make informed decisions about program modifications and changes.

C H A P T E R 11

POLITICS, STANDARDS, AND ETHICS

Evaluations within the social services are social activities and are influenced by the context within which they occur. The shape of all evaluations is molded by the beliefs, preferences, and biases of a program's various stakeholders. As we know from Chapter 1, these stakeholders include individuals who are directly involved in carrying out the evaluation (e.g., program workers, administrators), individuals interested in the evaluation's findings (e.g., funders, policy makers, the general public), and individuals who are evaluation participants (e.g., clients).

How evaluation plans are conceptualized and operationalized is also influenced by external factors such as societal trends, funding criteria, media events, political elections, fiscal reports, and the emergence of new social service programs. All of these influencing factors together make up the political context, or the *politics*, of program evaluation.

313

Throughout this book, we have provided a brief framework of how to plan, implement, and report simple evaluations. The strategies and approaches discussed provide a guideline of what a basic evaluation plan includes. When our modest straightforward ideas are tested in the actual human service world, however, the implementation of our ideas will not be a smooth process—owing to program politics, the topic to follow.

POLITICS OF EVALUATION

Program politics involve individuals and policies that govern human behavior, which, in turn, influence program decisions. Politics, by definition, include an element of self-interest, and it follows that political pressure usually exerts itself when uses of evaluation are considered. This section examines the politics of evaluation by discussing: (1) the nature of program politics, (2) appropriate uses of evaluation, (3) misuses of evaluation, and (4) political influences on evaluation decisions.

THE NATURE OF PROGRAM POLITICS

Program politics can be divided into internal and external politics. Politically charged situations can emerge within a program, in which case the individuals internal to the program are primarily involved. When the politics of a program extend beyond its boundaries, or when individuals outside the program impinge their views on the program's operations, external politics are at work.

INTERNAL PROGRAM POLITICS

Program administrators and staff are key players when it comes to internal politics. Program politics become apparent in situations that bring reason to reflect on the program's philosophy and how it delivers its services (i.e., goals, objectives, measures, and activities, see Figure 3.8). An evaluation must be prudent in dealing with internal politics since the views and opinions of administrators and staff can help or hinder any evaluative effort. When working in a program that has low staff morale, for example, we are faced with the challenge of getting staff to meaningfully anticipate—or, more specifically, to take ownership of—the evaluation process.

When staff morale is low, we have the double-edged task of motivating administrators to address staff issues, while designing, testing, and implementing the evaluation. When staff are feeling overworked, underpaid, and hopeless about the social problems affecting their clients, the monitoring approach to evaluation can be of some help. Assisting staff to focus their energies on improving client service delivery (given available resources and reasonable expectations for change) can also result in empowering those who work in difficult or financially depleted programs.

When staff morale is low due to personality conflicts with administrators or administrators' mismanagement of program resources, an evaluation is likely to exacerbate the conflicts. At a minimum, there must be consensus among program staff that a collective effort will result in improved services to clients.

EXTERNAL PROGRAM POLITICS

External politics come into play when individuals who are *outside* of the program feel they have a say about what is happening *within* the program. Some examples are: Clients who are dissatisfied with the services they received complain to the local newspaper; a house is purchased for a hospice program for AIDS patients in a residential area, much to the dislike of the neighbors; or, a funding agency announces that only social service programs that demonstrate good client outcomes will be funded in the next fiscal year. In the past decade, social service programs have faced considerable downsizing.

Programs also have been challenged by "accountability standards" to continue receiving public funds for ongoing operations. In some jurisdictions, programs have entered into a competition for limited funds in which they must demonstrate their level of effectiveness in producing client change. It is within this context that many program outcome evaluations are initiated. Senior administrators are compelled to show evidence that their programs' services, in fact, are beneficial to clients given the monies spent. Thus, many programs initiate evaluation activities because of outside pressures.

The danger in this case is that an administrator can become too focused on providing data as requested by the funders and not gather data that are optimally tailored to assist program decision making.

Politically charged situations develop when a program's staff and/or stakeholder groups hold different views about what events should take place and what program-based decisions ought to be made. The nature of the decisions being made, the invested interests of the respective parties, and the magnitude of potential client change can all influence the intensity of the political climate.

APPROPRIATE USES OF EVALUATION

Program politics also have a major impact on how evaluation findings are used. As a result, it is worth reviewing the appropriate uses of evaluations before launching into a more detailed discussion of program politics and their influence on program decisions. As discussed in previous chapters, evaluations are most appropriately used to guide internal and external decision making.

INTERNAL DECISION MAKING

The primary internal use of evaluation data is feedback. Evaluation findings provide information about the degree to which program objectives are being met. When these data are available in a timely fashion, administrators and workers alike can continually monitor the impacts of their decisions, and, where required, make adjustments to day-to-day activities and program operations.

At the case level, for example, evaluation data can provide an objective basis for making clinical decisions. As has been described throughout this book, selected practice objectives are measured repeatedly while the client is receiving service. These data are then used as feedback on client progress and become an important consideration in decisions to maintain, modify, or change treatment interventions.

At the program level, staff members are interested in a broader picture of how the program functions. The monitoring approach to evaluation, based on the aggregation of case-level data, allows a program to gather data continuously about its various components, practices, and procedures. The principal internal use for such data is developmental. The process is essentially as follows: Data are aggregated periodically, providing ongoing feedback about the functioning of various aspects of the program. Where the program is not performing as desired, administrators have the opportunity to make changes in structures, procedures, and practices. Subsequent data should then provide information about the impact of these changes. In this process, administrators can continually fine-tune and improve the program.

The most appropriate use of evaluation data is for developmental purposes. Individuals and workgroups can be provided data about the program's outcomes and challenged to do better. Since the evaluation's purpose is development, not judgment, people are more likely to take risks, innovate, and experiment. In such an environment, growth and development are more likely to occur. When staff members and teams feel encouraged to grow and learn, the program itself grows and learns.

Whether efforts are successful or not, in each instance, is not as important as whether individuals, workgroups, and the program have learned something in the process that can be applied to further development. Making effective use of feedback data is a distinguishing feature of effective workers and programs.

EXTERNAL DECISION MAKING

External uses of evaluation data usually involve funders, policy makers, evaluators, and other stakeholder groups. Appropriate uses include demonstration of accountability, program and policy decision making, and knowledge building.

Social service programs are, in a general sense, accountable to their clients, to their communities, and to other professional social service organizations. Specifically, they are always accountable to their funders. Accountability generally requires that a program demonstrate that its goal is consistent with community needs and that its services are being provided effectively and efficiently. One of the most common uses of evaluation data is to account for program activities (Chapter 5) and program results (Chapter 4).

At the policy level, it is sometimes necessary to make decisions between various ways of meeting particular social needs. Or, policy makers may decide to encourage the development of programs that are organized along certain intervention models. Currently, in many jurisdictions, the development of specialized-treatment foster homes is being encouraged while group-care facilities for young people are currently viewed as less desirable. At other times, funders face decisions regarding funding for a specific program. In all three cases, evaluation data can provide program-level information on which such decisions can be made.

Knowledge building for our profession is another way in which an evaluation's results may be used. Each completed evaluation study has the potential of adding to our knowledge base. Indeed, at times, evaluations are undertaken specifically for the purpose of acquiring knowledge. Because evaluations are conducted in real-life field settings, they are a particularly useful method for testing the effectiveness of treatment interventions.

Evaluations for external purposes are usually initiated by people outside the program, typically funding bodies such as governments, foundations, or the United Way. They are often also externally conducted by evaluation specialists on a project-by-project basis. When evaluations are externally imposed and externally conducted, there is a higher potential for problems in the evaluation process and the misuse of the evaluations' findings. This is because the external evaluator is likely to impose an evaluation framework that does not fit well with program operations or is not agreeable to program staff.

An effective safeguard is provided when administrators and staff are involved in all decisions relating to the planning and execution of the evaluation. An alternative to the externally conducted project evaluation is available to programs that establish internal evaluation systems. As discussed previously, the data collected through such systems may often satisfy many of the information needs of external stakeholders.

MISUSES OF EVALUATION

Internal and external politics can influence evaluation in a number of ways. The more highly charged the political situation in a program, the more likely it is that an evaluation will be misused.

Misuse of evaluation is a chronic and recurring problem in the social services. Some less credible purposes to which evaluations have been used are: (1) justification of decisions already made, (2) public relations, (3) performance appraisals, and (4) fulfilling funding requirements.

JUSTIFYING DECISIONS ALREADY MADE

Perhaps the most frequent misuse of evaluation data is justifying decisions that were made in advance of the evaluation. At the case level, for example, a worker may have decided, if only at the subconscious level, that a youngster in treatment foster care should be referred to a group-care program. The worker may then select a standardized measuring instrument (Chapter 6) that is likely to show that the youngster's functioning is highly problematic and use these data to justify the previously taken decision.

At the program level, an agency's senior administrator may already have decided that a certain program within the agency should be reduced in size. The executive board may then commission an evaluation in the hope that the results will show the program to be ineffective. Inevitably, any evaluation will uncover some shortcomings and limitations, and the administrator can then use these to justify the decision to reduce the size of the program. Similarly, outside funders who have already decided to cancel funding for a program may first commission an evaluation in the hope that the results will justify the preformed decision.

PUBLIC RELATIONS

Another misuse of evaluation is to distract attention from negative publicity. From time to time, incidents occur that bring a program unwelcome publicity. A worker in a group home, for example, may be indicted for sexual abuse of residents, or a preschooler may be returned from a treatment foster home to her natural home and be subsequently physically abused. These types of incidents inevitably attract intense media scrutiny.

With the occurrences of such incidents, some social service programs will immediately commission a large-scale evaluation and then decline any comment, pending the outcome of the evaluation. Although an evaluation may be an appropriate response in many such situations, it is even more important to take immediate steps to study the specific incident in detail and adjust procedures and practices to ensure that it will never again occur. But when an evaluation is commissioned merely to distract attention, much of the time, effort, and resources invested will be wasted, as there is unlikely to be any genuine interest in the results. The evaluation in this situation is a mere diversion.

PERFORMANCE APPRAISALS

Another serious misuse of evaluation occurs when it is used for purposes of worker performance appraisals. Data relating to client progress, for example, can be scrutinized inappropriately to document a worker's performance in terms of the attainment of his or her clients' practice objectives. Similarly, data can be aggregated inappropriately across a worker's caseload where "cumulative information" is then used for performance appraisal. At the program level, the contents of an evaluation report may be used to evaluate a supervisor or administrator. In all these cases, the evaluation's findings are likely to be used for political purposes, to specifically promote or undermine an individual worker and/or program.

Such misuses of the evaluative process are destructive, as administrators and workers alike will undoubtedly become defensive and concentrate their efforts on ensuring that evaluation data show them in the best possible light. These defensive efforts detract from the delivery of effective services to clients. Performance appraisals and program evaluations are two distinct processes with different purposes. Both are compromised if they are not kept separate.

FULFILLING FUNDING REQUIREMENTS

Funders are increasingly requiring an evaluation of some kind as a condition of a program's support, particularly of new, innovative, or demonstration projects. Staff members who are trying to set up a new program, or maintain an old one, may see the "evaluation requirement" component as a ritual without having direct relevance to them. They may thus incorporate an elaborate evaluation component into a program funding proposal, or graft evaluation activities onto an existing program, obediently jumping through hoops in order to satisfy funders that they are evaluating something or another.

Often, these facade evaluations plans are not implemented because they were designed for "show" and were not to be "realistic" in the first place. It is, of course, a serious misuse (not to mention a waste of time, effort, and resources) to undertake evaluations only to obtain program funds, without any thought of using the data derived from the evaluation to improve client service.

POLITICAL INFLUENCES ON EVALUATION DECISIONS

We have seen how internal and external politics can alter the reasons for conducting case- and program-level evaluations. It should be clear by now that politics severely influence the entire evaluative process—from beginning to end. We should also be aware, however, that politics influence evaluation decisions more subtly once the evaluation is underway. Individual beliefs, values, and biases of workers (internal politics), for example, may become more apparent when workers are asked to change their methods of recording client data. Or, program funders may interpret funding criteria more stringently in a particular year (external politics) as a consequence of the current fiscal situation. Such political pressures are continuously exerted throughout the entire evaluation process. Being aware of these pressures reduces their influence and the likelihood that an evaluation will stray.

We know that a social service program (including it's interventions) does not exist in a single static state. It exists in many states, or is multifaceted, and the particular state revealed by an evaluation depends on the purpose and focus of the evaluation and the methodology employed.

As evaluators, we must choose: (1) program objectives to be evaluated, (2) the design by which to evaluate them, (3) who will be included in the evaluation sample, (4) what data collection methods to use, (5) how to interpret the evaluation's findings, and (6) how to disseminate the evaluation's findings. These six choices are subject to political pressures, which sometimes have influence on an evaluation's findings and the distribution of the findings. As we will see shortly, evaluators have considerable latitude in making these choices. Let us now consider the six decision-making points in evaluation listed above and take a closer look at the politics that play within each.

PROGRAM AND PRACTICE OBJECTIVES

Many social service programs do not have clear and measurable program objectives. Likewise, not all workers develop specific and measurable practice objectives with their clients. How can a program (or an intervention) be evaluated if its objectives are not explicitly stated? What is to be evaluated in such a situation? If specific objectives are lacking, a program (or an intervention) can be in real trouble when it comes time for an evaluation, and the potential for misuse of an evaluation's findings is greatly increased.

At the program level, the selection of program objectives (discussed in Chapter 3) is somewhat complicated when a program is in existence. Because program objectives define the nature of client service delivery, many political factors influence how the objectives are expressed. Furthermore, the task of defining a program's objectives heightens the political context of the program. In reality, a program's objectives define the criteria on which the program is finally evaluated.

Administrators and workers who develop a program's objectives are influenced by variables such as individual preferences, past and current service delivery, longevity of staff, administrative style, and program resources. Pressures coming from outside the program that influence the selection of a program's objectives are variables such as the program's current reputation with different stakeholder groups, the existence of similar social service programs, funding criteria, and current community demands.

At the case level, the selection of practice objectives seems relatively straightforward when they are directly related to a program-level objective, but the choice of practice objectives is also affected by political factors. The duration of a program's services, for example, influences our expectations of client change. That is, practice objectives are different if the intervention is six hours long, as compared to six weeks or six months long. Other political influences may stem from the views of the client's family, the involvement of other social service programs or other helping professionals (e.g., physicians, teachers, church leaders), and whether any legal activity is involved.

EVALUATION DESIGN

The evaluation design chosen has a direct implication for how much knowledge will be gained from the evaluation efforts. Chapter 8 discussed the "ideal" program-level evaluation, which involves randomly assigning clients to an experimental or a control group. In some cases, random assignment to different groups is indeed a viable option. In our family preservation program, for example, it may be useful to randomly assign parents to two different types of parent-support groups. One group might have an educational focus, while the other might be more experiential in nature.

Given that parents receive support in either group, and assuming that no other research studies exist to help us decide which type of group is more effective, it is reasonable to give all parents an equal chance of being in either group. In this way, we permit the data to guide our future decision making about which type of support group to offer. While this argument favors random assignment in this specific circumstance (see Figure 8.1) some professionals are fundamentally opposed to assigning differential treatment interventions on the basis of "chance" alone.

As pointed out in Chapter 7, explanatory case-level evaluation designs involve the withdrawal of successful interventions and the possibility that such a withdrawal may be detrimental to the client. Under some circumstances, it may be possible to implement explanatory case-level evaluation designs without harm to clients. When a client leaves town for a period of time, for example, there may be no choice but to discontinue the intervention.

However, arrangements can be made to continue measuring the practice objective, and when the client returns, the intervention can be reintroduced. This would result in a powerful *ABAB* design that could support claims about the causal link between the intervention and client outcomes.

In most real-life social service programs, however, there is simply no meaningful justification for withdrawing a successful intervention. Furthermore, to discontinue a successful intervention solely for the purpose of implementing a powerful explanatory case-level evaluation design is unethical. Thus, a worker would have to forego the inferentially powerful withdrawal designs and use a less powerful descriptive or exploratory design.

SAMPLE SELECTION (UNIT OF ANALYSIS)

Whether we are conducting an evaluation of need (Chapter 2), outcome (Chapter 4), or process (Chapter 5), whom we select to include in an evaluation sample influences the data that are collected and, ultimately, the findings that are derived from the evaluative effort. Since all social service programs have a number of stakeholder groups, it is possible to gather evaluation data from many different perspectives, or data sources. In our family preservation program, for example, we could sample the program's workers (Data Source 1), other helping professionals involved with the clients (Data Source 2), the clients themselves (Data Source 3), or even the general public (Data Source 4) to obtain data in relation to the program's outcomes.

Clearly, different stakeholder groups—or data sources—have varying perspectives about the effectiveness of a program. As pointed out in Chapter 1, social service programs answer to multiple stakeholder groups. Thus, the group to which an evaluation should be tailored can sometimes turn into a political battle.

Politics continue to be a factor even after the sample is finally selected. Questions often arise about the criteria for sample inclusion. Suppose, for example, it was agreed in our family preservation program that the families would form the sample—or the unit of analysis. Evaluation results may be influenced considerably by how a "family" is defined. Are data collected from parents only, or are children included as well? Sometimes data are collected from *available* family members. Data for one family, for example, can be collected from the mother, while data for another family can be collected from both parents, the children, and a live-in grandparent.

Another consideration of sample inclusion is the timing of services. If all family members complete a self-administered "satisfaction with services standardized measuring instrument" at termination, for example, those families who have dropped out of the program previously and who are presumably dissatisfied will not be included. Thus, the results will reflect more satisfaction with the program than is really the case.

DATA COLLECTION METHODS

The methods used to collect data are also influenced by political factors. As it so happens, many participants of our family preservation program were also clients of the public welfare program. When a decision was made in Public Welfare to reduce the amount of monthly payments to welfare recipients, many clients in our family preservation program were also affected. Specifically, many clients could no longer afford telephones. The change in the public welfare program meant that our family preservation program could no longer reliably collect client follow-up data by telephone. An additional consideration was that clients who did not have phones may not have been doing as well as clients who were available through local telephone calls. Thus, follow-up data collected by this method may have tended to overstate the level of functioning of former clients.

The timing of data collection can also have a considerable effect on an evaluation's results. At both the case and program levels, different conclusions may be drawn about client success if progress is measured at the time of termination of services as opposed to some time after termination. In the case of group-care programs for children, for example, client deterioration and regression often take place subsequent to termination, because less structure and fewer social supports may be available in the community.

Outcome measures taken at the time of termination (as well as at follow-up) are both legitimate reflections of a program's objectives, but they represent different perspectives and may show different results. Clients, for example, may show positive change immediately after exiting the program (posttest), but may deteriorate (or improve further) three months later (follow-up).

Who actively collects data is another important decision to make. As discussed in previous chapters, many programs use front-line workers to collect data in an effort to keep costs at a minimum. As we know, the credibility of an evaluation's findings are enhanced when data are collected by individuals who are neutral to the intervention and evaluation process. Thus, program administrators are faced with the decision to spend limited program dollars on providing direct services to clients or evaluating services. Typically, the former choice wins out.

In this book, evaluation is described as a way of monitoring interventions, program processes, and outcomes in order to provide useful feedback so that continuous improvement and development are possible at the case- and program-levels. In both situations, evaluations merely reveal and record a single state of a process, much like a camera capturing the image of a static object. Thus, evaluation results give us a "snapshot" of a social service program, at best. This is an important fact to remember when interpreting evaluation findings. Programs and their interventions are complex entities, and different pictures may be presented at different points in time as a result of using different evaluation methods.

As we know, the degree to which a program achieves one of its objectives is a measure of success. However, it is often a matter of opinion whether a particular program's outcome should be deemed *successful*. Suppose for a moment that 60 percent of the graduates of a job-training program find employment. This figure may be interpreted as indicating success, in that *fully* 60 percent of graduates are employed or it may be taken to indicate failure, in that *only* 60 percent of graduates find work.

Moreover, such data as the percentage of former clients who find employment represent only a part of the evaluative picture. Relevant contextual factors must always be considered, such as the stability of the employment index, the income earned by former participants, and the level of job satisfaction experienced by them. The way in which an evaluation's findings are interpreted is a process known as *valuation*. Because criteria for a program's success are seldom predefined, evaluators often play an influential part in the valuation process; and depending on the judgment of an evaluator, the same result may be classified as either a success or a failure.

DISSEMINATION OF FINDINGS

The final stage of an evaluation is disseminating its findings. This stage consists of activities needed to ensure that an evaluation's findings are made available to all involved stakeholders.

At the case level, social service workers will have up-to-date information about the evaluation because they will most likely have been responsible for collecting some, if not all, of the data. Some clients may express an interest in what the data are showing, and it is usually appropriate to share this information with them. Indeed, progress (or lack of it) will be a continuing topic of discussion between workers, funders, administrators, and clients, and should enhance honesty and openness among all the groups. In general, the process of dissemination at the case level is an informal one and usually does not involve written reports.

Dissemination becomes a more formal activity at the program level. If an organization is using the monitoring approach to quality improvement, dissemination will be part of the day-to-day activities within the program. Decisions will undoubtedly have been made about the manner in which, and how often, evaluation findings are to be reported. Data can then be compiled and analyzed, and reports issued as scheduled.

It is particularly important that these periodic reports not be reserved for administrators, but be made available to the workers whose original data have been aggregated. These reports must be viewed as ongoing feedback. By disseminating reports widely (to staff at all levels of the program and other stakeholders) and immediately (upon printing), administrators can help create an environment in which the reports are viewed as information that in turn guides the ongoing development of the program.

In project evaluations, reports are usually not compiled until the latter stages of the evaluative effort. Again, it is important to disseminate these reports as early and as widely as possible. In particular, evaluators have a responsibility to ensure that each client who participated in the evaluation and who was promised a copy of the report is provided with one.

Generally, wide dissemination of evaluative findings fosters openness, honesty, and a constructive climate for future program development. In our society, information is power, and information provided by an evaluation can empower those who receive it, and disempower those who do not.

STANDARDS FOR EVALUATION

It is important that evaluators be alert to program politics and carry out evaluations in an appropriate and professional manner. There are various standards that exist to assist with the conceptualization and implementation of any kind of evaluation. This section provides an overview of general professional standards for evaluation and discusses six principles of evaluation practice that, when applied, will increase the likelihood that an evaluation will measure up to professional standards.

PROFESSIONAL STANDARDS

The most commonly accepted evaluation standards are those issued by the Joint Committee for Standards on Educational Evaluation. These standards were developed over a five-year period in the late 1970s and reflect the participation of 12 professional organizations and hundreds of professional program evaluators.

The Joint Committee identified four overlapping criteria against which evaluation practice should be judged: utility, feasibility, fairness, and accuracy. Although the committee's standards were written specifically as guidelines for program-level evaluations, they have considerable applicability to case-level evaluation as well. In either case, the four standards discussed below will be enhanced if all relevant stakeholder groups are consulted before an evaluation begins.

UTILITY

The utility criterion is intended to ensure that evaluations are carried out only if they will be potentially useful to one or more of the program's stakeholder groups (see Figure 1.1). In other words, evaluators are required to establish links between an evaluation's findings and the decisions to be derived from them. Data obtained from an evaluation must be relevant to decision makers and reported in a manner that decision makers can easily understand.

At the case level, the client and the front-line worker are, in most cases, joint decision makers. Because workers usually carry out case-level evaluations, they will be able to decide on the type of data to be gathered, the method of analyses, and the way in which evaluation findings will impact case-level decision making.

At the program level, evaluation findings are documented in a written report, which often provides program-level recommendations. To ensure that an evaluation has utility, the evaluator is responsible for determining beforehand, with as much clarity as possible, the decisions that are to be based on the evaluation's findings. The evaluator is also responsible for reporting results in a manner that can inform the decisions to be taken. It is obviously important that the report be comprehensible. Moreover, the evaluator's task is not limited to publishing the evaluation's findings.

The evaluator must also explain the findings to case- and program-level decision makers and to other interested stakeholder groups. When drafting recommendations, it is important that evaluators keep in mind the social, political, economic, and professional contexts within which recommendations will be implemented. The challenge is to provide recommendations that can result in meaningful and feasible improvement within existing constraints.

FEASIBILITY

A second criterion is feasibility. An evaluation should be conducted only if it is practical to implement within the budget and time available. Feasibility issues relate primarily to the selection of evaluation designs, a topic discussed earlier.

At the case level, feasibility requires that the selected evaluation design be compatible with day-to-day service delivery. Although it might be desirable from the perspective of "an objective evaluation" to implement an explanatory case-level design involving a withdrawal phase, it may be inadvisable (not to mention unethical) to do so. A less intrusive descriptive or exploratory design will likely be a more practical alternative.

At the program level, the questions to be answered may call for an explanatory program-level design requiring random assignment of clients to experimental and control groups. But it may not be possible to implement such a design without considerable disruption to service provision. Perhaps the evaluation questions can be answered through a descriptive or exploratory design; if not, the evaluation will have to be refocused or abandoned. Similarly, funding considerations or deadlines may limit the evaluation questions that can be addressed or the evaluation designs that can be implemented.

FAIRNESS

A third criterion is fairness. An evaluation should be undertaken only if it is conducted fairly. As discussed earlier, there is no one "accurate" picture of a program or an intervention within a program. There are multiple possible pictures, each representing a different perspective. Evaluators are responsible for creating fair and balanced representations, ones that take into account all relevant aspects of interventions or programs as well as all reasonable perspectives. Often, this means that no one picture will emerge and that evaluators will need to explain how the several perspectives fit together and how they relate to the overall social, economic, political, and professional contexts in which the program operates.

One area in which balance is particularly important is the competition between competing interests. Earlier in this chapter, the point was made that evaluations are susceptible to political influence. The term *politics,* in this sense, refers to attempts on the part of any particular group to coopt the evaluation process in an attempt to advance its own interests. It is particularly important for evaluators to avoid, or extricate themselves from, any position in which they are vulnerable to undue influence from any stakeholder group(s). If they are not careful to do so, evaluators increase the risk that the results of their efforts will be misused.

ACCURACY

The final criterion is accuracy. This has to do with the technical adequacy of the evaluation process and involves such matters as validity and reliability, standardized measurement instruments, samples, and comparisons of findings. The evaluator is also responsible for making clear any shortcomings in the evaluation's methodology, and the limits within which its findings can be considered to be accurate.

Although it is the evaluator's responsibility to ensure technical accuracy, this standard does not imply that the evaluator should unilaterally make design and data collection decisions. Rather, it is important that those who will use the evaluation findings participate in these decisions and so come to understand the strengths and limitations of the data.

PRINCIPLES OF MONITORING EVALUATION

Program politics are dynamic; that is, they are always changing and involve a multitude of factors. It is impossible to provide examples of all the possible problems (and solutions) that can occur in a social service program. Below are six principles of evaluation that, when practiced consistently, will lessen the influence of politics in an evaluation.

PRINCIPLE 1: EVALUATE PROGRAMS AND INTERVENTIONS, NOT PEOPLE

As we know, the primary purpose of a monitoring evaluation is to collect data that can be used for continuous improvement and development of programs and their respective interventions. We have already discussed why the use of data for appraising employee performance is a misuse of an evaluation. Thus, we know that it is inappropriate to use evaluation data to judge the performance of a single worker. It is just as important at the case-level that we do not judge individual clients according to the data collected.

Suppose, for example, that we monitored our interventions with a nine-year old girl experiencing behavior problems in the classroom. We note that after several interventions are attempted, her behavior deteriorates. Based on our data, we can only conclude that the interventions were not effective with the client, given the circumstances surrounding her situation. The data do not support us in making judgments about the client's character, such that she is "untreatable."

PRINCIPLE 2: EVALUATION AND INTERVENTION ACTIVITIES SHOULD BE INTEGRATED

We have advocated that evaluation and practice ought to be integrated for effective program operations and client service delivery. Stakeholders have a major interest in using data to assist them in answering questions about a program and the clients it serves. In turn, an evaluator must consider how well any evaluation activity fits with ongoing client service delivery. While the idea that "evaluation and service delivery go hand-in-hand" is easy enough to grasp intellectually, it is rarely practiced. Evaluators must make a special effort to advocate this position and help administrators and workers alike to see the utility of it. We have already discussed the many reasons why workers might fear evaluation (Chapter 1).

There are a number of things an evaluator can do to increase the likelihood of a program's accepting the concept of evaluation as an integral part of its service delivery structure. First, actively listen to program staff to determine whether they have taken ownership of the process. Do administrators say, "We want to give *you* full support to carry out the evaluation," or "How is *our* evaluation coming along?" Do administrators communicate information about the evaluation in person or by memo? How responsive are workers to evaluation requests? Do workers agree to take on evaluation tasks and then not follow through? By knowing the climate of the program, an evaluator can respond more sensitively to everyone's needs.

Second, be prepared to repeatedly send the "evaluation-practice integration" message to program staff. Successfully incorporating evaluation into client service delivery involves educating program administration *and* workers. Include the message in training and be prepared to repeat the message over and over (using different examples, of course). When workers express difficulty in managing their case load and the "additional" evaluation activity, take time to demonstrate the benefits of the integration of evaluation and practice.

PRINCIPLE 3: INVOLVE AS MANY STAKEHOLDER GROUPS AS POSSIBLE FROM THE BEGINNING

Because of the different points of view represented by the many stakeholder groups, and the possibility for hidden agendas to develop, it is important to involve members from each group early in the evaluation process. The benefit of including as many stakeholder groups as possible is that the evaluation plan will be open to scrutiny from a diverse range of perspectives. The downside of course is that "too many cooks can spoil the broth." Thus, while it is important to include as many stakeholder groups as possible, it is not necessary to involve all of them in every aspect of the evaluation effort. Each stakeholder group can be invited to periodic evaluation-planning meetings. Such meetings give the program an opportunity to show leadership in the evaluation plan and to provide a forum to hear and discuss the main interests and concerns of each stakeholder group.

After the update meeting, the evaluator can keep stakeholder groups involved at various levels. At a minimum, stakeholder groups can receive written or verbal information about the status of the evaluation. Reports can be printed in the form of a program newsletter, which can be as simple as a one-page update of current activities and decisions within the program. The evaluator can also invite responses to these reports.

In other cases, different stakeholder groups have different expertises that could be tapped to improve the evaluation plan. For example, a program board member may have legal expertise to assist in developing client consent forms; a group of clients can be asked to participate in a pilot study; neighborhood citizens could be surveyed about their attitudes toward clients living in a nearby group home.

PRINCIPLE 4: DEVELOP A RELIABLE AND ONGOING FEEDBACK SYSTEM

If an evaluation is guided by specific questions and has a clear time line for review, designing a system of feedback is relatively simple. It requires us to determine: (1) what data will be made available to whom, (2) at what times, and (3) who will be responsible for disseminating these data. The feedback system does not have to be elaborate. If workers are asked to record the type of interventions used with their clients over a period of time, for example, these data should be summarized and given back to the workers. Program staff simply need to know how feedback will be disseminated (e.g., memo to individual workers, group meeting), how often the data will be summarized (e.g., monthly, bimonthly, every three months), and who will collate and summarize the data (e.g., rotating responsibility among workers, administrator).

During the early phases of implementing a monitoring evaluation system, it is likely that feedback will give information about the completeness and consistency of data recording, rather than a comprehensive summary of the content being recorded. As with any new procedure, it takes time for staff to learn and practice new methods of data recording. If data-recording forms are incomplete, then the data summary will show major gaps. In this situation, the feedback is self-evident. Suppose workers in a family preservation program are expected to record their interventions with clients for each client contact, for example. Due to time limitations, however, workers only record data when they have sufficient time. Thus, the resulting summary list of interventions is incomplete. In this situation, the feedback must first focus on developing a system to gather complete, valid, and reliable data. Once these data are obtained, our analysis of the data will be more meaningful.

Clearly, a feedback system is complete only when the data collectors have the opportunity to respond to how the data are analyzed and summarized. Workers reviewing the summary of interventions, for example, could be asked to reflect on the "accuracy" of the list, or the "meaningfulness" of the data from their perspective.

PRINCIPLE 5: EVALUATION PROCEDURES ARE NOT PERSON DEPENDENT

Social service programs undergo a lot of change. Staff turnover, program downsizing, unstable funding, and administrative changes are just a few factors that can change program operations dramatically in a relatively short period of time. It is critical that an evaluation be able to withstand program interruptions and changes. When evaluation procedures are documented in an "easy to read" format, there will be less disruption when evaluation tasks are shifted from one individual to another. While it is important for each program staff member to take ownership of the evaluation process, the procedures of evaluation should be known to everyone.

PRINCIPLE 6: INVOLVE STAFF AT ALL LEVELS OF A PROGRAM

A constructive environment is one in which all staff are involved in the total evaluation process. A frequent mistake is to make the assumption that only senior-level staff members need the findings derived from an evaluation. This sends a clear message about the importance attached to the work of the staff members at other levels, unintentionally devaluing their work. Since many of these activities involve client service delivery, the program, in fact, implicitly devalues the very reason for its existence. At the same time, staff members at many levels in the program are required to operate without adequate feedback, which may decrease their effectiveness. In the process, the entire program suffers.

In well-functioning programs, evaluation and program decisions are made at all levels. Consequently, it is important that the evaluation system serve the needs of staff members at all levels, providing information for better-quality decisions throughout the program. Making decisions on the basis of an evaluation's findings is, as we have seen, a straightforward process. This feedback provides information about how well the program's objectives are being achieved and, based on these results, decisions can be made to continue existing activities, to modify them, or to switch to new ones.

ETHICAL GUIDELINES FOR EVALUATION

Ethics is concerned with the moral practice of evaluation or the "code of right and wrong" for deciding how to handle data, how to interact with clients, and, in a general sense, how to proceed in politically charged situations. A variety of ethical codes applicable to evaluation have been published. Although the ethical guidelines in existence have been written specifically to apply to program evaluations, many of the provisions apply to case-level evaluation as well. Most of the ethical guidelines and principles found in published codes can be organized around the four following themes: (1) purpose of the evaluation, (2) confidentiality, anonymity, and informed consent, (3) designing an ethical evaluation, and (4) informing others about an evaluation's findings.

PURPOSE OF THE EVALUATION

The purpose of an evaluation must be clearly spelled out to all those who are asked to participate, as well as to those who will be directly affected by the evaluation findings. Purpose includes information about who initiated and is funding the evaluation and the types of decisions to be based on the evaluation's findings. This is a time for clarity and frankness. If the purpose of an evaluation is to obtain objective data that can help in making decisions about funding, this should be clearly spelled out. If specific aspects of program functioning are the primary concern and it is hoped that evaluation data will shed light on relevant procedures and practices, this, too, should be explicitly stated.

Although this guideline may seem obvious, it is frequently violated. Evaluations are conducted ostensively to obtain data for program development, but it subsequently turns out that they were really intended to provide data for a funding decision. It is clearly unethical to engage in evaluations with hidden agendas.

CONFIDENTIALITY, ANONYMITY, AND INFORMED CONSENT

Confidentiality and anonymity specifically relate to how data are analyzed and reported. Confidentiality means that we have asked individuals providing us with data to trust us that we will keep the data private and restrict their use. Anonymity, on the other hand, refers to the practice of keeping data nameless. In case-level evaluations, we can guarantee confidentiality but not anonymity. In program-level evaluations, both conditions apply. The utmost care must be taken to preserve the promised anonymity and to keep confidential data out of the hands of unauthorized persons.

A promise that is of particular concern to many evaluation participants is that of anonymity. A drug offender, for example, may be very afraid of being identified; a person on welfare may be concerned whether anyone else might learn that he or she was on welfare. Also, there is often some confusion between the terms "anonymity" and "confidentiality." Some evaluations are designed so that no one, not even the person doing the evaluation, knows which evaluation participant gave what response. An example is a mailed survey form, bearing no identifying mark and asking the respondent not to give a name. In an evaluation like this, the respondent is *anonymous*.

However, it is more often the case that we do know how a particular participant responded and have agreed not to divulge the information to anyone else. In such cases, the information is *confidential*. Part of our explanation to a potential evaluation participant must include a clear statement of what information will be shared with whom.

As soon after data collection as practical, the identities of evaluation participants should be disguised by use of codes that make it impossible to associate specific data with any particular individual. Assigning codes will also provide an additional level of protection during the data analysis phase. The master code book, listing clients and their assigned codes, should be kept under lock and key, and preferably in a different location from the data (Grinnell & Stothers, 1991; Williams, Tutty, & Grinnell, 1995).

An important consideration in any evaluation is to obtain the participants' *informed* consent. The word "informed" means that each participant fully understands what is going to happen in the course of the evaluation, why it is going to happen, and what its effect will be on him or her. If the participant is psychiatrically challenged, mentally delayed, or in any other way incapable of full understanding, the evaluation must be explained to someone else—perhaps a parent, guardian, social worker, or spouse, or someone to whom the participant's welfare is important.

Informed consent means that the program participant has voluntarily agreed to participate in the evaluation, knows what will happen in the program, and fully understands any possible consequences. This applies equally to evaluations conducted at the case and program level.

Again, this provision seems self-evident, but there are well-known instances in which relevant information has been withheld from participants for fear that they would decline to participate or that their knowing the true purposes of the evaluation would compromise the reliability of measurements.

Participants should also be informed that they can withdraw at any time without penalty, and evaluators should recognize that, even when so assured, many clients do not feel free to do so. This is particularly likely to be true of children, as well as residents in group homes, institutions, hospitals, prisons, and senior citizens' homes. In such settings, it is the evaluator's responsibility to ensure that the consent obtained has not been coerced, either explicitly or implicitly.

It is clear that no evaluation participant may be bribed, threatened, deceived, or in any way coerced into participating. Questions must be encouraged, both initially and throughout the course of the evaluation. People who believe they understand may have misinterpreted our explanation or understood it only in part. They may say they understand, when they do not, in an effort to avoid appearing foolish. They may even sign documents they do not understand to confirm their supposed understanding, and it is our responsibility to ensure that their understanding is real and complete.

It is particularly important for participants to know that they are not signing away their rights when they sign a consent form. They can decide at any time to withdraw from the evaluation *without penalty*, without so much as a reproachful glance. The results of the evaluation will be made available to them as soon as it has been completed. No promise will be made to them that cannot be fulfilled.

All this seems reasonable in theory, but ethical obligations are often difficult to fulfill in practice. For example, there are times when it is very difficult to remove coercive influences because these influences are inherent in the situation. A woman awaiting an abortion may agree to provide private information about herself and her partner because she believes that, if she does not, she will be denied the abortion. It is of no use to tell her that this is not true: She feels she is not in a position to take any chances.

There are captive populations of people in prisons, schools, or institutions who may agree out of sheer boredom to take part in an evaluation study. Or, they may participate in return for certain privileges, or because they fear some penalty or reprisal. There may be people who agree because they are pressured into it by family members, or they want to please the social worker, or they need some service or payment that they believe depends on their cooperation. Often, situations like this cannot be changed, but at least we can be aware of them and try to deal with them in an ethical manner.

A written consent form should be only part of the process of informing evaluation participants of their roles and their rights as volunteers. It should give participants a basic description of the purpose of the evaluation, its procedures, and their rights as voluntary participants. All information should be provided in plain and simple language, without jargon.

A consent form should be no longer than two pages of single-spaced typing. All participants should be given a copy of the consent form. Questionnaires may have an introductory letter containing the required information, with the written statement that the completion of the questionnaire is the person's agreement to participate. In telephone surveys, the information below will need to be given verbally and must be standardized across all calls.

A written consent form should contain the following items, recognizing that the relevancy of this information and the amount required will vary with each evaluation project (Grinnell & Stothers, 1991; Williams, Tutty, & Grinnell, 1995):

1. A brief description of the purpose of the evaluation, as well as its value to the general/professional social work community (probability and nature of direct and indirect benefits) and to the participants and/or others.

2. An explanation as to how and/or why participants were selected and a statement that participation is completely voluntary.

3. A description of experimental conditions (if any) and/or procedures. Some points that should be covered are:
   a. The frequency with which the participants will be contacted.
   b. The time commitment required by the participants.
   c. The physical effort required and/or protection from overexertion.
   d. Emotionally sensitive issues that might be exposed and/or follow-up resources that are available if required.
   e. Location of participation (e.g., need for travel/commuting).
   f. Information that will be recorded and how it will be recorded (e.g., on paper, by photographs, videotape, audiotape).

4. Description of the likelihood of any discomforts and inconveniences associated with participation, and of known or suspected short- and long-term risks.

5. Explanation of who will have access to data collected and to the identity of the evaluation's participants (i.e., level of anonymity or confidentiality of each person's participation and information) and how long the data will be stored.

6. Description of how the data will be made public (e.g., final evaluation report, scholarly presentation, printed publication). An additional consent is required for publication of photographs, audiotapes, and/or videotapes.
7. Description of other evaluation projects or other people who may use the data.
8. Explanation of the participants' rights:
   a. That they may terminate or withdraw from the evaluation study at any point.
   b. That they may ask for clarification or more information throughout the evaluation effort.
   c. That they may contact the appropriate administrative body if they have any questions about the conduct of the individuals doing the evaluation or the evaluation's procedures.

DESIGNING AN ETHICAL EVALUATION

A necessary precaution before beginning an evaluation is to ensure that it is designed in an ethical manner. One of the more useful research designs, presented in Chapter 8, involves separating participants into control and experimental groups, and providing a treatment to the experimental group but not to the control group. The essential dilemma here is whether or not it is ethical to withhold a treatment, assumed to be beneficial, from participants in the control group. Even if control-group participants are on a waiting list and will receive the treatment at a later date, is it right to delay service in order to conduct the evaluation?

Proponents of this evaluation design argue that people on a waiting list will not receive treatment any faster whether they are involved in the evaluation study or not. Furthermore, it is only *assumed* that the treatment is beneficial; if its effects were known for sure, there would be no need to do the evaluation study. Surely, social workers have an ethical responsibility to test such assumptions through evaluation studies before they continue with treatments that may be ineffective or even harmful.

As mentioned before, the same kind of controversy pertains to an evaluation design in which clients are randomly assigned to two different groups, each receiving a different treatment intervention. Proponents of this design argue that no one is sure which treatment is better—that is what the evaluation study is trying to discover—and so it is absurd to assert that a client in one group is being harmed by being denied the treatment offered to the other group. Social workers, however, tend to have their own ideas about which treatment is better. Ms. Gomez's worker, for example, may believe that she will derive more benefit from behavioral than from existential therapy, and that it will be harmful to her if random assignment happens to put her in the existential group.

INFORMING OTHERS ABOUT AN EVALUATION'S FINDINGS

Another ethical consideration in an evaluation is the manner in which its findings are reported. It may be tempting, for example, to give great weight to positive findings while playing down or ignoring altogether negative or disappointing findings. There is no doubt that positive findings tend to be more enthusiastically received; but it is obviously just as important to know that two variables (i.e., the program and its outcomes) are not related as to know that they are.

All evaluation studies have limitations, because practical considerations make it difficult to use the costly and complex designs that yield the most certain results. Since evaluation studies with more limitations yield less trustworthy findings, it is important for us to be honest about an evaluation's limitations and for other social workers to be able to understand what the limitations imply.

Sometimes, the sharing of results will be a delicate matter. Staff may be reluctant to hear that the program is less effective than they thought. It will also be difficult, and often inadvisable, for us to share with research participants results that show them in an unfavorable light. For example, it may be honest to tell Mr. Yen that he scored high on the anxiety scale, but it may also be extremely damaging to him. Social workers wrestle every day with the problems of whom to tell, as well as how, when, and how much. The same difficulties arise in social work evaluation.

SUMMARY

This chapter presented various considerations that must be taken into account when evaluating a social service program. Because programs and interventions are complex entities, evaluation outcomes can be influenced through technical and other decisions. Often, evaluations also become politically charged, as one group of stakeholders or another tries to advance its interests. Consequently, evaluation principles, professional standards, and ethical guidelines for conducting evaluations are important. Ultimately, evaluations are most constructive when they are carried out in an organizational context that values growth and learning, and avoids judgment.

GLOSSARY

ACCOUNTABILITY A system of responsibility in which program administrators account for all program activities by answering to the demands of a program's stakeholders and by justifying the program's expenditures to the satisfaction of its stakeholders.

ACCURACY A standard of evaluation practice that requires technical adequacy of the evaluation process; includes matters of validity, reliability, measurement instruments, samples, and comparisons.

ACTIVITIES What practitioners do with their clients to achieve their practice and facilitative objectives.

AFFECTIVE PROGRAM OBJECTIVE An objective that focuses on changing an individual's emotional reaction to himself or herself or to another person or thing.

AGENCY   A social service organization that exists to fulfill a broad social purpose; it functions as one entity, is governed by a single directing body, and has policies and procedures that are common to all of its parts.

AGENCY GOAL   Broad unmeasurable outcomes the agency wishes to achieve; they are based on values and are guided by the agency's mission statement.

AGENCY OBJECTIVE   A program established to help in the achievement of the agency's goal.

ANONYMITY   The practice of keeping people nameless; people are identified using special codes.

AREA PROBABILITY SAMPLING   A form of cluster sampling that uses a three-stage process to provide the means to carry out a study when a comprehensive list of a population cannot be compiled.

ASSESSMENT   A professional activity that occurs prior to the intervention phase of practice in which a client's present level of functioning in relevant areas is assessed so that an appropriate intervention plan can be established.

AUDIT SHEET   A checklist of all data to be recorded for a particular client and the dates by which these data are due; usually located on the cover of each client file.

BASELINE MEASURE   A numerical label assigned to a client's level of performance, knowledge, or affect prior to any intervention; the first measure to be made in any series of repeated measurements; designated as the *A* phase in formal case-level designs.

BEHAVIORAL PROGRAM OBJECTIVE   An objective that aims to change the conduct or actions of clients.

CASE CONFERENCES   An informal, or nonempirical, method of case evaluation that requires professionals to meet and exchange descriptive client information for the purposes of making a case decision.

CAUSALITY In outcome evaluation, when a program is deemed the agent that brings about change for clients as measured by its objectives using explanatory evaluation designs.

CENSUS DATA A periodic governmental count of a population using demographic measurements.

CLASSICAL EXPERIMENTAL DESIGN An explanatory research design with randomly selected and randomly assigned experimental and control groups in which the program's objective (the dependent variable) is measured before and after the intervention (the independent variable) for both groups, but only the experimental group receives the intervention.

CLIENT A person who uses a social service agency—an individual, a couple, a family, a group, an organization, or a community.

CLIENT DATA In evaluation, measurements systematically collected from clients of social service programs; ideally, data are collected in strict compliance with the evaluation design and procedures.

CLIENT LOG A form whereby clients maintain annotated records of events related to their practice objectives; structured journals in which clients record events, feelings, and reactions relevant to their problem.

CLIENT SATISFACTION A program variable that measures the degree to which clients are content with various aspects of the program services that they received.

CLUSTER SAMPLING A multistage probability sampling procedure in which a population is divided into groups or clusters, and the clusters, rather than the individuals, are selected for inclusion in the sample.

COHORT ANALYSIS When data are collected from the *same* group of clients at all data collection points (e.g., program intake, termination, follow-up) in an evaluation.

COMPARISON GROUP POSTTEST-ONLY DESIGN A descriptive research design with two groups, experimental and comparison, in which the program's objective (dependent variable) is measured once for both groups, and only the experimental group receives the intervention (the independent variable).

COMPARISON GROUP PRETEST-POSTTEST DESIGN   A descriptive research design with two groups, experimental and comparison, in which the program's objective (the dependent variable) is measured before and after the intervention (the independent variable) for both groups, but only the experimental group receives the intervention.

COMPENSATION   Attempts by evaluators or staff members to counterbalance the lack of treatment for control-group clients by administering some or all of the intervention (the independent variable); a threat to internal validity.

COMPENSATORY RIVALRY   Motivation of control-group clients to compete with experimental group clients; a threat to internal validity.

COMPUTERIZED DATA SYSTEMS   An automated method of organizing single units of data to generate summarized or aggregate forms of data.

CONCEPTUALIZATION   The process of defining a social service program by a goal, objectives, measurements, and activities.

CONFIDENTIALITY   Keeping private and restricting the use of data that have been provided by individuals for the purposes of evaluation.

CONSTANTS   A characteristic that has the same value for all clients in an evaluation.

CONTEXTUAL DATA   Empirical or subjective data that reflect the circumstances of the problem and help to explain the outcome or score.

CONTROL GROUP   A group of randomly selected and randomly assigned clients in a study who do not receive the experimental intervention (the independent variable) and are used for comparison purposes.

CONVENIENCE SAMPLING   A nonprobability sampling procedure that relies on the closest and most available participants to constitute a sample.

COST-EFFECTIVE   When a social service program is able to achieve its program objectives in relation to its costs.

COST-EFFICIENT   When a social service program is able to achieve its program objectives at less cost, compared to another program striving for the same objectives.

CROSS SECTIONAL ANALYSIS When data are collected from a different group of clients at specified data collection points (e.g., program intake and exit) in an evaluation.

DATA Isolated facts, presented in numerical or descriptive form, on which client or program decisions are based; not to be confused with information.

DATA DISPLAY The manner in which collected data are set out on a page.

DATA SOURCES People or records that are the suppliers of data.

DECISION DATA CHART A chart that lists, in chronological order, decisions to be made, the data needed to make each decision, and the data actually collected; used to ensure that adequate links exist between the data collected and the decisions made.

DEMANDS In needs assessment, something that is so desired by people that they are willing to "march" for it; to be differentiated from *needs* and *wants*.

DEMORALIZATION Feelings of deprivation among control group clients that may cause them to drop out of the evaluation study; a form of mortality that is a threat to internal validity.

DEPENDENT VARIABLE A variable that is dependent on or caused by another variable; an outcome variable that is not manipulated directly but is measured to determine if the independent variable has had an effect; program objectives are dependent variables.

DESCRIPTIVE DESIGN A design that approximates a true experiment, but in which the worker does not have the same degree of control over manipulation of the intervention process; also known as quasi-experimental designs.

DIFFERENTIAL SELECTION The failure to achieve or maintain equivalency among the preformed groups; a threat to internal validity.

DIFFUSION OF TREATMENT Problems that may occur when experimental and control-group clients talk to each other about a study; a threat to internal validity.

DURATION RECORDING A method of data collection that involves direct observation and documentation of the practice objective by recording the length of time of each occurrence within a specified observation period.

EFFICIENCY ASSESSMENT   An evaluation to determine the ratio of effectiveness or outcome to cost; does not contain data that may explain why the program is or is not efficient.

EMPIRICAL DATA   Isolated facts presented in numerical or descriptive form that have been derived from observation or testing, as opposed to data derived from inference or theory.

EMPIRICAL EVALUATION   A method of appraisal based on the analysis of data collected by measuring instruments.

ETHICS   The moral practice of evaluation or the "code of right and wrong" for deciding how to handle data, how to interact with clients, and how to proceed in politically charged situations.

EVALUABILITY ASSESSMENT   An appraisal of a program's components and operations intended to determine whether a program can, in fact, be evaluated for outcome, efficiency, or process; mainly used to construct meaningful and measurable program objectives that are derived from the program's goal.

EVALUATION   A form of appraisal using valid and reliable research methods. There are numerous types of evaluations geared to produce data which in turn produce information that helps in the decision-making process. Data from evaluations are used in the quality improvement process.

EVALUATION DESIGN   A process used to evaluate some aspect of a program; intended to elicit data that are required in making some decision.

EXPERIMENTAL GROUP   In an experimental research design, the group of clients exposed to the manipulation of the intervention (the independent variable); also referred to as the treatment group.

EXPLANATORY DESIGN   An attempt to demonstrate with certainty that specific activities caused specific reported changes in practice objectives. The professional manipulates certain factors in the intervention to gain a greater degree of control over the proceedings; also known as experimental designs.

EXPLORATORY DESIGN A process in which a professional assesses the effects of an intervention process for the purpose of building a foundation of general ideas and tentative theories that can later be examined by more rigorous evaluative methods.

EXPRESSED NEEDS In needs assessment, the opinions and views of people who are directly experiencing a problem; also known as *felt needs*.

EXTERNAL EVALUATION An evaluation that is conducted by someone who does not have any connection with the program; usually an evaluation that is requested by the agency's funding sources. This type of evaluation complements an internal evaluation.

EXTERNAL VALIDITY The extent to which the findings of an evaluation study can be generalized outside the evaluative situation.

EXTRANEOUS VARIABLES Outside factors that occur at the same time as the intervention and thus may account for some of the measured change in practice objectives.

FACILITATIVE PRACTICE OBJECTIVE An objective that relates to the overall practice objective (it can be termed a practice subobjective); it also specifies an intended result and makes the achievement of the practice objective easier; constructed for the client's benefit.

FAIRNESS A standard of evaluation practice that requires evaluations to be conducted in a fair and ethical manner; includes the dissemination of evaluation results.

FEASIBILITY A standard of evaluation practice that requires evaluations to be conducted only under conditions that are practical and economically viable.

FIELD ERROR A type of nonsampling error in which field staff show bias in their selection of a sample.

FLOW CHART A diagram of client service delivery in which symbols are used to depict client movement throughout the service delivery system.

FOCUS GROUPS   A group of people brought together to talk about their lives and experiences in a free-flowing, open-ended discussion which typically focuses on a single topic; a semi-structured group interview.

FOLLOW-UP DATA   Collecting client data (as measured by a program's objectives) at specific points after clients have exited the program (e.g., three months, six months, one year).

FORMAL CASE-LEVEL EVALUATION   An empirical method of appraisal in which a single client is monitored via repeated measurements over time in order to examine change in a practice objective.

FORMATIVE EVALUATION   See *process evaluation.*

FREQUENCY RECORDING   A method of data collection involving direct observation and documentation in which each occurrence of the practice objective is recorded during a specified observation period.

GENERALIZABILITY   Extending or applying the findings of an evaluation study to clients or situations that were not directly evaluated.

GRAPHIC RATING SCALE   A type of measuring instrument that describes an attribute on a continuum from one extreme to the other, with points of the continuum ordered in equal intervals and assigned numbers.

HAWTHORNE EFFECT   Effects on clients' behaviors or attitudes attributable to their knowledge that they are taking part in an evaluation project; a reactive effect that is a threat to internal validity.

HISTORY IN RESEARCH DESIGN   Any event that may affect the second or subsequent measurement of the program's objectives (the dependent variables) and which cannot be accounted for in the evaluation design; a threat to internal validity.

HYPOTHESIS   A theory-based prediction of the expected results in an evaluation study; a tentative explanation of a relationship or supposition that a relationship may exist.

INDEPENDENT VARIABLE   A variable that is not dependent on another variable but is said to cause or determine changes in the dependent variable; an antecedent variable that is directly manipulated in order to assess its effect on the dependent variable. Interventions are independent variables.

INFORMATION   The interpretation given to data that have been collected, collated, and analyzed; Information is used to help in the decision-making process; not to be confused with data.

INFORMED CONSENT   Procedures in which clients, or evaluation subjects, are told in advance about the major tasks and activities they will perform during an evaluation study; clients then participate in the evaluation study only if they are willing to engage in these activities.

INSTRUMENTAL PRACTICE OBJECTIVE   An objective that bears no apparent relation to the practice objective, but when accomplished will remove practical impediments to the attainment of the practice objective; constructed for the client's benefit.

INSTRUMENTATION ERROR   Any flaws in the construction of a measuring instrument or any faults in the administration of a measuring instrument that affect the appraisal of program and practice objectives; a threat to internal validity.

INTAKE FORM   A data collection instrument that is administered to clients at or near the point of entry into a social service program. The form typically asks questions about client demographics, service history, and reasons for referral to the program.

INTERACTION EFFECT   Effects on the program's objective (the dependent variable) that are produced by the combination of two or more threats to internal validity.

INTERNAL EVALUATION   An evaluation that is conducted by someone who works within a program; usually an evaluation for the purpose of promoting better client services. This type of evaluation complements an external evaluation.

INTERNAL VALIDITY   The extent to which it can be demonstrated that the intervention (the independent variable) in an evaluation is the only cause of change in the program's objective (the dependent variable); soundness of the experimental procedures and measuring instruments.

INTERRUPTED TIME-SERIES DESIGN   A descriptive evaluation design in which there is only one group and the program objective (the dependent variable) is measured repeatedly before and after the intervention (the independent variable).

INTERVAL RECORDING   A method of data collection that involves continuous, direct observation and documentation of an individual's behavior during specified observation periods divided into equal time intervals.

KEY INFORMANTS   Individuals who are considered knowledgeable about the social problem that is being investigated and who provide new or original data through interviews. Examples are professionals, public officials, agency directors, social service clients, and select citizens.

KNOWLEDGE PROGRAM OBJECTIVE   An objective that aims to change a client's level of information and understanding about a specific social area.

LONGEVITY   In outcome evaluation, when client gains (as measured by a program's objectives) are maintained for a period of time after clients have exited the program (e.g., three months, six months, one year follow-up).

LONGITUDINAL CASE-STUDY DESIGN   An exploratory research design in which there is only one group and the program's objective (the dependent variable) is measured more than once; also referred to as a panel design, a cohort design, a developmental design, or a dynamic case study design.

MAGNITUDE RECORDING   A method of data collection that involves direct observation and documentation of the amount, level, or degree of the practice objective during each occurrence.

MAINTENANCE PROGRAM OBJECTIVE   An objective formulated in an effort to keep a program financially viable; constructed for the program's benefit.

MANUAL DATA MANAGEMENT   Noncomputerized method of organizing single units of data to generate summarized or aggregate forms of the data.

MATCHED PAIRS METHOD   A technique of assigning clients to groups so that the experimental and control groups are approximately equivalent in pretest scores or other characteristics, or so that all differences except the experimental condition are eliminated.

MATURATION   Any unplanned change in clients due to mental, physical, or other processes that take place over the course of the evaluation project and which affect the program's objective; a threat to internal validity.

MEASURE   A label, usually numerical, assigned to an observation that has been subjected to measurement.

MEASUREMENT   The process of systematically assigning labels to observations; in statistics, measurement systems are classified according to level of measurement and usually produce data that can be represented in numerical form; the assignment of numerals to objects or events according to specific rules.

MEASURING INSTRUMENTS   Instruments such as questionnaires or rating scales used to obtain a measure for a particular client or client group.

MISSION STATEMENT   A unique written philosophical perspective of what an agency is all about; states a common vision for the organization by providing a point of reference for all major planning decisions.

MONITORING APPROACH TO QUALITY IMPROVEMENT   An evaluation that aims to provide ongoing feedback so that a program (or project) can be improved while it is still underway; contributes to the continuous development and improvement of a human service program. This approach complements the project approach.

MONITORING SYSTEM   The evaluation design, protocols, and procedures that ensure systematic, complete, and accurate data collection; also includes a schedule for reporting and disseminating evaluation findings.

MORTALITY   The tendency for clients to drop out of an evaluation study before it is completed; a threat to internal validity.

MULTIGROUP POSTTEST-ONLY DESIGN   An exploratory research design in which there is more than one group and the program's objective (the dependent variable) is measured only once for each group.

MULTIPLE-TREATMENT INTERFERENCE   When a client is given two or more interventions in succession and the results of the first intervention may affect the results of the second or subsequent interventions; a threat to external validity.

MULTISTAGE PROBABILITY SAMPLING   Probability sampling procedures used when a comprehensive list of a population does not exist and it is not possible to construct one.

NEEDS   In needs assessment, something that is considered a basic requirement necessary to sustain the human condition; to be differentiated from *demands* and *wants.*

NEEDS ASSESSMENT   An evaluation that aims to assess the need for a human service by verifying that a social problem exists within a specific client population to an extent that warrants services.

NOMINAL GROUPS TECHNIQUE   A group of people brought together to share their knowledge about a specific social problem. The process is structured using a round-robin approach and permits individuals to share their ideas within a group but with little interaction between group members; a structured group interview.

NONEMPIRICAL EVALUATION   An informal method of appraisal that is not based on empirical data. It depends on theories and descriptions that a professional considers to be relevant to the case.

NONPROBABILITY SAMPLING   Sampling procedures in which all of the persons, events, or objects in the sampling frame have an unknown, and usually unequal, chance of being included in a sample.

NONREACTIVITY   An unobtrusive characteristic of a measuring instrument. Nonreactive measuring instruments do not affect the behavior being measured.

NONSAMPLING ERRORS   Errors in study results that are not due to sampling procedures.

NORM   In measurement, an average or set group standard of achievement that can be used to interpret individual scores; normative data describing statistical properties of a measuring instrument, such as means and standard deviations.

ONE-GROUP POSTTEST-ONLY DESIGN   An exploratory design in which the program's objective (the dependent variable) is measured only once; the simplest of all group evaluation designs.

ONE-GROUP PRETEST-POSTTEST DESIGN   A descriptive research design in which the program's objective (the dependent variable) is measured before and after the intervention (the independent variable).

ONE-STAGE PROBABILITY SAMPLING   Probability sampling procedures in which the selection of a sample from a population is completed in one single process.

OPERATIONALIZATION   The explicit specification of a program's objectives in such a way that the measurement of each objective is possible.

OUTCOME ASSESSMENT   See *outcome evaluation.*

OUTCOME EVALUATION   A program evaluation that is designed to measure the nature of change, if any, for clients after they have received services from a social service program; specifically measures change on a program's objectives; also known as *summative evaluation* and *outcome assessment.*

PERCEIVED NEEDS   In needs assessment, the opinions and views of people who are not directly experiencing a problem themselves.

PERFORMANCE APPRAISAL   The process of evaluating the efficiency and effectiveness of a staff person's work; a possible misuse of evaluation practice.

PHASE Any relatively distinct part of the contact between a professional and a client; *A* represents a baseline phase and *B* an intervention phase.

PILOT TEST Administration of a measuring instrument to a group who will not be included in the evaluation study to determine any difficulties respondents may have in answering questions and the general impression given by the instrument.

POLITICS Individual actions and policies that govern human behavior, which, in turn, influence program decisions. Politically charged situations usually have an element of self-interest.

PRACTICE OBJECTIVE A statement of expected change identifying an intended therapeutic result tailored to the unique circumstances and needs of each client; logically linked to a program objective. Practice objectives, like program objectives, can be grouped into affects, knowledge, and behaviors.

PRETEST-TREATMENT INTERACTION Effects of the pretest on the responses of clients to the introduction of the intervention (the independent variable); a threat to external validity.

PRINCIPLE OF PARSIMONY A principle stating that the simplest and most economical route to evaluating the achievement of the program's objective (the dependent variable) is the best.

PRIVATE CONSULTATIONS An informal method of case evaluation in which a social worker exchanges descriptive information about a client with another worker(s) to obtain solid advice.

PROBABILITY SAMPLING Sampling procedures in which every member of a designated population has a known chance of being selected for a sample.

PROCESS ANALYSIS See *process evaluation.*

PROCESS EVALUATION A type of evaluation that aims to monitor a social service program to describe and assess (1) the services provided to clients and (2) how satisfied key stakeholders are with the services provided. Data are used to provide ongoing feedback in order to refine and improve program service delivery; also known as *formative evaluation.*

PROGRAM An organization that exists to fulfil some social purpose; must be logically linked to the agency's goal.

PROGRAM DATA   In evaluation, measurements systematically collected about a program's operations. Ideally, the data are collected in strict compliance with the evaluation design and procedures.

PROGRAM GOAL   A statement defining the intent of a program that cannot be directly evaluated. It can, however, be evaluated indirectly by the program's objectives, which are derived from the goal. Not to be confused with program objectives.

PROGRAM MONITORING   A program activity comprised of the ongoing collection, analysis, reporting, and use of collected program data.

PROGRAM OBJECTIVE   A statement that clearly and exactly specifies the expected change, or intended result, for individuals receiving program services. Qualities of well-chosen objectives are meaningfulness, specificity, measurability, and directionality. Program objectives, like practice objectives can be grouped into affects, knowledge, and behaviors. Not to be confused with program goal.

PROGRAM STRUCTURE   Fixed elements of a program that are designed to support social service workers in carrying out client service delivery. Examples include: staff-worker ratio, supervision protocols, support staff, training, and salaries.

PROJECT APPROACH TO QUALITY IMPROVEMENT   Evaluations whose purpose is to assess a completed or finished program (or project); complements the monitoring approach.

PUBLIC FORUM   A group of people invited to a public meeting to voice their views about a specific social problem; an unstructured group interview.

PURPOSIVE SAMPLING   A nonprobability sampling procedure in which individuals with particular characteristics are purposely selected for inclusion in the sample; also known as judgmental or theoretical sampling.

QUALITATIVE DATA   Data that measure quality or kind.

QUALITY IMPROVEMENT PROCESS   An ethical commitment to continually look for and seek ways to make services more responsive, efficient, and effective; a process that uses the data from all types of evaluations to improve the quality of human services.

QUANTITATIVE DATA Data that measure quantity or amount in variables or constants.

QUOTA SAMPLING A nonprobability sampling procedure in which the relevant characteristics of a sample are identified, the proportion of these characteristics in the population is determined, and participants are selected from each category until the predetermined proportion (quota) has been achieved.

RANDOM ASSIGNMENT The process of allocating clients to experimental and control groups so that the groups are equivalent; also referred to as randomization.

RANDOM SAMPLING An unbiased selection process conducted so that all members of a population have an equal chance of being selected to participate in the evaluation study.

RANDOMIZED CROSS-SECTIONAL SURVEY DESIGN A descriptive research design in which there is only one group, the program's objective (the dependent variable) is measured only once, the clients are randomly selected from the population, and there is no intervention (the independent variable).

RANDOMIZED LONGITUDINAL SURVEY DESIGN A descriptive research design in which there is only one group, the program's objective (the dependent variable) is measured more than once, and clients are randomly selected from the population before the intervention (the independent variable).

RANDOMIZED ONE-GROUP POSTTEST-ONLY DESIGN A descriptive research design in which there is only one group, the program's objective (the dependent variable) is measured only once, and all members of a population have equal opportunity for participation in the evaluation.

RANDOMIZED POSTTEST-ONLY CONTROL GROUP DESIGN An explanatory research design in which there are two or more randomly selected and randomly assigned groups; the control group does not receive the intervention (the independent variable), and the experimental groups receive different interventions.

RATING SCALES A type of measuring instrument in which responses are rated on a continuum or in an ordered set of categories, with numerical values assigned to each point or category.

REACTIVE EFFECTS An effect on outcome measures due to the clients' awareness that they are participating in an evaluation study; a threat to internal and external validity.

RELIABILITY (1) The degree of accuracy, precision, or consistency of results of a measuring instrument, including the ability to reproduce results when a variable is measured more than once or a test is repeatedly filled out by the same individual, and (2) The degree to which individual differences on scores or in data are due either to true differences or to errors in measurement.

REPEATED MEASUREMENTS The administration of one measuring instrument (or set of instruments) a number of times to the same client, under the same conditions, over a period of time.

RESEARCHER BIAS The tendency of evaluators to find results that they expect to find; a threat to external validity.

RESPONSE BIAS The tendency for individuals to score items on a measuring instrument in such a manner that one score is reported for the majority of all items.

RESPONSE ERROR A type of nonsampling error in which the participants of an evaluation present themselves differently than they actually are, perhaps in a manner that is socially desirable.

RIVAL HYPOTHESIS A theory-based prediction that is a plausible alternative to the research hypothesis and might explain results as well or better; a hypothesis involving extraneous variables other than the intervention (the independent variable); also referred to as the alternative hypothesis.

SAMPLE A subset of a population of individuals, objects, or events chosen to participate in or to be considered in a study; a group chosen by unbiased sample selection from which inferences about the entire population of people, objects, or events can be drawn.

SAMPLING FRAME A listing of units (people, objects, or events) in a population from which a sample is selected.

SAMPLING THEORY   The logic of using methods to ensure that a sample and a population are similar in all relevant characteristics.

SECONDARY DATA ANALYSIS   A data utilization method in which available data that predate the formulation of an evaluation study are used to answer the evaluation question or test the hypothesis.

SELECTION-TREATMENT INTERACTION   The relationship between the manner of selecting clients to participate in an evaluation study and their responses to the intervention (the independent variable); a threat to external validity.

SELF-ANCHORED RATING SCALE   A type of measuring instrument in which respondents rate themselves on a continuum of values, according to their own referents for each point.

SELF-REPORT Measuring Instrument   Instruments such as questionnaires or rating scales in which clients answer questions about their individual experiences and perspectives.

SIMPLE RANDOM SAMPLING   A one-stage probability sampling procedure in which members of a population are selected one at a time, without chance of being selected again, until the desired sample size is obtained.

SNOWBALL SAMPLING   A nonprobability sampling procedure in which individuals selected for inclusion in a sample are asked to identify additional individuals who might be included from the population; can be used to locate people with similar points of view (or experiences).

SOCIAL DESIRABILITY   (1) A response set in which respondents tend to answer questions in a way that they perceive as giving favorable impressions of themselves, and (2) The inclination of data providers to report data that present a socially desirable impression of themselves or their reference groups; also referred to as impression management.

SOLOMON FOUR-GROUP DESIGN   An explanatory evaluation design with four randomly assigned groups, two experimental and two control. The program's objective (the dependent variable) is measured before and after the intervention (the independent variable) for one experimental and one control group, but only after the intervention for the other two groups, and only the experimental groups receive the intervention.

SPECIFICITY OF VARIABLES An evaluation project conducted with a specific group of clients at a specific time and in a specific setting which may not always be generalizable to other clients at a different time and in a different setting; a threat to external validity.

SPOT-CHECK RECORDING A method of data collection that involves direct observation and documentation of the practice objective at specified intervals rather than continuously.

STAKEHOLDER A person or group of people having a direct or indirect interest in the results of an evaluation.

STANDARDIZED MEASUREMENT INSTRUMENT A paper-and-pencil tool, usually constructed by researchers and used by human service professionals, to measure a particular area of knowledge, behavior, or feeling; provides for uniform administration and scoring and generates normative data against which later results can be evaluated.

STATISTICAL REGRESSION The tendency for extreme high or low scores to regress, or shift, toward the average (mean) score on subsequent measurements; a threat to internal validity.

STRATIFIED RANDOM SAMPLING A one-stage probability sampling procedure in which the population is divided into two or more strata to be sampled separately, using random or systematic random sampling techniques.

SUBJECTIVE DATA Isolated facts, presented in descriptive terms, that are based on impressions, experience, values, and intuition.

SUMMATED SCALE A multi-item measuring instrument in which respondents provide a rating for each item. The summation of items provides an overall score.

SUMMATIVE EVALUATION See *outcome evaluation*.

SURVEY A method of collecting evaluation data in which individuals are asked to respond to questions that are designed to describe or study them as a group; can be conducted by mail or telephone.

SYSTEMATIC RANDOM SAMPLING A one-stage probability sampling procedure in which every person at a designated interval in the population list is selected to be included in the study sample.

TARGETS FOR INTERVENTION   A unit of analysis (e.g., individuals, groups, organizations, and communities) that is the focus for change in an evaluation. Criteria used to define targets include demographics, membership in predefined groups, and social conditions.

TESTING EFFECT   The effect that taking a pretest might have on posttest scores; a threat to internal validity.

USER INPUT   In evaluation, when the persons responsible for completing a measuring instrument are involved in its creation; for example, when program workers have a say as to how the program intake form is developed.

UTILITY   (1) A characteristic of a measuring instrument that indicates its degree of usefulness (e.g., how practical is the measuring instrument in a particular situation?), and (2) A standard of evaluation practice that requires evaluations to be carried out only if they are considered potentially useful to one or more stakeholders.

VALIDITY   The degree to which a measuring instrument accurately measures the variable it claims to measure.

VALUATION   Interpretation given to data produced by evaluations; the degree to which results are considered a success or failure.

VARIABLE   A characteristic that can take on different values for different individuals; any attribute whose value, or level, can change; any characteristic (of a person, object, or situation) that can change value or kind from observation to observation.

WANTS   In needs assessment, something that is so desired by people that they are willing to "pay" for it; to be differentiated from *demands* and *needs*.

REFERENCES AND FURTHER READING

Alreck, P.L., & Settle, R.B. (1985). *The survey research handbook.* Homewood, IL: Irwin.

Alter, C., & Evens, W. (1990). *Evaluating your practice: A guide to self-assessment.* New York: Springer.

American Psychological Association. (1973). *Ethical principles in the conduct of research with human participants.* Washington, DC: Author.

American Psychological Association. (1977). *Standards for providers of psychological services.* Washington, DC: Author.

American Psychological Association. (1981). *Specialty guidelines for the delivery of services by counseling psychologists.* Washington, DC: Author.

Austin, M.J., & Crowell, J. (1985). Survey research. In R.M. Grinnell, Jr. (Ed.), *Social work research and evaluation* (2nd ed., pp. 275–305). Itasca, IL: F.E. Peacock Publishers.

Babbie, E. (1992). *The practice of social research* (6th ed.). Belmont, CA: Wadsworth.

Bailey, K.D. (1992). *Methods of social research* (3rd ed.). New York: Free Press.

Barlow, D.H., & Hersen, M. (1984). *Single-case experimental designs: Strategies for studying behavior change* (2nd ed.). Elmsford, NY: Pergamon.

Barlow, D.H., Hayes, S.C., & Nelson, R.O. (1984). *The scientist-practitioner: Research and accountability in applied settings.* Elmsford, NY: Pergamon.

Baugher, D. (1981). *Measuring effectiveness.* San Francisco: Jossey-Bass.

Beck, R.A., & Rossi, P.H. (1990). *Thinking about program evaluation.* Thousand Oaks, CA: Sage.

Beckman, D. (Ed.). (1987). *Using program theory in evaluation.* San Francisco: Jossey-Bass.

Bell, A. (1983). *Assessing health and human service needs.* New York: Human Sciences Press.

Bisno, H., & Borowski, A. (1985). The social and psychological contexts of research. In R.M. Grinnell, Jr. (Ed.), *Social work research and evaluation* (2nd ed., pp. 83–100). Itasca, IL: F.E. Peacock Publishers.

Blase, K., Fixsen, D., & Phillips, E. (1984). Residential treatment for troubled children: Developing service delivery systems. In S.C. Paine, G.T. Bellamy, & B. Wilcox (Eds.), *Human services that work: From innovation to standard practice.* Baltimore: Paul H. Brooks.

Bloom, M., Fischer, J., & Orme, J. (1994). *Evaluating practice: Guidelines for the accountable professional* (2nd ed.). Englewood Cliffs, NJ: Prentice-Hall.

Blythe, B.J., & Tripodi, T. (1989). *Measurement in direct practice.* Thousand Oaks, CA: Sage.

Booth, A., & Higgins, D. (1984). *Human service planning and evalua-tion for hard times*. Springfield, IL: Charles C. Thomas.

Borowski, A. (1988). Social dimensions of research. In R.M. Grinnell, Jr. (Ed.), *Social work research and evaluation* (3rd ed., pp. 42–64). Itasca, IL: F.E. Peacock Publishers.

Boruch, R.F., & Cecil, J.S. (Eds.). (1983). *Solutions to ethical and legal problems in applied social research*. New York: Academic Press.

Boruch, R.F., & Pearson, R.W. (1985). *The comparative evaluation of longitudinal surveys*. New York: Social Science Research Council.

Borus, M.E., Tash, W.R., & Buntz, C.G. (1982). *Evaluating the impact of health programs*. Cambridge, MA: MIT Press.

Bryk, A.S. (1983). *Stakeholder-based evaluation*. San Francisco: Jos-sey-Bass.

Buros, O.K. (Ed.). (1978). *The eighth mental measurements yearbook* (2 vols.). Highland Park, NJ: Gryphon Press.

Campbell, D., & Stanley, J. (1963). *Experimental and quasi-experi-mental designs for research*. Chicago: Rand McNally.

Carley, M. (1981). *Social measurement and social indicators*. Lon-don: Allen & Unwin.

Carter, R.K. (1983). *The accountable agency*. Thousand Oaks, CA: Sage.

Catterall, J.R. (Ed.). (1985). *Economic evaluation of public programs*. San Francisco: Jossey-Bass.

Chambers, D.E., Wedel, K.R., & Rodwell, M.K. (1992). *Evaluating social programs*. Boston: Allyn & Bacon.

Chelimsky, E., & Shadish, W.R. (1997). *Evaluation for the 21st Cen-tury: A resource book*. Thousand Oaks, CA: Sage.

Ciarlo, J.A. (Ed.). (1981). *Utilizing evaluation: Concepts and manage-ment techniques*. Thousand Oaks, CA: Sage.

Collins, D., & Polster, R. (1993). Structured observation. In R.M. Grin-nell, Jr. (Ed.), *Social work research and evaluation* (4th ed., pp. 244–261). Itasca, IL: F.E. Peacock Publishers.

Compton, B.R., & Galaway, B. (1989). *Social work processes* (4th ed.). Belmont, CA: Wadsworth.

Connor, R.F., Altmas, D.G., & Jackson, C. (Eds.). (1984). *Evaluation studies review annual.* Thousand Oaks, CA: Sage.

Connor, R.F., Clay, T., & Hill, P. (1980). *Directory of evaluation training.* Washington, DC: Pintail Press.

Corbeil, R. (1992). Evaluation assessment: A case study of planning an evaluation. In J. Hudson, J. Mayne, & R. Thomlison (Eds.), *Action-oriented evaluation in organizations* (pp. 107–134). Middletown, OH: Wall & Emerson.

Corcoran, K.J. (1988). Selecting a measuring instrument. In R.M. Grinnell, Jr. (Ed.), *Social work research and evaluation* (3rd ed., pp. 137–155). Itasca, IL: F.E. Peacock Publishers.

Crane, J.A. (1982). *The evaluation of social policies.* Boston: Kluwer-Nijhoff.

Davis, B.G. (Ed.). (1986). *Teaching of evaluation across the disciplines.* San Francisco: Jossey-Bass.

Davis, B.G., & Humphreys, S. (1985). *Evaluating intervention programs.* New York: Teachers College Press.

Deshler, D. (1984). *Evaluation for program improvement.* San Francisco: Jossey- Bass.

Dillman, D.A. (1978). *Mail and telephone surveys: The total design method.* New York: Wiley.

Edelstein, B.A., & Berber, E.S. (1987). *Evaluation and accountability in clinical training.* New York: Plenum Press.

Epstein, I. (1988). Quantitative and qualitative methods. In R.M. Grinnell, Jr. (Ed.), *Social work research and evaluation* (3rd ed., pp. 185–198). Itasca, IL: F.E. Peacock Publishers.

Evaluation Research Society. (1980). *Standards for program evaluation.* Potomac, MD: Evaluation Research Society.

Feldman, E.J. (1981). *A practical guide to the conduct of field research in the social sciences.* Boulder, CO: Westview Press.

Ferber, R., & Hirsch, W.Z. (1982). *Social experimentation and economic policy.* Cambridge, MA: Cambridge University Press.

Fetterman, D.M., & Pitman, M.A. (1986). *Educational evaluation.* Thousand Oaks, CA: Sage.

Fink, A. (1993). *Evaluation fundamentals: Guiding health programs, research, and policy.* Thousand Oaks, CA: Sage.

Fink, A. (1995). *The survey kit* (2nd ed.). Thousand Oaks, CA: Sage.

Finsterbusch, K. (Ed.). (1983). *Social impact assessment methods.* Thousand Oaks, CA: Sage.

Fischer, J. (1993). Evaluating positivistic research reports. In R.M. Grinnell, Jr. (Ed.), *Social work research and evaluation* (4th ed., pp. 347–366). Itasca, IL: F.E. Peacock Publishers.

Fitz-Gibbon, C.T., & Morris, L.L. (1987). *How to design a program evaluation.* Thousand Oaks, CA: Sage.

Forehand, G.A. (1982). *Applications of time series analysis to evaluation.* San Francisco: Jossey-Bass.

Gabor, P., & Ing, C. (1997). Sampling. In R.M. Grinnell, Jr. (Ed.), *Social work research and evaluation: Quantitative and qualitative approaches* (5th ed., pp. 237–258). Itasca, IL: F.E. Peacock Publishers.

Garvin, C.D. (1981). Research-related roles for social workers. In R.M. Grinnell, Jr. (Ed.), *Social work research and evaluation* (pp. 547–552). Itasca, IL: F.E. Peacock Publishers.

Gilchrist, L.E., & Schinke, S.P. (1988). Research ethics. In R.M. Grinnell, Jr. (Ed.), *Social work research and evaluation* (3rd ed., pp. 65–79). Itasca, IL: F.E. Peacock Publishers.

Gilgun, J. (1997). Case designs. In R.M. Grinnell, Jr. (Ed.), *Social work research and evaluation: Quantitative and qualitative approaches* (5th ed., pp. 298–312). Itasca, IL: F.E. Peacock Publishers.

Gochros, H.L. (1988). Research interviewing. In R.M. Grinnell, Jr. (Ed.), *Social work research and evaluation* (3rd ed., pp. 267–299). Itasca, IL: F.E. Peacock Publishers.

Green, G.R., & Wright, J.E. (1979). The retrospective approach to collecting baseline data. *Social Work Research and Abstracts, 15,* 25–30.

Greenwald, R.A., Ryan, M.K., & Mulvihill, J.E. (1982). *Human subjects research.* New York: Plenum Press.

Grinnell, R.M., Jr. (1985). Becoming a practitioner/researcher. In R.M. Grinnell, Jr. (Ed.), *Social work research and evaluation* (2nd ed., pp. 1–15). Itasca, IL: F.E. Peacock Publishers.

Grinnell, R.M., Jr. (1993). Group research designs. In R.M. Grinnell, Jr. (Ed.), *Social work research and evaluation* (4th ed., pp. 118–153). Itasca, IL: F.E. Peacock Publishers.

Grinnell, R.M., Jr. (Ed.). (1997). *Social work research and evaluation: Quantitative and qualitative approaches* (5th ed.). Itasca, IL: F.E. Peacock Publishers.

Grinnell, R.M., Jr. (1997). The generation of knowledge. In R.M. Grinnell, Jr. (Ed.), *Social work research and evaluation: Quantitative and qualitative approaches* (5th ed., pp. 3–24). Itasca, IL: F.E. Peacock Publishers.

Grinnell, R.M., Jr., & Siegel, D.H. (1988). The place of research in social work. In R.M. Grinnell, Jr. (Ed.), *Social work research and evaluation* (3rd ed., pp. 9–24). Itasca, IL: F.E. Peacock Publishers.

Grinnell, R.M., Jr., & Stothers, M. (1991). *Research in social work: A primer.* Itasca, IL: F.E. Peacock Publishers.

Grinnell, R.M., Jr., & Unrau, Y. (1997). Group designs. In R.M. Grinnell, Jr. (Ed.), *Social work research and evaluation: Quantitative and qualitative approaches* (5th ed., pp. 259–297). Itasca, IL: F.E. Peacock Publishers.

Groves, R.M. (1989). *Telephone survey methodology.* New York: Wiley.

Guba, E.G., & Lincoln, Y.S. (1981). *Effective evaluation.* San Francisco: Jossey-Bass.

Hornick, J.P., & Burrows, B. (1988). Program evaluation. In R.M. Grinnell, Jr. (Ed.), *Social work research and evaluation* (3rd ed., pp. 400–420). Itasca, IL: F.E. Peacock Publishers.

Hoshino, G., & Lynch, M.M. (1985). Secondary analyses. In R.M. Grinnell, Jr. (Ed.), *Social work research and evaluation* (2nd ed., pp. 370–380). Itasca, IL: F.E. Peacock Publishers.

House, E.R. (1981). *Evaluating with validity.* Thousand Oaks, CA: Sage.

House, E.R. (1993). *Professional evaluation: Social impact and political consequences.* Thousand Oaks, CA: Sage.

Hudson, J., & Grinnell, R.M., Jr. (1989). Program evaluation. In B. Compton & B. Galaway (Eds.), *Social work processes* (4th ed., pp. 691–711). Belmont, CA: Wadsworth.

Hudson, J., Mayne, J., & Thomlison R. (1992). (Eds.), *Action-oriented evaluation in organizations.* Middletown, OH: Wall & Emerson.

Hudson, W.W. (1981). Development and use of indexes and scales. In R.M. Grinnell, Jr. (Ed.), *Social work research and evaluation* (pp. 130–155). Itasca, IL: F.E. Peacock Publishers.

Hudson, W.W. (1985). Indexes and scales. In R.M. Grinnell, Jr. (Ed.), *Social work research and evaluation* (2nd ed., pp. 185–205). Itasca, IL: F.E. Peacock Publishers.

Hudson, W.W. (1993). Standardized measures. In J. Krysik, I. Hoffart, & R.M. Grinnell, Jr. *Student study guide for the fourth edition of Social work research and evaluation* (pp. 243–263). Itasca, IL: F.E. Peacock Publishers.

Ihilevich, D., & Gleser, G.C. (1982). *Evaluating mental health programs.* Lexington, MA: Lexington Books.

Isaac, S., & Michael, W.B. (1980). *Handbook in research and evaluation.* San Diego, CA: EDITS.

Jackson, G.B. (1980). Methods for integrative reviews. *Review of Educational Research, 50,* 438–460.

Joint Committee on Standards for Education Evaluation. (1981). *Standards for evaluations of educational programs projects and materials.* Toronto, Ontario, Canada: McGraw-Hill.

Jordan, C., Franklin, C., & Corcoran, K. (1997). Measuring instruments. In R.M. Grinnell, Jr. (Ed.), *Social work research and evaluation: Quantitative and qualitative approaches* (5th ed., pp. 184–211). Itasca, IL: F.E. Peacock Publishers.

Kettner, P.M., Moroney, R.M., & Martin, L.L. (1990). *Designing and managing programs: An effectiveness-based approach.* Thousand Oaks, CA: Sage.

Kidder, L.M., & Judd, C.M. (1986). *Research methods in social relations* (5th ed.). New York: Holt, Rinehart & Winston.

Krueger, R.A. (1997). *Focus groups: A practical guide for applied research.* Thousand Oaks, CA: Sage.

Krysik, J., Hoffart, I., & Grinnell, R.M., Jr. (1993). *Student study guide for the fourth edition of Social work research and evaluation.* Itasca, IL: F.E. Peacock Publishers.

Krysik, J., & Grinnell, R.M., Jr. (1997). Quantitative approaches to the generation of knowledge. In R.M. Grinnell, Jr. (Ed.), *Social work research and evaluation: Quantitative and qualitative approaches* (5th ed., pp. 67–105). Itasca, IL: F.E. Peacock Publishers.

Kyte, N.S., & Bostwick, G. (1997). Measuring variables. In R.M. Grinnell, Jr. (Ed.), *Social work research and evaluation: Quantitative and qualitative approaches* (5th ed., pp. 161–183). Itasca, IL: F.E. Peacock Publishers.

Lavrakas, P.J. (1987). *Telephone survey methods: Sampling, selection, and supervision.* Thousand Oaks, CA: Sage.

LeCroy, C.W., & Solomon, G. (1993). Content analysis. In R.M. Grinnell, Jr. (Ed.), *Social work research and evaluation* (4th ed., pp. 304–316). Itasca, IL: F.E. Peacock Publishers.

Levin, H.M. (1983). *Cost-effectiveness: A primer.* Thousand Oaks, CA: Sage.

Lidz, C.S. (Ed.). (1987). *Dynamic assessment.* New York: Guilford Press.

Lincoln, Y., & Guba, E. (1985). *Naturalistic inquiry.* Thousand Oaks, CA: Sage.

Love, A.J. (1991). *Internal evaluation: Building organizations from within.* Thousand Oaks, CA: Sage.

Madaus, G.F., Scriven, M., & Stufflebeam, D. (Eds.). (1983). *Evaluation models.* Boston: Kluwer-Nijhoff.

Maloney, D.M. (1984). *Protection of human research subjects: A practical guide to federal laws and regulations.* New York: Plenum.

Mayne, J. (1992). Establishing internal evaluation in an organization. In J. Hudson, J. Mayne, & R. Thomlison (Eds.), *Action-oriented evaluation in organizations* (pp. 306–317). Middletown, OH: Wall & Emerson.

Mayne, J., & Hudson, J. (1992). Program evaluation: An overview. In J. Hudson, J. Mayne, & R. Thomlison (Eds.), *Action-oriented evaluation in organizations* (pp. 1–19). Middletown, OH: Wall & Emerson.

McMurtry, S.L. (1997). Survey research. In R.M. Grinnell, Jr. (Ed.), *Social work research and evaluation: Quantitative and qualitative approaches* (5th ed., pp. 333–367). Itasca, IL: F.E. Peacock Publishers.

Mindel, C.H. (1997). Designing measuring Instruments. In R.M. Grinnell, Jr. (Ed.), *Social work research and evaluation: Quantitative and qualitative approaches* (5th ed., pp. 212–234). Itasca, IL: F.E. Peacock Publishers.

Mindel, C.H., & McDonald, L. (1988). Survey research. In R.M. Grinnell, Jr. (Ed.), *Social work research and evaluation* (3rd ed., pp. 300–322). Itasca, IL: F.E. Peacock Publishers.

Mohr. L.B. (1995). *Impact analysis for program evaluation* (2nd ed.). Thousand Oaks, CA: Sage.

Morgan, D. (1988). *Focus groups as qualitative research.* Thousand Oaks, CA: Sage.

Moss, K.E. (1988). Writing research proposals. In R.M. Grinnell, Jr. (Ed.), *Social work research and evaluation* (3rd ed., pp. 429–445). Itasca, IL: F.E. Peacock Publishers.

Mullen, E.J. (1988). Constructing personal practice models. In R.M. Grinnell, Jr. (Ed.), *Social work research and evaluation* (3rd ed., pp. 503–533). Itasca, IL: F.E. Peacock Publishers.

Murray, J.G. (1980). *Needs assessment in adult education.* Ottawa, Ontario, Canada: National Library of Canada.

Mutschler, E. (1979). Using single-case evaluation procedures in a family and children's service center: Integration of practice and research. *Journal of Social Service Research, 2,* 115–134.

Nelsen, J.C. (1988). Single-subject research. In R.M. Grinnell, Jr. (Ed.), *Social work research and evaluation* (3rd ed., pp. 362–399). Itasca, IL: F.E. Peacock Publishers.

Newman, D.L., & Brown, R.D. (1996). *Applied ethics for program evaluation.* Thousand Oaks, CA: Sage.

Nowakowski, J. (Ed.). (1987). *The client perspective on evaluation.* San Francisco: Jossey-Bass.

Nurius, P.S., & Hudson, W.W. (1993). *Human services: Practice, evaluation, and computers.* Belmont, CA: Brooks/Cole.

Palumbo, D.J. (1987). *The politics of program evaluation.* Thousand Oaks, CA: Sage.

Patton, M.Q. (1982). *Practical evaluation.* Thousand Oaks, CA: Sage.

Patton, M.Q. (1987). *Creative evaluation* (2nd ed.). Thousand Oaks, CA: Sage.

Patton, M.Q. (1990). *Qualitative evaluation and research methods* (2nd ed.). Thousand Oaks, CA: Sage.

Patton, M.Q. (1996). *Utilization-focused evaluation: The new century text* (3rd ed.). Thousand Oaks, CA: Sage.

Pecora, P.J., Fraser, M.W., Nelson, K.E., McCroskey, J., & Meezan, W. (1995). *Evaluating family-based services.* New York: Aldine.

Polster, R.A., & Collins, D. (1988). Measuring variables by direct observations. In R.M. Grinnell, Jr. (Ed.), *Social work research and evaluation* (3rd ed., pp. 156–176). Itasca, IL: F.E. Peacock Publishers.

Polster, R.A., Collins, D., & Coleman, H. (1997). Structured observation. In R.M. Grinnell, Jr. (Ed.), *Social work research and evaluation: Quantitative and qualitative approaches* (5th ed., pp. 315–332). Itasca, IL: F.E. Peacock Publishers.

Polster, R.A., & Lynch, M.A. (1985). Single-subject designs. In R.M. Grinnell, Jr. (Ed.), *Social work research and evaluation* (2nd ed., pp. 381–431). Itasca, IL: F.E. Peacock Publishers.

Posavac, E.J., & Carey, R.G. (1992). *Program evaluation: Methods and case studies* (4th ed.). Englewood Cliffs, NJ: Prentice-Hall.

Price, R.H., & Politser, P.E. (1980). *Evaluation and action in the social environment.* New York: Academic Press.

Ramos, R. (1985). Participant observation. In R.M. Grinnell, Jr. (Ed.), *Social work research and evaluation* (2nd ed., pp. 343–356). Itasca, IL: F.E. Peacock Publishers.

Raymond, F.B. (1985). Program evaluation. In R.M. Grinnell, Jr. (Ed.), *Social work research and evaluation* (2nd ed., pp. 432–442). Itasca, IL: F.E. Peacock Publishers.

Reamer, F.G. (1979). Fundamental ethical issues in social work: An essay review. *Social Service Review, 53,* 229–243.

Reamer, F.G. (1982). *Ethical dilemmas in social service.* New York: Columbia University Press.

Reamer, F.G. (1983). Ethical dilemmas in social work practice. *Social Work, 28,* 31–35.

Reid, W.J. (1993). Writing research reports. In R.M. Grinnell, Jr. (Ed.), *Social work research and evaluation* (4th ed., pp. 332–346). Itasca, IL: F.E. Peacock Publishers.

Reid, W.J., & Smith, A.D. (1989). *Research in social work* (2nd ed.). New York: Columbia University Press.

Rossi, P.H. (1982). *Standards for evaluation practice.* San Francisco: Jossey-Bass.

Rossi, P.H., & Freeman, H.E. (1993). *Evaluation: A systematic approach* (5th ed.). Thousand Oaks, CA: Sage.

Royse, D. (1991). *Research methods in social work.* Chicago: Nelson-Hall.

Royse, D., & Thyer, B.A (1996). *Program evaluation: An introduction* (2nd ed.). Chicago: Nelson-Hall.

Rubin, A. (1993). Secondary analysis. In R.M. Grinnell, Jr. (Ed.), *Social work research and evaluation* (4th ed., pp. 290–303). Itasca, IL: F.E. Peacock Publishers.

Rubin, A., & Babbie, E. (1997). Program-level evaluation. In R.M. Grinnell, Jr. (Ed.), *Social work research and evaluation: Quantitative and qualitative approaches* (5th ed., pp. 560–587). Itasca, IL: F.E. Peacock Publishers.

Rush, B., & Ogborne, A. (1991). Program logic models: Expanding their role and structure for program planning and evaluation. *The Canadian Journal of Program Evaluation, 6,* 95–106.

Rutman, L. (1980). *Planning useful evaluations.* Thousand Oaks, CA: Sage.

Schinke, S.P. (1985). Ethics. In R.M. Grinnell, Jr. (Ed.), *Social work research and evaluation* (2nd ed., pp. 101–114). Itasca, IL: F.E. Peacock Publishers.

Schinke, S.P., & Gilchrist, L.D. (1993). Ethics in research. In R.M. Grinnell, Jr. (Ed.), *Social work research and evaluation* (4th ed., pp. 79–90). Itasca, IL: F.E. Peacock Publishers.

Schuerman, J.R. (1983). *Research and evaluation in the human services.* New York: Free Press.

Scriven, M. (1991). *Evaluation thesaurus* (4th ed.). Thousand Oaks, CA: Sage.

Seaberg, J.R. (1988). Utilizing sampling procedures. In R.M. Grinnell, Jr. (Ed.), *Social work research and evaluation* (3rd ed., pp. 240–257). Itasca, IL: F.E. Peacock Publishers.

Shadish, W.R., Cook, T.D., & Leviton, L.C. (1991). *Foundations of program evaluation.* Thousand Oaks, CA: Sage.

Siegel, D.H. (1988). Integrating data-gathering techniques and practice activities. In R.M. Grinnell, Jr. (Ed.), *Social work research and evaluation* (3rd ed., pp. 465–482). Itasca, IL: F.E. Peacock Publishers.

Siegel, D.H., & Reamer, F.G. (1988). Integrating research findings, concepts, and logic into practice. In R.M. Grinnell, Jr. (Ed.), *Social work research and evaluation* (3rd ed., pp. 483–502). Itasca, IL: F.E. Peacock Publishers.

Silkman, R.H. (Ed.). (1986). *Measuring efficiency.* San Francisco, CA: Jossey-Bass.

Smith, D.A. (1992). The evaluation of program efficiency. In J. Hudson, J. Mayne, & R. Thomlison (Eds.), *Action-oriented evaluation in organizations* (pp. 180–194). Middletown, OH: Wall & Emerson.

Smith, M.J. (1990). *Program evaluation in the human services.* New York: Springer.

Smith, N.J. (1988). Formulating research goals and problems. In R.M. Grinnell, Jr. (Ed.), *Social work research and evaluation* (3rd ed., pp. 89–110). Itasca, IL: F.E. Peacock Publishers.

Stufflebeam, D., & Shinkfield, A. (1984). *A systematic evaluation.* Boston: Kluwer Nijhoff.

Suchman, E.A. (1967). *Evaluative research.* New York: Russell Sage Foundation.

Taylor, S., & Bogdan, R. (1984). *Introduction to qualitative research methods: The search for meanings.* New York: Wiley.

Thyer, B.A. (1993). Single-system research designs. In R.M. Grinnell, Jr. (Ed.), *Social work research and evaluation* (4th ed., pp. 94–117). Itasca, IL: F.E. Peacock Publishers.

Toseland, R.W. (1993). Choosing a data collection method. In R.M. Grinnell, Jr. (Ed.), *Social work research and evaluation* (4th ed., pp. 317–328). Itasca, IL: F.E. Peacock Publishers.

Tripodi, T. (1974). *Uses and abuses of social research in social work.* New York: Columbia University Press.

Tripodi, T. (1983). *Evaluative research for social workers.* Englewood Cliffs, NJ: Prentice-Hall.

Tripodi, T. (1985). Research designs. In R.M. Grinnell, Jr. (Ed.), *Social work research and evaluation* (2nd ed., pp. 231–259). Itasca, IL: F.E. Peacock Publishers.

Tripodi, T., Fellin, P.A., & Meyer, H.J. (1983). *The assessment of social research: Guidelines for the use of research in social work and social service* (2nd ed.). Itasca, IL: F.E. Peacock Publishers.

Trochim, W.M. (1984). *Research design for program evaluation: The regression- discontinuity approach.* Thousand Oaks, CA: Sage.

Tutty, L.M., Grinnell, R.M., Jr., & Williams, M. (1997). Research problems and questions. In R.M. Grinnell, Jr. (Ed.), *Social work research and evaluation: Quantitative and qualitative approaches* (5th ed., pp. 49–66). Itasca, IL: F.E. Peacock Publishers.

Tutty, L.M., Rothery, M.L., & Grinnell, R.M., Jr. (1996). *Qualitative research for social workers: Phases, steps, and tasks.* Boston: Allyn & Bacon.

Unrau, Y.A. (1993). A program logic model approach to conceptualizing social service programs. *The Canadian Journal of Program Evaluation, 8,* 33–42.

Unrau, Y.A. (1997). Implementing evaluations. In R.M. Grinnell, Jr. (Ed.), *Social work research and evaluation: Quantitative and qualitative approaches* (5th ed., pp. 588–604). Itasca, IL: F.E. Peacock Publishers.

Unrau, Y.A. (1997). Selecting a data collection method and data source. In R.M. Grinnell, Jr. (Ed.), *Social work research and evaluation: Quantitative and qualitative approaches* (5th ed., pp. 458–472). Itasca, IL: F.E. Peacock Publishers.

Unrau, Y.A., & Coleman, H. (1997). Qualitative data analysis. In R.M. Grinnell, Jr. (Ed.), *Social work research and evaluation: Quantitative and qualitative approaches* (5th ed., pp. 501–472). Itasca, IL: F.E. Peacock Publishers.

Washington, R.O. (1980). *Program evaluation in the human services.* Lanham, MD: University Press of America.

Watts, T.D. (1985). Ethnomethodology. In R.M. Grinnell, Jr. (Ed.), *Social work research and evaluation* (2nd ed., pp. 357–369). Itasca, IL: F.E. Peacock Publishers.

Webb, E., Campbell, D., Schwartz, R., & Sechrest, L. (1966). *Unobtrusive measures: Nonreactive research in the social sciences.* Chicago: Rand McNally.

Weinbach, R.W. (1988). Agency and professional contexts of research. In R.M. Grinnell, Jr. (Ed.), *Social work research and evaluation* (3rd ed., pp. 25–41). Itasca, IL: F.E. Peacock Publishers.

Weinbach, R.W., & Grinnell, R.M., Jr. (1996). *Applying research knowledge.* (2nd ed.). Boston: Allyn & Bacon.

Weinbach, R.W., & Grinnell, R.M., Jr. (1998). *Statistics for social workers* (4th ed.). White Plains, NY: Longman.

Weiss, C.H. (1972). *Evaluation research: Methods of assessing program effectiveness.* Englewood Cliffs, NJ: Prentice-Hall.

Williams, D.D. (1986). *Naturalistic evaluation.* San Francisco: Jossey-Bass.

Williams, M., Grinnell, R.M., Jr., & Tutty, L.M. (1997). Research contexts. In R.M. Grinnell, Jr. (Ed.), *Social work research and evaluation: Quantitative and qualitative approaches* (5th ed., pp. 25–46). Itasca, IL: F.E. Peacock Publishers.

Williams, M., Tutty, L., & Grinnell, R.M., Jr. (1995). *Research in social work: An introduction* (2nd ed.). Itasca, IL: F.E. Peacock Publishers.

Witkin, B.R., & Altschuld, J.W. (1995). *Planning and conducting needs assessments.* Thousand Oaks, CA: Sage.

INDEX